D1571394

SOCIO-POLITICAL THEATRE IN NIGERIA

Editorial Inquiries:

Mellen Research University Press
534 Pacific Avenue
San Francisco, California 94133

Order Fulfillment:

The Edwin Mellen Press
Box 450
Lewiston, New York 14092

SOCIO-POLITICAL THEATRE IN NIGERIA

I. Peter Ukpokodu

MELLEN RESEARCH UNIVERSITY PRESS
San Francisco

Library of Congress Cataloging in-Publication Data

This book has been registered with the Library of Congress.

ISBN 0-7734-9963-6

Copyright © 1992 I. Peter Ukpokodu

Printed in the United States of America

Dedicated,
In Ultimate Affection,
To my Wife, Nelly,
To my Sons, Evar and Loy,
For Endurance.

CONTENTS

ACKNOWLEDGMENTS

I would like to express my gratitude to the numerous publishers and authors without whose works a historical and critical work of this nature would have been impossible:

Oxford University Press for extracts from Wole Soyinka's *Collected Plays 1*, *Collected Plays 2*, Ebun Clark's *Hubert Ogunde: The Making of Nigerian Theatre* and Sonny Oti's *The Old Masters*.

Ibadan University Press for extracts from Femi Osofisan's *The Chattering and the Song*, J. P. Clark's *The Ozidi Saga*, Irele and Ogunba's *Theatre in Africa* and Ogunba's *The Movement of Transition*.

Heinemann Educational Books for extracts from *African Plays for Playing 2*, *Nine African Plays for Radio*, Ola Rotimi's *If*, and Zulu Sofola's *King Emene*.

Onibonoje Publishers for extracts from Rasheed Gbadamosi's *Echoes from the Lagoon*, Elechi Amadi's *Peppersoup* and *The Road to Ibadan*.

Ethiope Publishing Corporation for extracts from Ezenta Eze's *The Cassava Ghost*.

Thomas Nelson (Nigeria) for extracts from Wale Ogunyemi's *Langbodo*.

Kole Omotoso for extracts from *Shadows in the Horizon*.

Femi Osofisan for extracts from *Once Upon Four Robbers*.

University Press Limited for extracts from Zulu Sofola's *Old Wines are Tasty*.

Longman Drumbeat for extracts from Bode Sowande's *Farewell to Babylon and Other Plays*.

W. W. Norton & Company for extracts from Wole Soyinka's *Death and the King's Horseman*.

Indiana University Press for extracts from Wole Soyinka's *Opera Wonyosi*.

Orisun (Acting) Editions for extracts from Wale Ogunyemi's *Ijaye War* and Wole Soyinka's *Before the Blackout*.

John Agetua for extracts from *Six Nigerian Writers* and *When the Man Died*.

University of London Press for extracts from James Ene Henshaw's *Dinner for Promotion* and *This is Our Chance*.

Faber and Faber for extracts from Michael Crowder's *The Story of Nigeria*.

Hutchinson & Co. (Publishers) for extracts from Michael Etherton's *The Development of African Drama*.

The Macmillan Press for extracts from R. N. Egudu's *Modern African Poetry and the African Predicament*.

Penguin Books for extracts from Frantz Fanon's *The Wretched of the Earth* and Paulo Freire's *Pedagogy of the Oppressed*.

Routledge and Kegan Paul for extracts from *The Morality of Art*.

Northwestern University Press fro extracts from Claude Welch, Jr.'s *Soldier and State in Africa*.

New Horn Press for extracts from Femi Osofisan's *Kolera Kolej* and Wole Soyinka's *Art, Dialogue and Outrage*.

Antola Esko for extracts from "The Roots of Domestic Military Interventions in Black Africa".

Nigeria Magazine for extracts from Ebun Clark's "The Nigerian Theatre and the Nationalist Movement" and "Ogunde Theatre: The Rise of Contemporary Professional Theatre in Nigeria 1946-72"; from Abiola Irele's "Negritude–Philosophy of African Being"; and from Yemi Ogunbiyi's *Drama and Theatre in Nigeria*.

Publishers of *Headlines, Daily Times, Nigerian Opinion*.

All publishers and authors who appear in my Notes and Bibliography

Paul and Michelle Rabbideau for book design.

FOREWORD

I

Too many of us long grounded in the so-called "canon" of Western theatre and drama often, in our narrow-sightedness, come to believe that the tradition of Sophocles, Shakespeare, Racine, Goethe, Ibsen, Stanislavsky, Chekhov, Copeau, O'Neill, Brecht, Artaud, Pinter, Grotowski, et al. is the *only* tradition or the *best* tradition. This is an exaggeration, of course, but sometimes it's more comfortable for those of us in theatre to ignore manifestations of theatre that are unfamiliar. Sometimes it might be more healthy and enlightening for us to take a multicultural view or a feminist view or maybe even a masculinist view in order to "see" the canon more clearly.

Some of the rich theatrical traditions often ignored, because they are outside the parameters of Western culture, are those of the Middle East, Asia, and Africa. Perhaps these cultures have something very important to teach us about the theatre: how theatre arises, why it sometimes becomes political in the uncertainties and stresses of a culture (particularly in the Third World); how it has the capacity to enliven political and social arguments in its immediate metaphors and symbols. Often, as we know from Western culture, important theatre has emerged in periods of cultural stress: the Soviet Golden Age of the 1920s, the 1960s and early 1970s in Europe and the United States.

In Africa, for example, the theatre is rooted in the political and social moment. I. Peter Ukpokodu is a native Nigerian, well-trained in and well-aware of the Western theatrical canon. But also, as a Nigerian, he has been directly a part of the revolutionary political movements, riots, and stresses of Nigerian society.

In this book, Ukpokodu focuses on his native theatre and drama essentially in the period since independence (from colonial rule) in the 1960s to the present. He is presently contemplating up-dating this book to deal with the early twenty-first century, which, of course, has not yet occurred.

While those grounded in the Western canon cannot fully have ignored the names of playwrights such as Wole Soyinka or John Pepper Clark, Ukpokodu presents us with numerous others: Hubert Ogunde, Wale Ogunyemi, Femi Osofisan.... He also discusses the Negritude movement, the problem of leadership, the bloody civil war, the wave of Marxist ideology. These influences are traced in the development of Nigerian dramatic literature and its performances by actors.

Ukpokodu's book, thus, deals with the recent history of an unsettled culture and the theatre emerging as a result of that unsettlement. Those committed to the Western canon, and particularly those interested in moments of theatre developed in periods of revolution--the Reformation, the rise of the romantic movements in the late eighteenth and late nineteenth centuries, the 1960s, etc.--should find much by analogy to reflect upon in Ukpokodu's discussion of recent Nigerian theatre. His discussion of the Nigerian dilemma is informed, sensitive, and precise.

Robert Findlay
Professor of Theatre/ Film
University of Kansas

II

The circumstances of history puts Africa in the foreground of international interest and Nigeria is a key focus because of its place and role in that history.

What makes Nigeria is not its name in history but the differing attempts being made by the various peoples over the years to consolidate the socio-political content of the name as an exemplar for posterity. This is the imperative of Dr. Peter Ukpokodu's study of "the house that Britain built" as seen through the concerned efforts of artists and intellectuals following in the wake of tradition.

Because of the force and scope of the study, it is appropriate to relate to the statistical fact that by its population one in every five black and African is a Nigerian. It is of note that the geographical location of Nigeria in West Africa makes such a distinction a testimony of its role in contemporary political history of Africa and why developments in it need the attention of the world.

Nigeria is the confluence of the streams of dispersals of peoples and civilizations from the Upper Nile Valley and ancient Western Sudanic empires:

> Within its frontiers were the great kingdoms of Bornu, with a known history of more than a thousand years; the Fulani Empire which for the hundred years before its conquest by Britain had ruled most of the Savannah of Northern Nigeria; the kingdoms of Ife and Benin, which had produced art recognized amongst the most accomplished in the world; the Yoruba Empire of Oyo, which had once been the most powerful of the states of the Guinea Coast; the city states of the Niger Delta, which had grown in response to European demands for slaves and palm oil; as well as the loosely organized Ibo peoples of the Eastern region [which encloses the culture of Igbo Ukwu] and the small tribes of the plateau [amongst whose terrain the Nok culture, one of the oldest in Africa, was located]. (Excerpt from Michael Crowder, *The Story of Nigeria*, London: Faber and Faber, 1962, p. 19).

Socio-Political Theatre in Nigeria is a study which translates a historical discourse of creativity into a living force. As a critical analysis of works by playwrights and

viii

dramatists– all of them theatre practitioners, the study explores their achievable goals and provides a range of available options through a systematic analysis and treatment of the socio-political temperament of the nation state. Beginning from developments at the ancient Oyo Yoruba Empire of the fifteenth and nineteenth centuries where the Alarinjo Theatre originated, first as an agency of state governance for socio-political awareness and edification, and later, as an instrument of mass appeal and social action, the study traverses time to focus on the literary theatre of contemporary Nigeria.

The dynamics of the theatre in Nigeria have always been re-inforced by artistic and intellectual elements and these have mutually shaped the socio-political climate considerably. The popular theatre of the late Hubert Ogunde (1916-1990) was in the vanguard of the struggle for Nigeria's independence from British colonialism even as the literary theatre of Wole Soyinka, the first African to be awarded the Nobel Prize for Literature, became a veritable platform for the intelligentsia to hear the varied voices of artistic realism and vision proffered to actually shape events in society. The study brings together and analyses the attempts of a sizeable number of the playwrights and dramatists (male and female) whose works, written in English, the *lingua franca* of Nigeria, do not merely serve the theatre audience as 'fleshpots for escapist indulgence', but function to all intents and purposes as a twinge of conscience. To this extent the study traces political developments through artistic accomplishments and aesthetic qualities of stagecraft and viewpoint.

Crucial to the study is the quest for political leadership and the attendant violence and impropriety in politics. The cry for a revolutionary social change is presumed to demand a new breed leadership that would over-ride the *status-quo* and harness all forces to a new art of government for the well-being of the masses and the tightening of the loose ends of the cord of unity in a country with disparate peoples, cultural affiliations, linguistic differences and religious practices. We are given a historical perspective developed in

the various plays spotlighting the following classes of
leadership:

the Traditional Ruling Class
the Priestly Class
the Peasant Class
the Intellectual Class
the Armed Forces Class and
the Artist

The importance and effectiveness of these classes of rulers
are weighed against the role of professional politicians who
consciously take to politics as business.

As the crystallization of national consciousness begins
to reveal the extent to which the people can be mobilized by
effective leadership, the study concentrates on and exposes
the contradictions and faults which exist in the different
leadership postures.

Any progression that channels African culture into
different pathways without trace of or alignment to its base
component is bound to fail because of inherent ambiguities
and the context of alienation which naturally develops as a
consequence. Many of such plays are identified and the
extent to which the playwrights and dramatists project a
political system or ideology as a *modus operandi* for the
benefit of society. Amongst the various strategies, the study
pays a particular attention to the plays of Wole Soyinka and
those of the newbreed playwrights and dramatists whose
Marxist preoccupations only show in their zeal to impact
students in the campuses of the various universities of
Nigeria with the prospect of a new life-rhythm, mores and
social organization through the means of theatre. The
ideologues, in particular, attempt through their plays to
impose a superstructure without a base.

Soyinka is skeptical about leadership by intellectualism.
His treatment of this phenomenon is in the portrait of the
Professor in his play, *The Road*, who absentmindedly
pursues the riddle of death instead of the substance of the
brass tacks of life needed by the downtrodden who rally

around with hope but encounter the ambiguities contained in his kind of leadership directions.

The study however, identifies Soyinka's social vision– one that uses satire and myth to tear through the speculative projections of intellectualism. Soyinka contends with the Marxist ideologues who themselves seemed lost on negative contradictory definitions. Art as an instrument of political change must need be expressed through the heart and mind of the masses, springing forth from the cultural base of their social existence. The radicalism of Frantz Fanon, Che Gueverra or Chairman Mao so much paraded on the university campuses, tends to befog rather than clarify the sign posts of the times. We are given Soyinka's posture through his plays that the dramatist should be more of an analyst and critic of the socio-political culture including the excrescences of certain African Heads of State.

The onset of dictatorship in Africa is treated and exemplified in the works of the new playwrights but it is Soyinka who identifies the trend as a criminal act in his *Opera Wonyosi*, based on a fusion of John Gay's *The Beggars Opera* and Bertolt Brecht's *The Three Penny Opera*. Soyinka is convinced that it is the people's apathy toward their erstwhile "messiahs" that encourages dictatorship. As a writer, he uses his play, *Kongi's Harvest*, to identify with Kongism– a system of governance which sets out to reconstruct traditional dictatorship (Oba Danlola's citadel of power) for the purpose of installing a new social order. Kongism captures the spirit of traditional African authoritarianism of the philosopher or priestly king, but the significance of Kongism is attested to in the method by which the transfer of the 'old image' of traditional rulership is replaced by a new scheme of governance. Kongism distinguishes between the dictatorship of the charismatic individual and the dictatorship of the proletariat. Soyinka's preference is clear. The stalemate at the end of the play is evidence of his open-mindedness about the option. Kongism is an untested phenomenon in Africa that still holds sway, be it in the civilian or military regimes.

Socio-Political Theatre in Nigeria is a significant analysis of trends in Nigeria as an emerging polity whose unity and survival depend on a number of factors. Dr. Ukpokodu provides the insights of playwrights and dramatists to the happenings only as a kernel example of what exists in Third World Africa. The search for a socio-political formula of governance then will knit together the disparate groups (in language and culture) that inhabit each independent colonially delimited African country through diverse experiments has become the concern of artists and intellectuals. Toward this the study presents a coherent analysis and prospects for Nigeria. Dr. Ukpokodu's study provides a perspective which brings the theatre to the fore front of social change in an important country of Africa.

Joel A. Adedeji, Ph.D.
Langston Hughes Visiting Professor
Theatre/Film and
African/American Studies
University of Kansas

PREFACE

I am amazed that even as I write a Preface to this study, I am already thinking of writing on the socio-political theatre in Nigeria from the 1990s to the end of the century as a follow up. Perhaps, this stems from my strong conviction that such theatre has an eternal existence and that one can know much about Nigeria and Africa through it. New dramatists of socio-political leaning have arisen–Tunde Fatunde, Tess Onwueme, Samson Amali, Atiboroko Uyovbukerhi, Akanji Nasiru, Sam Ukala–who must go through the crucible of self and theatre criticism, and hopefully, will reach maturity and assert their presence in the late 1990s. By that same period, Soyinka's successors–Femi Osofisan, Zulu Sofola, Bode Sowande–will be at their dramatic zenith, while the older dramatists–Wole Soyinka, John Pepper Clark, Ola Rotimi–will still have great intensity even as they wane. One of these three will become the living "father of Nigerian theatre" in succession to Hubert Ogunde, the irrepressible, energetic capsule of theatricality who died last year.

Socio-political theatre in Nigeria as it emerges and will emerge in the decades ahead, is important to me but will by no means be my only preoccupation. I am currently working on two manuscripts– "Continental African Theatre" and "African Proverbs Explained". Indeed extracts from the former which I presented at the Mid-American Theatre Conference in Kansas City, Missouri, and at the Alums Conference of Theatre and Film at the University of Kansas, Lawrence, in March and April this year, were so highly demanded that for my own selfish motives, I have decided to make them unavailable until they appear in the forth-coming book. "Essays On African masterpiece Drama" is also an envisaged work. These projected works encompass the totality of Africa, North, South, East and West, Africa as a continent unfragmented into North or South of the Sahara as opportunistic politicians and scholars do for their convenience.

But my present concern is this book, *Socio-Political Theatre in Nigeria*, which is mostly a study of Nigerian drama, from the eve of her independence from Britain in 1960 to the present, with supportive material from the larger Nigeria's socio-political history. Its first chapter examines the appropriateness and usage of the term "Nigerian Drama" and sets limits on its meaning. It also looks at what influences the Negritude movement and independence had on Nigerian drama, and why it is important to study Nigerian drama of socio-political concern.

While Chapter 2 looks at the precursors of socio-political theatre in pre-colonial "Nigeria" and in Nigeria on the eve of her independence, Chapter 3 examines the drama that reflects social and political malpractices of the newly independent Nigeria. Style of politics and electioneering that marked the first Republic is discussed in detail. This is the period of Guerilla Theatre.

Among other things, Chapter 3 portrays the absence of any worthwhile leadership. Chapter 4, therefore, discusses what seems to be a central preoccupation of drama throughout this post-independence period: the quest for right leadership. Representative leaders are brought forward and scrutinized. The chapter concludes with the examination of the attributes of the true leader the period demands.

Political impropriety and lack of true leadership that greeted the new nation led to a bloody civil war. chapter 5 looks at this war, and its aftermath, as it is represented in drama. Included in this discussion is the issue of military leadership. Chapter 6 examines the theme of dictatorship in Africa.

Chapter 7 focuses attention on the best known Nigerian colonial struggle–the Aba Women's Riot of 1929–in drama to discuss nationalist struggle in Africa in general. The chapter compares this drama to plays written in territories where such struggles actually take place in Africa. It draws on liberation theology and on liberation theories of Frantz Fanon, Paulo Freire and Jean-Paul Sartre for corroboration.

While Chapter 8 studies the new wave of Marxist ideology in Nigerian theatre practice, Chapter 9 is preoccupied with national unity. But it transcends Nigerian national unity to discuss black unity with reference to World Black and African Festival of Art and Culture (FESTAC) held in Nigeria in 1977.

The study concludes with a chapter that summarizes what has been the role of theatre in the Nigerian socio-political situation and to project what might happen in future dramaturgy. Appendices give plot synopses of the major plays, biographics of playwrights and glossary.

This kind of study poses a particular problem: how to work within a historical concern and yet be faithful to drama. Somehow my approach was not in vain, as the report from an external assessor for Longman Nigeria Limited shows:

> Peter Ukpokodu's *Socio-Political Theatre in Nigeria* is a commendable work in many respects. The sheer historical breadth of the manuscript attests to the ambitious nature of the undertaking which the writer set out to accomplish–a broad historical review of the path of growth of socio-political theatre in Nigeria from the pre-colonial to the post-colonial era. The very nature of this kind of undertaking makes it imperative for the writer to have a critical awareness not only of the nature of socio-political theatre but also of most of the plays written and/or produced in Nigeria over that extensive period of time. The dilemma here is that an excessive concern with the historical is likely to diminish the concentration on the plays. And in this regard the author manages to strike a balance in the ten chapters that make up this work. (p. 1)

While this book says a lot of the dramas and dramatic techniques of the period, not much is said about the theatrical techniques. There was not much of the latter that could be specifically called socio-political theatrical technique. But some outstanding ones must be mentioned.

Hubert Ogunde's Theatre was more production-bent than script-oriented. Perhaps as a way to survive hostile government reaction to scathing anti-government pieces, to avoid censorship and litigation which could only be proved when there is a script, Hubert Ogunde simply produced his plays–a mixture of dance, music, acrobatics and dialogue–instead of writing them. His theatrical method called for a lot of improvisation and dexterity from the performers. His was a performance-oriented theatre and what we have as his written "plays" are the synopses, scenarios and songs which appeared in the program notes that were give to the audience. Hubert Ogunde's Theatre could perform anywhere–village square, market place, city hall–and still have an audience.

In the turbulent socio-political period of the early 1960s, Wole Soyinka gave birth to a guerrilla form of staging and performance. Called the Guerrilla Theatre, performances took place on streets that were blocked off to motorists. The productions were sudden, improvised and pungent. Because of the guerrilla tactics of attacking corrupt, but powerful politicians, the theatre was always on the run. No performance was repeated for the same audience at the same spot, and a performance was hurriedly advertised only in the manner of an African town-crier some minutes before production. Since it was a street theatre–and in Nigeria people are always in the streets–audience was readily available to witness the event. The sketches of the Guerrilla Theatre are recorded for posterity in *Before the Blackout* (1965), though before this was *The New Republican* (1964). The sketches of the latter exist now mostly in the former. The Guerrilla Theatre was short-lived, but there has been a call for its revival. Florence Adetoun Oni, a former member of that theatre, has, since 1986, advocated a resurgence of the guerrilla form of theatre that will use Nigeria's indigenous languages (*Prime People*, Vol. 1, No. 16, September 1986). This will supposedly correct some of the mistakes of the Guerrilla Theatre whose effectiveness was attenuated by the crucial factor that the performances were in English before a street audience that mostly spoke a Nigerian indigenous language of Ife.

The Ahmadu Bello University Community Theatre unit has on-going activities often referred to as the Samaru Projects. The theatrical process here involves the cooperative efforts of the University theatre faculty and students on the one hand and the communities around the university on the other. The purpose is to help the communities solve some of their problems by first using theatre to elucidate these problems and their solutions. First is the period of information research in which the theatre faculty and students go into selected communities in Northern Nigeria to identify some pressing issue and problem in those communities. Interviews are conducted with the people who are affected by the problem. The problem is then analyzed. Play-making through improvisation using some people from the communities is carried out. This is to make the people feel that the unfolding theatrical event is theirs. Those who are not actively engaged in the production are involved in the discussion and evaluating that follow every rehearsal. Every member of the communities involved is encouraged to attend the final performance. This performance is followed by a discussion–a kind of people's parliament–in which they discuss and decide finally what concrete steps in actual life they must take to alleviate their particular problem. The theatrical event is theirs, the decision is theirs, but it remains for the University Community Theatre to pay them visits as a follow-up of the production to make sure that the people are actually implementing the decision they have arrived at to solve their problem. The first projects took off in 1980 though the theoretical framework was laid earlier.

Similar to the Samaru Projects is the Katsina-Ala Project organized by the Benue State Government Council for Arts and Culture, Makurdi. Begun in 1982, the Katsina-Ala Project tried to train theatre workers, social workers and students of the College of Education on how to use theatre for social development. It also sought to awaken the consciousness of the rural communities to their plight so that they could do something to improve their lot. The theatrical technique was similar to that of the Samaru Projects. It was a street theatre that provided entertainment in the indigenous language or pidgin about affairs relating directly to their prospective audiences. A small road that led to a square with private compounds around it was cut off to traffic; a tarpaulin was erected as a backdrop and the actors in the dust facing the setting sun to illuminate the "stage" performed to a semicircle of audience.

In Ibadan, Benin and later in Ife, Femi Osofisan began writing and producing using Brechtian technique. But his Brechtian technique is only so in name for Osofisan has imbued it with his own unique style of presentation in which socialist or Marxist ideology is modified in an entirely Nigerian and African tactile audience participation, music, dance, poetry, sparse props and sets, a Grotowskian interpretation of traditional mythology, a true "endlessness" as in *The Chattering and the Song* (1977) and a playwright's Marxist self-criticism as in the first version and production of *Eshu and the Vagabond Minstrels* at the University of Benin, 1985. The play was directed by me. The epilogue of this 1985 version of this latter play is a good material for students of dramatic theory and criticism, and could be put on the same classic pedestal as Aristophanes' *The Frogs* in this regard. *Eshu and the Vagabond Minstrels* was directed by the playwright at the University of Ife (now Obafemi Awolowo University) in 1986; it holds the record of the longest continuous 'running-production' in Nigerian theatre history.

In the theory and criticism of socio-political drama in Nigeria, there was abundant ground for antagonism as the critics, most of them playwrights, felt at ease in criticism and countercriticism. Alliances of criticism were no sooner formed than abandoned as accusations as to the fidelity or otherwise to newly erected or newly embraced canons of criticism were made. But is was a most impressive galaxy of critics and theorists: Biodun Jeyifo, Niyi Osundare, Femi Osofisan, Kole Omotoso, Chinweizu, G. G. Darah, O. Onoge, Molara Ogundipe-Leslie, Tunde Fatunde and Wole Soyinka. Soyinka's pate became oftentimes the whetstone for sharpening critical swords by the Ibadan-Ife Group but Soyinka had an impervious skull and dispersed his assailants when he drew his blazing sword. By constantly charging at each other the critics and playwrights kept themselves at their best in their vocation. Tar Ahura, Salihu Bappa and Oga Abah put into practice their theories of mass social transformation through drama in Northern Nigeria. While they were thus engaged I had begun my own projects on drama therapy through the auspices of CENSCER (Center for Social, Cultural and Environmental Research) of the University of Benin, and in a paper, "Beyond the Pleasure Principle: Drama for Social Rehabilitation" (CENSCER 1986), I strongly pointed out what new redemptive role theatre should play in Nigeria.

These theories and criticisms are treated in this book as they relate to the plays discussed but they belong in a much bigger, more detailed forthcoming work entitled "Continental African Theatre". This in no way reduces the importance and scope of the present work. Since my cultural upbringing sees self-praise and grandiose self-assessment as vain, it suffices for me to quote from what the Longman assessor says of *Socio-Political Theatre in Nigeria*:

> The book is rich in content, orderly in organization and extremely relevant because there is no single book on Nigerian Theatre which gives such a comprehensive overview of Nigerian drama of socio-political aspiration. It also provides an appendix which will be very endearing to students because it gives plot synopsis of very many plays and provides adequate biographical information on the playwrights. The language and style of presentation are also immediately accessible ....
> *Socio-Political Theatre in Nigeria* is capable of fulfilling the long felt need for a book which takes a comprehensive look at this area of our national [Nigerian] theatrical heritage. Academics and students alike will welcome it because it fills a vacuum which has remained embarrassingly unfilled for a long time. (pp. 3-4)

Much as O. A. Atinmo, editor for Longman Publishers (Nigeria), wanted to publish this book in 1988, I had to leave Nigeria partly because of the academic hostility and persecution perpetrated by the Ibrahim Babangida military administration. Under the smiling machiavellianism of Babangida, Jubril Aminu, the anti-academic Minister of Education, presided over the slaughtering of Ahmadu Bello University students, the harassment of student union leaders, the proscription of ASUU (Academic Staff Union of Universities) and the detention without trial of its leaders, and the installation of puppet vice-chancellors instead of those elected by the various senates to run the universities.

Mediocrity became a criterion for becoming head of an academic department, and fawning mediocres there were in great plenitude. For once the happy mediocre inherited the unhappy universities. The universities literally burned as one crisis followed another and the government responding by indefinitely closing one university after another. In the reign of academic terror that ensued, top academics and theatre practitioners fled the nation. M. J. C. Echeruo, Molara Ogundipe-Leslie, Biodun Jeyifo, Huma Ibrahim, Emmanuel Obiechina, Niyi Osundare, Isiodore Okpewho, Vincent Ike, Joel Adedeji, Femi Euba, Femi Osofisan, Rashida Abubakar and the peripatetic Nobel Laureate Wole Soyinka are in various degrees of domicile outside Nigeria at the moment of writing. An outstanding poet, philosopher, author and member of ANA (Association of Nigerian Authors), General Mamman Vatsa, wanted to turn things around in an allegedly planned military coup d'etat; General Babangida's administration, which itself came to power through a coup d'etat in 1985, summarily executed Mamman Vatsa. The times were so inauspicious, so "out of joint", that I could only talk in metaphors of foreign plays. I directed Athol Fugard's *Sizwe Bansi is Dead* to show that Nigeria was no much better than South Africa in terms of respect-disrespect of human lives, and just before I left the country in 1988, I directed Samuel Beckett's *Waiting for Godot* to indicate that a Godot needed an appearance to save Nigeria from imminent suicide. In a journal article on the production, Muyiwa Awodiya, now head of Theatre Arts, University of Benin, wrote:

> The production of *Waiting for Godot* ... at this time is very relevant to the Nigerian situation: prevalent unemployment, hunger, disease, homelessness, hostility, deprivation of liberty, social insecurity ...! The tramps in the play experience all these threats to man's survival to the extent that they need each other and the presence of Godot to confirm that they do exist. (*The Guardian*, Saturday, May 21, 1988, p. 14)

Here was my friend inadvertently publicly unveiling the veiled. I can now say, in retrospect, that I have always been socio-politically conscious. In my secondary education at Saint Paul's, Benin City, I was a senior prefect (a leadership position) and in my stint at the Catholic Major Seminary of Saints Peter and Paul, Ibadan, I was an elected Sports Secretary and Secretary-General of SRC (Students Representative Council). Then came my undergraduate career at the University of Ibadan. The 1975/76 academic year there was an eventful one for me. Not only did I participate as an actor in such productions as Wale Ogunyemi's *The Ijaiye War*, Eugene O'Neill's *The Emperor Jones* and Neville Nkoli's *Home to the River*, my political inclination erupted to involving in student unionism. I campaigned and got elected, for the Office of Sports Commissioner for Independence Hall. I became also a member of the Hall Executive Council, Hall Management Committee and the University Sports Council–great political and managerial responsibilities for an undergraduate that eventually earned me a Distinguished Service Award. I was also the Secretary-General of Etsako Students Union. During the campaigns for the Office of Sports Commissioner, I went so late to *The Ijaiye War* rehearsal (I had a major role–Reverend Adolphus Mann) that the director was furious at my excuse and asked me what theatre had to do with politics. I guess this book answers that question in some detail.

As a student politician, I was in a position of leadership, and in those turbulent years I did participate actively in some of the student riots against unpopular military government decrees and activities. My year as a producer and presenter of such radio programs as Meditation, Youth Scene, Book Review and Theatre-on-the-air in Ogun State Broadcasting Corporation, Abeokuta, and my engagement with the National Youth Service Corps brought me further into close acquaintance with social and political issues in Nigeria. Over all these looms my own experience as a Nigerian national who witnessed the civil war, military coups some dastardly some salvific, and the punishment of political opponents by those in power.

The discussion in this book then is that of one informed in both the theatre and the socio-political history of Nigeria. But the form the study takes now would have been impossible had it not been for the untiring help and inspiration of my academic friends and colleagues: Robert Findlay, Joel Adedeji, John Gronbeck-Tedesco, William Kuhlke, Dapo Adelugba, Jed Davis, Ron Willis and Muyiwa Awodiya—all professors of Theatre. Professors Findlay and Adedeji bore patiently my encroachment on their time and talent and undertook to write a foreword to this book from different perspectives at a very short notice from me. I have no apologies to them. I was their student at the Universities of Ibadan and Kansas and it is all their fault that they gave me a sublime education that now pushes me to write this book and forthcoming ones. But I am immensely grateful to them for I keep on learning from their immense worldly and academic experiences.

Robert Cobb, Professor of English, an Africanist and former Executive Vice-Chancellor of the University of Kansas, and his wife gave me and my wife an overwhelming support academically and materially. From June to October, 1990, the key to Prof. Cobb's office was in my possession as I used the comfort of his office and his library to revise portions of this book. His criticism of the work was gentle and thorough just as Mrs. Cobb's cooking was always refreshing, invigorating and exquisite.

The family of Prof. and Mrs. Tom Erb, my host family in Lawrence, gave me and my family the support conducive to the completion of this work. They always gave me the timely relaxation I needed, and my family always felt at home with them. Thanks to Mrs. Karen Erb's patient tutoring, I now can eat raw vegetables!

Paul and Michelle Rabbideau, the couple with computer wizardry, must be commended for their unique secretarial touch. They energetically did a perfect and taxing job without being Shylock; rather they became good smiling friends of mine willing to put in the changes I always made. For this, the book is much theirs as it is mine.

Nelly Ukpokodu gave that unique and invaluable response which only a wife can give. And thanks to Evar and Loy: their ill-timed disturbances often turned out to be healthful and restorative.

To all these people and to those I cannot point out individually for lack of space and time, I acknowledge my indebtedness. Let this work be a living proof of their assistance and let what escapes the banal in it be an honor to them and a mark of their ingenuity.

I. Peter Ukpokodu
Lawrence, Kansas
April, 1991

NIGERIA
AND
SOCIO-POLITICAL DRAMA

•1•

The use of English makes them [plays] transcend tribal boundaries and imbues them with a national character, for even though English is not Nigeria's mother tongue, it gives the nation and language a sense of unity and makes the dramas available for international consumption.

Because this research is an ambitious one in that it aims at transcending national scholarship in its treatment of Nigerian drama of socio-political concern, it becomes imperative to look at the word "Nigeria" and the phrase "Nigerian drama." The concern with both national and international dimensions is inherent in the dual nature of "Nigeria" itself as a land of its native inhabitants and as a child of British overseas adventures. It is not one of those countries that can boast of one people, nor is it one of those nations, like Israel, that can lay claims to its original nationhood through divine architecture.[1] Nigeria, as a nation, is the creation of Britain, and thus of man. But if man's creation cannot rival divine masonry in perfection, the house built by Britain is, nevertheless, a most imperfect one.

Nigeria was never a nation state in the usually accepted meaning of nation as a people who share a common ancestry, history, tradition, language and belief. Before Britain, Germany and France began their scramble for West Africa, the territory now known as Nigeria "contained not just a multiplicity of pagan tribes, but a number of great kingdoms that had evolved complex systems of government independent of contact with Europe."[2] As Michael Crowder clearly points out:

> Within its frontiers were the great kingdom of Bornu, with a known history of more than a thousand years; the Fulani Empire which for the hundred years before its conquest by Britain had ruled most of the savannah of Northern Nigeria; the kingdoms of Ife and Benin, which had produced art recognized amongst the most accomplished in the world; the Yoruba Empire of Oyo, which had once been the most powerful of the states of the Guinea Coast; the city states of the Niger Delta, which had grown in response to European demands for slaves and palm oil; as well as the loosely organized Ibo peoples of the Eastern region and the small tribes of the plateau.[3]

Although there were cultural and commercial connections between these peoples, such connections were not tight enough as to induce a homogeneous nation. Whatever occasional friendship existed between them was one of convenience and was often times sporadic. Not only were there wars and rivalries between these various kingdoms, there were civil wars within each kingdom. Especially with the growth of the lucrative trade in slaves in the southern kingdoms and the Jihad (Islamic Holy War) of Uthman dan Fodio in the north, belligerence became a powerful characteristic of pre-colonial Nigeria. Some of these kingdoms were so powerful that they challenged the British government even when Protectorates had been formed in Nigeria. For example, in the Eastern part of Nigeria, Britain had to lead military expeditions against the famous Arochuku oracle of the Iboland, not only because it encouraged slave trade which had been abolished but that it was also a rival to British authority. It was this group of fiercely independent warring kingdoms that Britain brought together to make Nigeria when Lord Lugard amalgamated the Southern and Northern Protectorates of Nigeria in 1914.

What is baffling in pre-colonial "Nigeria" is the fact that even those kingdoms that claimed the same descent were not united politically. The erstwhile Hausa states, for example, which have a legend of common origin, were not united until the opening years of the nineteenth century. And although the former Yoruba kingdoms have traditions of origin that attempt to explain their common language, political institutions and culture from a common descent, they were never united under a single political entity. They often fought against themselves and in this weakness the Benin empire to their East had a number of tributary Yoruba states. And while the policy of these kingdoms was one of conquest and expansion under a king, we learn from the *Nigeria Handbook, 1978-1979*, that:

> Other peoples such as the Nupe, Borgu ... also evolved large independent kingdoms in the course of their history, but among other peoples inhabiting the eastern and middle areas of Nigeria, the political system was quite different. These peoples, ... the Igbo, the Ijaw, etc., preferred to live in autonomous village communities ruled by elders and family heads. Among them, economic and socio-political institutions such as common markets, exogamous marriages and oracles were adopted which extended their range of association beyond their villages.[4]

With the amalgamation of north and south, the area occupied by all these different peoples became Nigeria. The territory achieved independence from Britain in 1960; when it became a Federal Republic in 1963, the birth of Nigeria was complete. Thus today, Nigeria has within its boundaries a "large number of tribal groups ranging in size from a few thousand to many million, speaking between them several hundred languages or dialects." There exists a bewildering "variety of customs, language and social organization." Although attempts have been made by some linguists and sociologists to classify the different tribal linguistic groups into wider cultural affiliations, some theorists have proved that "linguistic affiliation does not necessarily imply common descent, since contact between two very different groups can result in the assimilation of the linguistic system of one by the other."[5]

This brief excursion into the labyrinth of Nigeria is useful as a background to the limits I intend to set on the term "Nigerian drama." It leads one to an appreciation of the difficulty involved in trying to talk of a Nigerian drama. In a country with disparate peoples, cultural affiliations, linguistic groups, religious practices and vegetation, the single most important unifying "Nigerian" factor is the territory the people called Nigerians occupy. Thus "Nigerian drama," as used in the study, refers to any play written by anyone whose origin is from anywhere within the geographical boundaries of Nigeria and is a Nigerian citizen. And, at the risk of rousing the bitter curses of the Nigerian chauvinist, let me further limit "Nigerian drama" to that written in English.

There are myths of creation in Nigeria. Perhaps, the most notable is that which claims Ile-Ife, a city in the Oyo state of the Yoruba tribe of Nigeria, as the place where life began on earth. According to the myth, Olodumare, the Supreme Being, looked upon the earth he had created and saw that it was a mass of water. So he decided to do something about it. He sent his son, Oduduwa, down on a chain bringing with him a palm nut, a fowl and a handful of sand. Oduduwa went to work immediately. He poured the sand over the water, presumably still hanging on to the chain his father held for him, and the fowl was let loose to scatter it with its claws over the water. The scattered sand became land. The palm nut was thrown on the land and it grew to a palm tree with sixteen branches.[6] After that Olodumare decided to create man.

Some people have interpreted the sixteen branches of the palm tree as representative of the people who grew from one stock to spread to other parts of Nigeria. In Nigeria, traditional numbers are not tied down to strict rules. Sixteen could be an exact number or it could be a metaphor for many people that came to be at the beginning of God's creative activities. Whatever interpretation one gives the number is not as interesting to me as the possibility that this creation story could very well stand for the Tower of Babel from which grew the myriad of tongues and lingual unintelligibility that is characteristic of Nigeria.

Nigeria is no melting pot—at least of languages and dialects. For political reasons, it has been impossible to adopt one of the many Nigerian languages as an official Nigerian indigenous language. But what I suppose is the fundamental barrier to adopting a Nigerian language in official matters is the inability of getting one that is understood throughout the country. Nigerians have, therefore, found it easier to operate in the language of their colonial master than in their own indigenous languages, especially if they are matters that have to do with the whole country.

Yet, even the use of English in Nigeria has a limitation. Although it is spoken throughout the country, it is not a language spoken by everyone. Its use is restricted to those who have gone through formal Western education. An adulteration of English called "pidgin" has become more popular. There is no formal education in pidgin; it is simply the language of business or commerce and is understood and applied alike by those who have and those who have no formal education.

The importance of English in a definition of Nigerian drama can be seen by illustrating with two of Nigerian playwrights—Wole Soyinka and John Pepper Clark. Concerning Wole Soyinka, Oyin Ogunba points out that:

> Soyinka's literary playground is essentially the Yoruba culture of Western Nigeria, his own indigenous culture. There he feels at home to choose his situations and characters not only among fellow human beings in a contemporary context, but also among gods, spirits and demons as well as dead ancestors, illustrious and otherwise.[7]

One of Soyinka's plays deeply imbued with Yoruba culture is *Death and the King's Horseman*.[8] It is a strange ritual play in which "the dramaturgical accent ... is ... on the all-pervading personality of Iku, Death itself, celebrated like a primordial deity. It is ... on the seemingly immutable tribal ethos of traditional Yorubaland."[9] And in an Author's Note, Soyinka himself explains that:

The confrontation in the play is largely metaphysical, contained in
the human vehicle which is Elesin and the universe of the Yoruba
mind—the world of the living, the dead and the unborn, and the
numinous passage which links all: transition ... [The play] can be
fully realized only through an evocation of music from the abyss of
transition.[10]

Let us look at the Yoruba world view on death that
Soyinka applies within the artistic limits of the play.
     When an Oba (King) dies, as he does in *Death and the
King's Horseman*, special funeral ceremonies are
performed. To announce his death, an attempt is made to
alter the appearance of things: big, well-known, vital trees
are cut down or trimmed, market days are cancelled,
festivities are rescheduled. The rationale behind this is to
indicate that the leader of the people is gone and that things
must go topsy-turvy in a world without a leader. It is said
that the Oba's corpse is not buried in one place; it is
dismembered for burial in different places, for he is more
than an ordinary man. And, most appalling to contemporary
sensibility, the heart of the Oba is preserved and given to the
succeeding ruler to eat. Says J. O. Awolalu:

It is illuminating that, according to Yoruba belief as among several
other nations, royalty never dies; and the way in which this is
symbolized among the Yoruba is to give the heart of the deceased
king to the succeeding one to eat; the genius of kingship thus
continues.[11]

Days of rituals accompany such death.
     Other important events mark Yoruba funeral ceremony
in general. Of these, the Egungun is of vital importance, and
Soyinka does not hesitate to make use of it in the play.
Sango, now deified as the god of thunder and of lightning,
is usually credited with the formation of the Egungun, a
form of ancestral worship in which a deceased head of a
lineage is evoked to make a temporary reappearance in the
world in a costumed figure.
     According to J. A. Adedeji, Sango had tried in vain to
secure the remains of his father, Oranyan, the founder of

Oyo, for burial there after the latter had died at Ife. He was told that the body of his father was not available because it had undergone an inexplicable change of form and had disappeared. The undaunted Sango decided, as an alternative to normal burial ceremonies, to design new obsequies for his father. Through a special ceremony, he is said to have brought the reincarnated spirit of his father to the outskirts of Oyo. There he set up a mausoleum for his worship, and appointed a keeper whose duty it was to bring forth Oranyan's spirit as a masquerade through an invocation. This ceremony was later enlarged and formalized as a common and permanent feature of the Yoruba funeral ceremony in the form of the Egungun society with a hierarchy of officers and priests.[12]

It is believed that a living person who puts on the Egungun costume also carries the spiritual powers of the ancestor whom he represents. When he wears the costume, he is regarded as a creature from the abode of the gods and of departed spirits, an "ara orun," a "citizen of heaven." So the costumed figure is treated with great respect and men who meet it must remove their caps and pay homage to it. Women are banned from coming near it, except the initiated few who have entered their menopause.[13]

But at the core of Soyinka's play is ritual death. Variously called in the play as "ritual murder," "ritual suicide," and "to commit death" or "die the death of death," ritual death and its associate, human sacrifice, were the highest form of offering in the Yoruba tribe. It has been explained away that ritual death was not carried out from mere sadistic pleasure and devaluation of man's life: it was conceived that man himself was the greatest sacrifice a community could offer to the gods to achieve anything from them. There was a pervading principle that it was better for one man to die than that a whole people perish. The suffering and death of the victim brought new life to the community.[14]

Though some ritual deaths were violent, the death of Elesin in *Death and the King's Horseman* was to be peaceful and graceful. It was to be executed through his own psychic power when the moon and the secret cult responsible for the affair announced the time. By such corporeal death brought in through metaphysical means, he would accompany the dead king to the ancestral world. However, through his own mental weakness and the intervention of the District Officer, Elesin fails in this duty. This brings far-reaching consequences.

A second example is from another Nigerian playwright, J. P. Clark, who belongs to the Ijaw tribe of the Delta area of Nigeria and whose plays are based on the riverine culture of this tribe. His play, *Ozidi*, for example, "is based on the Ijaw native epic drama of Ozidi, performed in seven nights to dance, music, mime, and ritual."[15] As he points out in *The Ozidi Saga*:

> There is no fixed text to the work. All that each teller of the story has is the plot ... which he proceeds to give body and full expression ... by his reconstruction of a dramatic narrative that is the public property of an audience very much aware of its proprietary rights ... The audience, in full possession of the facts, participates in the act, constantly cheering or jeering as at a concert recital of popular pieces that have become part of the cultural consciousness of the public. The queries and questions punctuating the performance are mostly from the young in the audience, while corrections and modifications of forms and facts come from among the adult members who know the score inside out and maintain accordingly a constant watch over it, citing tradition to back up their interventions.[16]

As an epic, *The Ozidi Saga* covers many areas of the traditional life of the Ijaw people. Myth, beliefs, religious practices, philosophy and art are covered in its scope. For example, there are many songs in the epic which are organic to the piece; yet others are mere pieces for war and wrestling. What begins as a family vengeance against its enemies achieves a greater dimension of ridding a city or a state of its adversaries, celebrating and enacting traditional beliefs in witchcraft, sorcery, the military power of the tribe in the past and the eradication of sickness and diseases. But amidst this entirely secular dramatic nature is the infusion of religious aspects:

> The production of the Ozidi drama ... begins each day with a round up of seven virgin girls, as special sacrificial offerings are gathered at the compound of the story-teller-protagonist. This sets at once the religious tone of the drama and story. After worshipping before his household and personal gods, the story-teller-protagonist, supported by ... the town-owner, and other leading citizens, leads a solemn song procession of the seven virgins to the stream ... There sacrifice is offered in homage to spirits of the water without whose help the enterprise on land cannot prosper. It is well to note here that the prayer is not for art alone but also for life so that the people may have their own fair share of women, children and money apparently flowing to enrich life elsewhere and without which there can be no real enjoyment of art anywhere. The worship over, the party returns, in a recession dance to the square at a brisk pace of song and dance.[17]

What is most interesting is that this religious approach does not distract the performers from its essential dramatic ingredient which is the universal theme of a son avenging the unlawful death of his father:

> In the epic proper, the worthiness and sanctity of the hero's mission clearly is self-evident in that he has to find ultimate rest for his father murdered by treacherous colleagues ... Such a violent unhappy death, the Ijo believe, deprives a dead man of the privilege of joining his ancestors. If he has heirs with any sense of honor, these certainly will ask the community for an inquest which usually takes the form of warlike preparations, followed by restitution and rites of purification. Only when these motions have been gone through, an expensive process, can the dead be deemed properly buried.[18]

I have used extended examples from these two playwrights who have gained both national and international recognition to point out the difficulty involved in trying to understand their works. Both are Nigerians yet they use only the cultural backgrounds familiar to them and their tribes. Moreover, the factual accounts from which they

draw materials for the plays cited in these examples already
exist in traditional forms. Wole Soyinka's *Death and the
King's Horseman* exists in a way in Duro Ladipo's *Oba
Waja* while J. P. Clark's *Ozidi* is a miniature of the original
native Ijo epic drama of Ozidi. The importance of this
comparison is that *Oba Waja* and the Ijo original of Ozidi are
fine dramas, yet they remain local, unknown and
inaccessible to other parts of Nigeria because they are written
or performed in their particular ethnic and cultural languages
only; they cannot be understood to speakers of other
Nigerian languages. On the other hand, *Death and the
King's Horse-man* and *Ozidi* are readily available and
known to other communities because they are written in
English which, though not the mother tongue, is the official
language of Nigeria. Whereas *Oba Waja* and the Ijo original
of Ozidi, cannot be read, understood and performed outside
their cultural birthland, *Ozidi* and *Death and the King's
Horseman* can be read and produced in any part of Nigeria.

Thus plays written in English carry a more national
outlook in the sense that the audiences they draw are spread
throughout the country whereas plays written in one of the
Nigerian indigenous languages are limited to the ethnic
group that speaks the language. Aware of the national and
international scope of their writings, some of the playwrights
who write in English have gone further than writing plays.
They have evolved some means of explaining the difficult-
to-understand cultural backgrounds of their plays to their
large national and international audiences. Wole Soyinka,
for example, has written, among other theories, "The Fourth
Stage," which attempts to explain the origin of Yoruba
tragedy through the mysteries of Ogun, "God of creativity,
guardian of the road, god of the metallic lore and artistry.
Explorer, hunter, god of war, Custodian of the sacred oath,"
and draws comparative and contrastive examples with
Greek, Christian and Buddhist cultures and Nietzsche.[19]   J.
P. Clark does a similar thing in *The Ozidi Saga*, a book that
explains the dramatic and cultural background of the Ozidi
play. English makes these works available to every Nigerian
who can read and redeems them from ethnic closure. The

use of English makes them transcend tribal boundaries and imbues them with a national character, for even though English is not Nigeria's mother tongue, it gives the nation and language a sense of unity and makes the dramas available for international consumption. English becomes, then, an important definitive aspect of Nigerian drama.

Two great historical events have affected Nigerian drama, and their overpowering influence has tended to make them essential parts of the definition of Nigerian drama. These two events—Negritude and Independence—are so important to the shaping of Nigerian artistic endeavors that they cannot be overlooked in a study of this nature. Negritude and Independence led to cultural dramas that overshadowed those of socio-political concern. There are still some people who would equate Nigerian drama with Nigerian cultural display today.

Coined by Aimé Césaire, a West Indian poet from the island of Martinique, "Negritude" has over the years, accumulated so many meanings and ideas that it has come to mean almost all things to all men.[20] Its hallmark nevertheless remains the same—it was a reaction by the blacks in Africa and the West Indies to European colonialism, especially that of France. Its British equivalent was that of "African personality," but Negritude was so powerful that it became more popular and eventually even the meaning of African personality fell under its canopy. Revivalist forms of Negritude are even current today, one of the most recent being that of "African Authenticity" in which the propounder and adherent, the President of the Congo, changed his name from Joseph Mobutu to Mobutu Sesse Sekou, and that of his country from Congo to Zaire.

Negritude was, in its origin, a reaction to "evolué" or "assimilation," as a governing principle of French colonialism in Africa and the black world. Assimilation was a principle superficially attractive but with devastating consequences. It aimed at making Frenchmen out of black Africans. Its proclamation was that black Africans could achieve any social and political status in France if they "assimilated" French culture. This Frenchification of blacks meant a mental, and to those who went to Paris, an environmental change. It meant that for the Africans to enter the French modus vivendi, they must forsake their indigenous socio-cultural values. But even if they succeeded in evolving to Frenchmen and reached the promised land, the blacks, as Professor Egudu points out, did not taste of the promised milk and honey:

> That these Africans assimilated French culture is a certainty, but whether they gained equal social status and recognition with Frenchmen is a different matter. Assimilation was not aimed at elevating the African but at devaluing his culture, and that was why it was thought necessary to strip him of his true cultural self and put on him a foreign one which he was later to revolt against. The contemptuous attitude of the French toward the African and his world was vindicated by their discrimination between 'metropolitan France'—the original, undefiled France—and 'France Overseas' which was there only for economic purposes. Thus there was cultural and economic domination behind assimilation. There could not be 'equality' for the African while his humanity and culture were not recognized and the process of Frenchification went on. Furthermore, the principle of equality in political, social and economic spheres was not practicalized, since there were 'contradictions' here and there.[21]

If the French rape of Africa was mainly that of culture and economy, that of the West Indies included the rape of history. The slave trade which originally wrenched the blacks in the West Indies from Africa denied them family life, thus preventing as much as possible, a cultural and historical continuity. Even after general manumission of slaves and the total abolition of slave trade, French "evolué" policy prevented common black culture, language, and an unbiased educational system. The black West Indians notably in Haiti, Martinique, Trinidad and Tobago, looked to France for a pattern of life. "To Africa, to their past, even to their skin color, they were made to look in shame and discomfort," and until recently, "African tribesmen on the screen excited derisive West Indian laughter."[22]

Reaction to this attitude gave birth to the movement called Negritude. According to Aimé Césaire, the originator and first user of the term, "Negritude is the simple recognition of the fact of being black, and the acceptance of this fact, of our destiny as black people, of our history, and of our culture."[23] But what began as the reaction of only French-speaking countries in the black world soon took on a Pan-African (and later Pan-Negro) attitude to history and culture in the hands of Leopold Sedar Senghor, the poet and President of the West African country of Senegal. He became its most vocal adherent and exponent and he gave the term wider dimensions and definitions, ranging from a somewhat indiscriminatory eulogy of black culture in his poems to high intellectuality in his observations.

Abiola Irele explains that Senghor's intellectual effort is aimed at showing the "human value and significance of traditional African values" as well as establishing the appropriateness of these values to the modern African context and to contemporary man. He points out that Senghor does not call for a "simple return to outmoded customs and institutions ... but rather to an original spirit which gave meaning to the life of the individual in traditional African society."[24]

Whether Senghor called for embracing an "outmoded" culture—for which he has been criticized heavily—or not, the point is that Negritude did awake in Africa a eulogy of the past and a nostalgic glorification of the African culture. Its impact was felt in the whole of Africa. And Nigeria was in the cultural grip of Negritude when it attained independence from Britain in 1960. The impact of the two factors—Independence and Negritude—on drama was enormous; Negritude simply added energy to the euphoria that accompanied Independence to favor drama that luxuriated in cultural display. For Nigeria has a variety of culture almost equivalent to its many languages. There exists abundant material for any culture-oriented playwright, and this was what most playwrights seized upon.

What is noteworthy is that even in the midst of this euphoria, when culture was all that was in the thought of most dramatists, there were echoes, though faint, of social and political concern in some works. Some of these echoes were stifled to obscurity by the predominant cultural sounds but a few gained intensity and grew to disturbing noises. Within a decade of independence the socio-political concern of Nigerian drama had shown that it was a force to be reckoned with. By then the civil war had come and gone and a notable playwright had been imprisoned for his political activity. Perhaps it is too early to ask whether drama can actually bring forth social and political changes, and whether it has ever brought such changes. It is difficult to cite any particular drama that did make such changes in the socio-political spheres of a nation. But dramatists have been involved personally in trying to shape the political and social destiny of nations.   Wole Soyinka, Nigeria's leading playwright, is one of these.

His first noteworthy political involvement outside the campus of the University was in 1965 when he is said to have gone to the radio station of Western Nigeria Broadcasting Service and seized the recorded speech of the Premier of that region. The recorded speech was that of election victory, and it was Soyinka's belief that the balloting was not fair. After seizing the tapes, Soyinka is said to have broadcast his own message to the people, calling for a condemnation of the elections and encouraging the populace to demand fair and just elections.[25] Then in 1967, he got himself involved directly in the politics of the Civil War and was arrested. He himself talks of his activities that led to his arrest:

> My arrest and my framing were two entirely different affairs. The one was prompted by the following activities: my denunciation of the war in the Nigerian papers, my visit to the East [the secessionist region of Nigeria], my attempt to recruit the country's intellectuals within and outside the country for a pressure group which would work for a total ban on the supply of arms to all parts of Nigeria; creating a third force which would utilize the ensuing military stalemate to repudiate and end both the secession of Biafra, and the genocide-consolidated dictatorship of the Army which made both secession and war inevitable.

I was framed for my activities in gaol. I was framed and nearly successfully liquidated because of my activities inside prison. From Kiri-kiri [Nigeria's maximum security prison], I wrote and smuggled out a letter setting out the latest proof of the genocidal policies of the government of Gowon. It was betrayed to the guilty men; they sought to compound their treason by a murderous conspiracy.[26]

What we see then is that in spite of an overwhelming cultural fervor generated by Negritude and Independence, signs of a strong socio-political drama, even if pursued only by a few dramatists in its beginning, had begun to emerge. Three decades after Independence, Nigeria seems in a position to boast of the most lively, forceful and critical socio-political drama in Africa. The survival of this form of drama seems assured by the emergence of young playwrights like Bode Sowande, Femi Osofisan, Kole Omotoso, Ola Rotimi, O. O. Amali, Tunde Fatunde, Tess Onwueme, Akanji Nasiru, Sonny Oti, Zulu Sofola and Atiboroko Uyovbukerhi.

THE
STATE OF AFFAIRS
BEFORE
INDEPENDENCE

•2•

The king did not release these "ghost actors;" he kept them in his palace to entertain him and he surprised his councillors when during a banquet he called in the "ghosts" to wait upon their creators, the members of the King's Council.

Joel A. Adedeji

For lack of written accounts, it cannot be ascertained when socio-political drama began in Nigeria. Perhaps the first documented evidence of what could be called socio-political drama occurred in the Yorubaland towards the end of the sixteenth century. The erstwhile powerful Oyo Empire had been over-run by the Nupe warriors from the North and the rulers of Oyo had sought safety in exile. Later, events had begun to turn in their favor, and with the sudden abandonment of the anti-Oyo belligerence by the Nupes,[1] Abipa, the last of the Oyo kings in exile, decided in about 1590 to return his people to the ancient capital. This attempt to return to Oyo Ile met a chilly and unfavorable, almost hostile, response from Abipa's subjects, and especially, from the nobles in the King's Council. Most of these people had been born in exile and had come to accept their capital in exile, Igboho, as a home. Even those who had been involved in the early wanderings and wars felt reluctant to move to their original home. Their exile home had given them the firm security they wanted and they were "unwilling to abandon their farms and houses."[2] But the king was adamant and the members of the King's Council decided to use "the element of disguise as a stratagem to foil the attempted move."[3] J. A. Adedeji writes that the Alapini was "the brain behind the dramatic strategy."

> At his initiative, the Oyo-Mesi [the King's Council] planned to stop the King's move. They knew that, as was customary, the king would send emissaries to inspect the abandoned sites, propitiate the gods, and make sacrifices before the final move-in took place. As they were resolved on thwarting the King's will, they thought the move could be stopped by frightening the emissaries off the old sites by a company of ghost-mummers. They got masked actors (or ghost-mummers) ready and secretly despatched them to Old Oyo to precede the King's emissaries.[4]

These masked actors performed the roles of six stock-characters—the hunchback, the dwarf, the albino, the cripple, the leper and the prognathus—all unfortunate, handicapped characters referred to as 'people of the gods' because they are said to have been created by the Yoruba arch-divinity, Obatala or Orisanla, when he was drunk.[5] When the royal messengers arrived at the site of the former palace that had been razed to the ground when the capital was sacked, they purified themselves in preparation to offer sacrifices to their gods and ancestors, as they had been instructed. But no sooner had they put down things to begin the offerings than "these odd creatures [appeared and] roamed all night over the nearby Ajaka hill with torches in their hands, hooting and shrieking 'ko si aiye, ko si aiye' ('no room, no room'). The terrified messengers hastened back to tell the Alafin [King] of their adventure."[6]

Someone soon betrayed the councillors' strategy to the much depressed king. The latter sent brave and powerful hunters to the site to investigate the report about the ghosts and to capture them if they were really masked human beings. The "bogus phantoms" were soon rounded up, earning the king the title "Oba M'oro", "the king who caught ghosts."[7] The king did not release these "ghost actors;" he kept them in his palace to entertain him and he surprised his councillors when during a banquet he called in the "ghosts" to wait upon their creators, the members of the King's Council.[8]

This story, which is still re-enacted during the installation ceremony of a new king in Oyo, and which has been used as a plot in a folk opera by Duro Ladipo, seems the earliest historically dated evidence of socio-political drama in Nigeria. Here, in the use of costumed figures and stock-characters to act as ghosts to frighten away the King's emissaries and, therefore, to influence an important political decision, drama is employed as a political weapon to fight against an unpopular government decision. In his position as 'God's Deputy' or 'second (in command) to the gods,' the King carried both secular and religious powers and could not be effectively resisted by ordinary, secular, revolutionary means. He could not be disobeyed. Therefore, the only real effective opposition would have to come from the supernatural world of gods and spirits to whom he is a representative—hence the dramatic use of "ghosts" to alter his decision. For if the area he wanted to move to has been inhabited by supernatural beings, he cannot take his people there for man cannot exist on the same plane as supernatural beings. The "ghosts" had cried "no room, no room" for human habitation there and if he had violated their warning he and his people would have headed for an ignominious downfall. It was a master plan, then, that the Councillors hatched; but for its betrayal it would have been a successful use of dramatic means to alter the unique political decision of a king in power.

That the drama of the "Ghost Catcher"[10] is the first historically recorded illustration of drama with socio-political concern does not mean that it is the first of that type. There are others which existed in pre-colonial Nigeria like the "Efa" of Uzairue in the Edo language group of Bendel State and the "Ozidi" epic drama of the Ijaw tribe of the Niger Delta. The Efa has no record of its beginning, but it is still used today as a form of social correction and of political advice to the ruler of the Uzairue clan. Of the Ozidi, recent scholarship permits us to say something more. But whether they are earlier or more recent than the "Ghost Catcher" cannot be ascertained.

The Ijo epic drama of Ozidi, says J. P. Clark, is "told and acted in seven nights to dance, music, mime and ritual. The age of this work itself is unknown, but this seems immaterial, for where there are no written chronicles time becomes meaningless..."[11] Though the drama contains a lot of cultural elements like the belief in witchcraft and sorcery, supernatural forces and the use of rituals, masquerades, trance and wrestling, these are not what gives the drama its organic unity. They are more meaningful when seen in the political context of the play which essentially is that of disruption of the unity of a state and the vengeful attempt to bring back justice, order and unity. According to J. P. Clark, the play, *Ozidi*,

> ... begins with the treason and treachery committed by a group of warlords in the city-state of Orua against the brothers Temugedege, who is king, and Ozidi, the leading general of the state. The rest of the epic tells of the posthumous birth of the general's son, the extra-ordinary manner of his growing up under the magic wings of his grandmother Oreame, and of the numerous battles the hero does with all manner of men and monsters to regain for his family its lost lineal glory. In this process, he oversteps the natural bounds set to his quest, and it is not until he has received divine visitation from the small-pox king that he emerges purged and is received back into the society of men.[12]

Furthermore, Clark sees Ozidi as "a supreme warrior who had to perform a number of seemingly impossible feats to reach a destined end"—the reestablishment of the rightful authority and of bringing the people together again, although this mission is colored by "a personal sense of wrong, the settlement of which determines the future course of public affairs in a powerful state."[13] Here we see an undertaking that is at one and the same time personal and public, as in *Hamlet*, in which the avenger's killing of the usurper king is both a duty to a murdered father and a "purge" of the elements that have made "the time out of joint." In fact, Clark sees Ozidi as "a straight instrument of justice," and his grandmother, Oreame, as a woman of supernatural powers who performs the role of fate and a goading conscience to him.[14]

The socio-political connotation of *Ozidi* is reinforced on the seventh and closing night of the performance. The drama ends with joyful song that celebrates "Oh new town..!"[15] —a firm reminder that the drama is about the restoration of peace and the reunification of the town ("town" in the wider connotation of "city-state") after treason and warfare had occurred, and not really about one individual, Ozidi, although he, more than anyone else, brought about the peace and unity. Though the story of Ozidi has a tragic tone, its performance usually ends with a glorification of the past, the remembrance of those days when the Orua clan, or by extension, the Ijaw tribe, dominated other city-states and demanded tributes from them. The song that ends the performance imbues them with that sense of unity which allowed them to accomplish such feats and makes them proud that in spite of some rancor that might exist, they are still a united political entity.

These examples—the Ghost Catcher, Efa and Ozidi— show that socio-political dramas existed in pre-colonial Nigeria. Although only one of them can be historically dated, we do know that they existed before the onset of British colonization of Nigeria. They existed in the traditional form of Nigerian drama which is a fusion of many elements—dance, song, music, mask, masquerade, mime, and ritual, performed wherever there is space, usually a village square, and not necessarily tied to words and formal theatre architecture. With the arrival of Britain and the introduction of western form of drama and concert, a new approach to drama began to be adopted in Nigeria. If drama, even in its traditional, mostly non-verbal, form could be tied to social and political affairs, the western form of drama that Western missionaries and Britain brought to Nigeria was bound to be used by Nigerians in the politics of colonialism. In the forefront of this was Hubert Ogunde, often referred to as a "father figure" and as "the grand old man of Nigerian theatre."[16] In his hands, drama became a megaphone for decrying British colonialism and social injustice and a weapon for a peaceful nationalist struggle. A detailed treatment of Hubert Ogunde becomes necessary since he is the true precursor of the socio-political dramas that exist today in Nigeria.

The background to Ogunde's socio-political dramas is found in the beginnings of Nigerian cultural nationalism. At the beginning of the twentieth century, educated Nigerians had begun to disengage themselves from dependence on European firms established in Lagos, Nigeria, and those professionally qualified, especially in the medical sciences, had begun independent practices rather than accept discrimination in the civil service of the colonial administration. When racial discrimination reared its head in the church also, fierce anti-missionary attacks were directed at the church rather than at the British administration.

According to E. A. Ayandele, "the educated Africans saw the white man's 'invasion' of Nigeria in the spectacles of missionary enterprise. British rule and the economic exploitation of the country were not seen as isolated events, but as the effects of missionary activity."[17] Africans saw the relationship between Christian missionary enterprise and European colonialism and civilization as that of cause to effect, root to branch. Therefore, because missionary activities "aimed at uprooting Nigerian customs and institutions, they were believed to have imperialist motives ... to render Africans a prey to the exploitation of traders and the unpleasant aspects of the political domination of the administrators."[18]

In some instances, both the missionaries and their converts carried their practices to the point of absurdity. It was the belief by most of the missionaries that a genuine convert to Christianity must wear Western dresses, drink tea and adopt European names and manners. "For adoption of European culture was an outward sign of the inward transformation from the 'pagan' to the Christian state."[19] Indeed, Adolphus Mann, one of the early missionaries, is reported to have been so indignant at the idea of renouncing European names for African names at baptism that he considered anyone who had such an idea and practiced it as "guilty of 'Anglophobia' and Anti-English 'monomania.'"[20]

But the converts even exceeded missionary expectations as they nursed contempt for their vernacular and became disrespectful to their 'pagan' parents.   They deluded themselves with the idea that the less African they became the more Christian they were.   "Instances were not wanting of converts educated in England who on coming back to Nigeria pretended that they did not understand the vernacular,   and   when   spoken   to,   spoke   through interpreters." To them England became the 'mother country' and 'home' and "it was a difficult task ... to persuade an educated African that he was not a European." It is said that even by 1887, "anglicized Africans lamented that Nigerians were not eating with their wives" while some called West African Christianity "a sham because converts were not going out for a walk with their wives."[21]

At the turn of the century, that is after 1895, this attitude had begun to change.   Educated Nigerians began to take pride in African customs and institutions.   This pride ushered in new ways of "Independent thinking which made them assess and criticize more strongly than before missionary enterprise, British administration and the trading pattern of the country."[22] This attitude was revolutionary and the reasons for it are not far-fetched.

Educated Africans were disappointed at not being accepted into the European community in Nigeria on the basis of equality. This experience was contradictory to the hope that had been stirred in them by missionary preaching of a cosmic fraternity and human equality before God. Though they had acquired British degrees and labor experience, the Africans found themselves placed under less qualified Europeans. They also discovered that they were paid less than the Europeans with whom they did the same work. They were also excluded from conditions of service, such as gratuities, promotions and retirements.   Racial separatism began to infest social institutions such as hospitals, churches, and transportation. Relations between Africans and Europeans underwent such a deterioration that in 1907 Egerton, the Governor of Southern Nigeria, implored all officials to treat their "African subordinates in a humane manner," although a year later, he himself expropriated the land and property of about two thousand native inhabitants for official European residences and "announced that henceforward 'native' buildings must not be near to European quarters."[23]

Ayandele further points out the dilemma of the educated African and the irony of the entire situation in which he found himself. The educated African's attempt to imitate the Europeans did not flatter the latter; rather it made him their "laughing stock." To these colonial administrators and missionaries, the educated African had become a ridiculous imitator who in attempting to be what he could not "also lost the virtuous characteristics of the uncontaminated tribesman" and had been turned into "an unrecognizable human being." Not only could he not find a firm footing in the world of his European master but even the missionaries had failed to provide him with "membership in a group with clear moral standards and obligations." He found himself also isolated from "the moral and social solidarity of the tribal life." He lacked "corporate feeling." There was a pathetic realization that the "Europeanized African" had become a "tertium quid" between the true tribal African and the European and was "a geographical, a physiological and a psychological monstrosity, ... like pictures in a phantasmagoria."[24]

Moreover, as the African Church shows in a report of its proceedings at this time, European secularity and religiosity had become intertwined. Christianity was to suffer from this union, since the African now failed to distinguish between the two. The report shows that European Christianity had devolved towards emptiness and "delusive fiction," a "dangerous thing" that debauched the African with intoxicants and promoted immoral and pharisaic attitudes. It was a "religion which points with one hand to the skies, bidding you 'lay up for yourselves treasures in heaven,' and while you are looking up grasps all your worldly goods with the other hand, seizes your ancestral lands, labels your forests, and places your patrimony under inexplicable legislation."[25]

All these experiences and feelings led to cultural nationalism. As a movement in opposition to the culture and behavior of the ruling masters, cultural nationalism became political. Indeed, as James S. Coleman points out, cultural and political nationalisms are "two aspects of a single phenomenon."[26] The educated African assumed leadership in this opposition, becoming the spokesman for all Nigerians. Hubert Ogunde was one such leader, and, though of limited education, he was to make his impact on the Nigerian political scene through drama, having begun participation in some dramatic activities at the early age of eight. After his education he became a teacher and an organist in a Protestant Church. He was involved in pious, religious dramas at first, but with maturity and awareness of the political situation—he was a policeman for a short period—he directed his energy towards nationalist sentiments, in his plays.

In Nigeria, the period of intense political activities against British rule could be said to have begun in 1944 when various organizations decided to form a National Front to demand Independence. It was also the beginning of the intense anti-colonial, political dramas of Hubert Ogunde. As Ebun Clark brings to our awareness, there was, during this period, "a remarkably great interest in the existence and survival of the theatre as a channel providing political as well as cultural education for the masses."[27] Not only was the theatre considered an instrument capable of fostering "the theory and practice of association between citizens,"[28] it was seen as a powerful institution that needed the encouragement and patronage of the people. Says an editorial of one of the nationalist papers:

> There is no reason why the theatre should not have a future despite the invasion of Hollywood and Elstree films, which are often vehicles for expressing a foreign way of life and brandishing that same way to us neglected colonials. If we are to be independent, and eventually we shall, it is essential that we should preserve our

national identity. The Nigerian theatre is one way of developing that personality.[29]

More than any other theatre of this period, Ogunde's was closely allied to the political situation. Ogunde's dramas, some of which were in the form of opera, were often controversial because of his frequent attacks on the colonial government. These embarrassed the government and made Ogunde and his theatre targets of official harassment. From a total of about nineteen plays written by Ogunde during this period (1945-1950), thirteen are politically influenced, although only six are overtly political. These overtly political plays—the same could be said of all his plays—cannot be critically examined here because they were never published and made available to the public. They were simply created for his theatre. Much of the information we have about them comes from the newspapers of the period and, especially, from what Ogunde himself made available to Ebun Clark, who has studied the Ogunde theatre extensively. The six undisguised political plays were aimed at demanding that freedom be granted unconditionally or at exposing what Ogunde considered to be evil or inhuman in the colonial administration of Nigeria. The plays are *Worse than Crime* (1945), *Strike and Hunger* (1945), *Tiger's Empire* (1946), *Herbert Macaulay* (1946), *Towards Liberty* (1947), and *Bread and Bullet* (1950). Then upon the attainment of independence, he wrote the *Song of Unity* (1960) and *Yoruba Ronu* (1964).

The play, *Worse than Crime*, is usually considered Ogunde's first real political play. It is a dramatization of the slave trade as it occurred between Europe and Africa. While it is silent about the African who in the first instance sold the fellow African to the Europeans, it depicts how black Africans were forcibly removed from their native land by the Europeans to a foreign land where they did all the slavish jobs. But the play also gives credit to the European slaver who eventually realized the inhumanity involved in both slave trade and slavery and declared both abolished and illegal. The greatest blessing of the abolition of slave trade was the total liberation of erstwhile slaves; these returned to their native lands—that is, those who could still remember where they were uprooted from—and brought back and taught to their people at home the new ways of life, especially Christianity, that they had learned while in slavery. Though the play focuses on slavery, its political meaning was deeper than concern with the mere historical slave trade. It was a declaration that colonialism was a form of slavery, and that whatever form or shape it took, it was "worse than crime." The meaning was clear to the British administrators of Nigeria and the police were quick in putting Ogunde and another member of his theatre into custody for two days.

Written in the same year as *Worse than Crime* is *Strike and Hunger*. An authoritarian foreign king, Yejide, comes from the seas, spreading conquest and displacing the native ruler. After successfully subduing all resistance, he places the local inhabitants under a most severe rule. There is scarcity of work and anyone who wants to survive in a bare existence must work for the king. While there is unheard of starvation,

> Yejide [the foreign ruler] eats butter
> The blackman eats leather from animals
> Yejide eats bread
> The blackman eats beniseed
> Yejide eats sugar
> The blackman drinks peppery water.[30]

The merciless Yejide, unsurpassed in evil machination, also demands that whatever foodstuff the people have be forcibly brought to his magnificent palace. There he keeps the whole food of the land and resells it to those who can buy at an exorbitant price. The poor, and the infirm who come to this "market of hunger" are turned away after being beaten and abused. Tearfully, these downtrodden subjects sing as they go away:

> The government of the world has turned on its head
> The government of the world is becoming old

The government of the world is falling into the pit
The government of the world is becoming old
The day of weeping is at hand
The day of weeping is at hand
The day of weeping is near
It is entering life
Yejide, the king, power of life,
Is reigning as if the leopard is reigning
Over the animals in the forest
Is reigning, as if Satan is governing
Over the fishes in the lagoon
Eh! the Lord Almighty that created you
Created us
And He does not create us
To become your slaves
God Almighty shall judge, the dead shall judge
The Head of our fathers in sky that died
Shall fight the murderers
We are hungry, we that feed in agony
Old people die of hunger
In the house of the poor
Children die of hunger
In the house of the poor
Mothers die of hunger
In the house of the poor
Their pregnant women give birth in suffering
They are giving birth at the market of hunger
God Almighty shall judge
The dead shall judge
The heads of our fathers that die
Shall fight the murderers
We workers do not have money to feed
And we do not have clothes, nor garments
We walk 'naked like monkeys'
Yejide the King is eating, Yejide the King is drinking
He forgets that the day of recompensation is coming
God Almighty shall judge
The dead shall judge
The head of our fathers that die
Shall fight the murderers.[31]

When the hunger and subhuman treatment reach unbearable proportions the people revolt against working for their new ruler. Yejide finds that the only way to quell the seething rebellion by the formerly docile, long-suffering workers is to increase their salaries to meet the inflation. He does this and the people live happily ever after.

Yejide, though a Nigerian name, refers to the exploitative British colonial ruler. Though tyrannical, he is credited to be wise, so that he knows how to meet the people's demand before a full-scale uncontrollable revolt. The play's ending shows that since the king is wise and devises means to make the people live happily, it would be difficult, almost impossible, to throw him out of the land that does not belong to him. What Ogunde seems to be saying is that the nationalist must look for subtle means to match the ruler's wisdom if he is to throw off the rule, but that it would take a long time before it is realized since the people are happy and apparently satisfied after the wage increase.

The play has a historical background. In 1945, the year it was written, about thirty thousand workers belonging to about seventeen unions went on strike for over a month to demand wages equivalent to the rising cost of living. Says James Coleman:

> The cost-of-living allowance granted to most workers in 1942 was not considered adequate, and as the cost of living continued to mount, labour unrest kept pace. By 1945, workers claimed that the cost of living had gone up 200 percent with no corresponding relief in wage.[32]

Then in 1946, Hubert Ogunde wrote *Tiger's Empire* and *Herbert Macaulay*. *Tiger's Empire* depicts the arrival of European colonizers in Nigeria. They come in a very subtle manner, not as sword-wielding and trigger-happy conquerors, but as pious missionaries and sincere merchants. They are quick to win the trust and affection of the local ruler with whom they sign a peaceful treaty of preaching the good news of their religion and of participating in commercial enterprises. But all is a show of ostentation for no sooner do they find their ways into the hinterland than their accompanying military 'brothers' come in, accusing the local inhabitants of killing the missionaries and traders. The soldiers are ruthless in conquering the tribes and soon declare themselves masters and sole governing body of the land.

In *Tiger's Empire*, Ogunde links the missionaries with the evil perpetrated by colonialism. But it must be pointed out that this is the only play in which he does so, and even in it there are no such inimical intentions as those held by some native politicians and intellectuals of this pre-independence, colonial period. To this end, the observation of Ebun Clark is noteworthy:

> It is important to note that Ogunde's attacks on the white man were directed solely at the political masters, namely, the official agents of colonial rule; not once did he direct his attacks at missionaries [solely]. Ogunde objected vehemently, as many Southern Nigerians did, to political subjection and all the evils of colonial domination. For him, however, the missionaries brought nothing but good to Africa. With them came Western education and the beginning of advancement in technology and industry. They introduced the Christian religion, a religion which in spite of itself did not obliterate the traditional religions of Africa but introduced yet another good religious philosophy to Africa. Indeed his praise of Christianity knows no bounds ... It would be wrong therefore to state that Ogunde considered the white men totally evil. According to him, some were often humane and understanding. There were those whose consciences could not abide the practice of slave trade, and who therefore fought to abolish it. For their actions he thanked them, saying [in *Worse than Crime*]:
> We give thanks in life—you council!
> The council of the white people
> That promulgated a difficult law
> that no one should serve as
> Slaves in life.33

Ogunde's *Herbert Macaulay* is not so much an attack on a foreign administration and the evil in colonialism as it is a tribute to the man that bears the name of the play. It is a historical account of the life of one of Nigeria's "major architects of independence."[34] Herbert Macaulay was the grandson of the first African bishop, Samuel Ajayi Crowther. One of those who evolved the philosophy that

Nigerians should use the press as a medium for nationalist outpourings, he denounced segregation in Church and State and resigned from the Civil Service rather than be discriminated against. And when Bishop Herbert Tugwell and Governor Egerton wanted a church built for British citizens only, Macaulay stigmatized the venture as an effort to create an "official temple of white Christians" and led a strong opposition to it.[35] He conducted some tours of the Yoruba hinterland in which he educated the traditional rulers to ward off both the Colonial Office's threat to land tenure and the Christian missionaries' anti-liquor engagement. Perhaps, Herbert Macaulay's most memorable deed was his publication of a pamphlet, *Governor Egerton and the Railway (1908)*, in which he alleged a financial mismanagement and misappropriation by the administration in regard to the Nigerian railway construction. He pointed out that the mishandling of funds had plunged the government into a "hopeless abyss of a gigantic Public Debt which will create a good cause for Land and Capitation Taxes in the near future." His fear was that the innocent citizens would be made to bear "the nasty brunt of an imminent HEAVY PUBLIC DEBT with all its concomitant political evils."[36] The issues involved in the life of *Herbert Macaulay* are political, although Ogunde has always insisted that it is not one of his political plays.[37]

Like some of his other plays, the script of *Towards Liberty* has not survived. What we know is that the play explicitly calls for political freedom from British colonialism. Referred to as "the greatest political play ever produced by Hubert Ogunde", it calls for unity of the various movements as a step towards total freedom from colonialism.[38]

Ogunde's *Bread and Bullet* is a historical play about the killing of some miners by the government police when they protest for more pay. These are people who, on asking for "bread," have been given "bullets." In his book, *The Second World War and Politics in Nigeria, 1939-53*, G. O. Olusanya gives the historical background of the play:

This incident [the shooting and killing of the coal miners] is of major significance in Anglo-Nigerian relations because it was one of the first breaks in the tradition of peaceful if passionate verbal conflict and paper warfare between the Nigerians and the British. On 8th November, 1949, the Nigerian miners at the Enugu Colliery adopted a "go-slow tactic" in protest against the Government's refusal of their demand for a daily wage of 5s. 10p and welfare facilities. This led to a "sit down" strike on 15th November. On 18th November, the Government, fearing that explosives might be used by the miners for rioting purposes, sent a detachment of police to remove the explosives. While the police were discharging their duty, a crowd of miners carrying crowbars and picks, which they used in their day-to-day labour, surrounded them. The officer-in-charge lost his nerve and ordered his men to open fire. Eighteen men were killed and 31 wounded, two of whom died later. This incident produced an out burst of indignation and protest from Nigerians.[39]

But for an inclusion of a romantic scene between the hero and his woman, Ogunde's *Bread and Bullet* is historically accurate, indeed so accurate that it was thought powerful enough to incite Nigerian citizens against the colonial administration. The play was banned in the major cities of the northern part of Nigeria, and in one of these cities Ogunde was accused of sedition in a magistrate court and fined six pounds for putting up posters of the play without the permission of authorities.[40] There was abundant grounds for fear of public riot on the part of the government. The incident had already given birth to a certain Zikist Movement that militantly declared colonial rule evil and unmindful of public interest, and under the auspices of this movement riots, in which more shootings and deaths took place, had occurred.[41] Such fear might have engendered the attitude of the government toward Ogunde's *Bread and Bullet.*

With Independence from Britain in 1960, Ogunde wrote the *Song of Unity.* Nothing is really politically important in this play apart from its celebration of independence and a call for the unity of the various ethnic groups in Nigeria. But for his *Yoruba Ronu* (or *Yoruba Think*), perhaps his last effective and most important political play, a lot can be said.

Written between 1963 and 1964, *Yoruba Ronu* is both a bitter attack on the political imbroglio of Western Nigeria, the home of the Yoruba tribe, and a call to reason. Its historical root is the quarrel between two powerful Yoruba politicians which had led to a split in the party—the Action Group—to which both belonged. One of these men, Chief Obafemi Awolowo had been imprisoned for treason and the other, Chief Akintola, had led a splinter group to form the Nigerian National Democratic Party and won the regional elections. A period of unrest had followed in which the Yoruba people suffered as the antagonism between the rival parties grew more and more fierce. It was at this time that the ruling political group, the Nigerian National Democratic Party, commissioned Herbert Ogunde to write a play for the inaugural ceremonies of the cultural wing of the party.

While the song of the play asks the "Yoruba people to unite once again to become one of the most powerful and prosperous groups in Nigeria," the play per se, according to Ebun Clark,[42]

> ... is an allegorical story depicting how a traditional ruler, Oba Fiwajoye, was betrayed to his enemy Yeye-Iloba by his deputy. The King's enemy later found a way of imprisoning him together with two of his senior chiefs. The Deputy then installed himself as the King and subjected his people to harsh rule. Eventually, the people killed the usurper, Oba Fiwajoye was released from prison to join his people; and peace and prosperity reigned forever more in the kingdom.[43]

The play was produced for the political party that asked for it in 1964. In attendance was the Premier of Western Region and the political leader of the Nigerian National Democratic Party, Chief Akintola. He had to leave the play before it concluded for he saw it as an attack on him and his government. "Oba Fiwajoye was obviously seen as Chief Awolowo, and the Oba's Deputy who sold him to his enemy as Akintola. .." Chief Akintola replied to the production by declaring Ogunde's theatre an "unlawful society" whose intentions were "dangerous to the good government of Western Nigeria.[44] Thus was Ogunde banned from the region that was the primary cultural and political milieu of his plays and audience.

The ban came as a shock and most of the Nigerian newspapers were displeased at this turn of events. They made the ban their headline news. The *Daily Times*, echoing the view of the Action Group, saw it shameful that it was a native government, and not the former colonial, British government that encroached on the "constitutional rights of Mr. Hubert Ogunde." It appealed to the Nigerian President to "repeat his admonition that all functionaries of the Governments should ensure that the freedoms entrenched in our constitution are not trampled underfoot."[45] But the reactions of the people and of the newspapers can be summarized in extracts from the editorial of the *West African Pilot*:

> The play has picked some people sorely. But TRUTH IS BITTER. One would think that there is a remedy in law for all those who feel that they have been unjustly slandered or libelled. To apply the weight of Government in settlement of personal grievances would be out of tune with democratic concepts. We would like to feel that this is not the case in Western Nigeria.
>
> For twenty years Hubert Ogunde and his concert party have entertained the people of Nigeria and they are quite a success. To think of this group as anything other than strictly artistes is to believe that the Omnipotent can be evil. The Western Nigeria Government can work itself up to the point where it believes that the concert party is an unlawful body. We doubt if ... the populace shares this belief.
>
> The Criminal Code Law as it relates to unlawful societies, many will say, is being applied for the first time to a transparently innocent party. Hitherto, it had been applied to secret cults and organizations who engender disorder. Lawyers will argue that the makers of the law never intended it to be applied to a group of artistes who by their words and gimmicks please or make their audience sad. It is true enough!
>
> By declaring the concert party an unlawful body, the Government is clearly restricting the right of this body to pursue a trade. They are denying the group a means of livelihood. Ogunde's plays are

written in the vernacular and acted by Yoruba 'native' artistes. His
main audience, therefore, are the people of the Yoruba West. If he
cannot reach this audience, he and his artistes will disband for want
of work.[46]

Chief Akintola and his government remained
implacable, and Ogunde replied to the ban with a protest
play, *Otito Koro (Truth is Bitter)*. Ebun Clark records the
venomous opening lines of the play as Ogunde recreated it
for her:

We do not kill a dog because it barks
And we do not kill a ram because it butts
What have I done that you withhold my daily bread from me?
L - I - F - E!
Help me ask from the worthless elder
Help me ask from the wicked one
The evil doer thinks that other people talk about him
The evil doer runs away, even when no one pursues him
We have made a promise to our God
That we shall tell the truth, even if it is bitter
If you have not done ill, why did you stop the play?
If you are not treacherous, why are you afraid of my songs?
The world loves a liar
The honest man is tied down like a horse
The world hates truth
Truth is hard, truth is bitter
You have told the people of the world that I have spoiled
    the town
I will make a report of you to all the sons and daughters
    of Oduduwa.[47]

Oh yes! you have fed on lies
You fraud!
You break down other people's houses to build your own
You appear like a gentle ram
If you are bought by some people
You can be bought out by others
Hawk feeds on cursed foods
Feeds on anything
The world loves a liar
The honest man is tied down like a horse

The world hates the truth.

We that are banned
We wait on the Lord
We leave everything to God—the Silent
Judge to fight on our behalf
It is yours, yours, yours
What is more
You cannot walk at noonday
Because of the passion of the world
You have become like the rhino
That walks only in darkness
It is yours, yours
What is more
The day of vengeance is coming, we know, it is very near
The day of vengeance is coming, we know, it is very near.[48]

The Government of Western Nigeria never made any effort to lift the ban on Ogunde and his theatre. Indeed, it extended the ban to broadcasting any of Ogunde's works in the government radio and television. It was not till the soldiers took over the government in a bloody coup d'etat that the ban was lifted in 1966. Perhaps the experience wrought a change in Ogunde, for ever since then his force has been felt mainly in cultural drama.

There were other theatre groups that produced some political dramas in pre-Independence Nigeria but none of them had the force exerted by Ogunde theatre. Layeni, for example, did write a play on the historical shooting of coal miners by a group of nervous policemen, just as Ogunde did in his *Bread and Bullet*. But his *Enugu Miners* was not as dramatically involving as Ogunde's *Bread and Bullet*.

Then there was the group led by the fiery Miss Adunni Oluwole. Her interest extended beyond political drama to real politics. Later in life, she was to abandon the former for the latter as she became increasingly disillusioned with the manner with which politicians sought independence from British rule. It is noted that she made her feelings about political malpractices known through the medium of drama, but that when she found this ineffective, she mounted the soapbox and harangued the political leaders. By 1954, she

had completely disbanded her theatre to form The
Commoners' Liberal Party.   She astonished other
nationalists by opposing the call for independence in 1956
because she wanted "the ordinary man ... to choose whether
he wanted the best form of colonial rule with a policy of
gradualism towards successful self-government or the worst
form of home rule with its evils of nepotism, disunity,
victimization and 'life more abundant' for a few." Enigmatic
both in politics and theatre, she was also a religious leader.
She knew the minds of people well, especially of politicians
whom she disrespected for toying with the lives of the
people whose welfare they professed to protect, and for
abusing their vocation.   She died of tetanus while on a
political tour in 1957.[49]

All these dramatists, no matter how minimal their
output, had opened the road for others to follow in their
dramatic pursuit.   Hubert Ogunde, though he wrote a
political play at Independence, had curtailed his political
theatre to the advantage of cultural drama perhaps because of
the suffering he underwent when his theatre was banned.
But he, and the others, did show a way that the theatre could
be employed, and with Independence and the maturity of
some Nigerian dramatists, the example set by the precursors
was to be furthered.

VIOLENCE AND IMPROPRIETY IN POLITICS

•3•

When the writer in his own society can no longer function as conscience, he must recognize that his choice lies between denying himself totally or withdrawing to the position of chronicler and postmortem surgeon.

Wole Soyinka

The path that socio-political drama would follow in the independent Nigeria had been carved out even before Nigeria attained independence from Britain. There had been a gradual realization that freedom from colonial rule might not be the arrival of tortured, famished children in a promised land of milk and honey. By 1954, for example, a notable dramatist, Adunni Oluwole, had perceived the hypocrisy in indigenous politicians as they paid lip services to the welfare of the people. She, therefore, employed the theatre as a means to harangue the politicians. Her deep feeling of disillusionment and pessimism was such that she decided that something more than persuasion through drama was necessary to alter the direction of events. She went into realpolitik and tried to persuade the people not to rush into a bad form of self-rule. She pointed out that the politicians were simply pursuing their self-interests, planning how to despoil the nation with ease. Unfortunately,[1] she did not live long to pursue her goal through dramatic and political involvement. But her insights were prophetic, as we shall see in this chapter.

Nigeria did achieve her independence from Great Britain in 1960. The celebration and festivities that occurred were unprecedented in spending spree, pomp, pageantry and jubilation. Cars which had earlier been imported for the occasion were given suitable registration by the politicians and placed at the use of foreign dignitaries who graced the occasion. But no sooner had the celebrations ended than these cars vanished; when they reappeared, they had been ingenuously converted to be the personal possessions of the politicians.[2] Little consideration, if any, was given to the populace, most of them illiterate, who albeit barely had an inkling of what the celebrations were all about and whose concept of independence, of self-rule and of the territorial geography of Nigeria was "just as intelligible as some mathematical symbol to the non-numerate" nevertheless accepted with patience and magnanimity the taxation and sacrifices that the era demanded. While the political elites made their parties a living spring of champagne and other imported wines and "squabbled for the newest make in Mercedes cars," it did not matter any more whether there was no "adequate transport to get basic foods to the markets" and that the deprived of the society, "the wretched of the earth"—to use Frantz Fanon's phraseology—had "no banquets, no joy rides, no national honors,"[3] no good houses and no good roads. What Adunni Oluwole had accused the politicians of in her drama and politics had become very obvious, but she had died before the attainment of independence. Other dramatists, however, did rise up to the challenge and captured the political impropriety and violence of the period in plays. The most influential of these dramatists is Wole Soyinka whose book, *Before the Blackout*, is singularly most useful as a text for the study of the politics of the period because of its avowed political nature. A selection of satirical sketches, *Before the Blackout* is a salad of sour taste that serves both as an antidote and an indicator to everything volatile, ambivalent, angst-ridden and schizophrenic in the Nigerian political situation of the First Republic. It is a cornucopian presentation of alarming scenarios for disaster.

As a prelude to a thorough analysis of the socio-political situation of the period that gave birth to *Before the Blackout*, a brief run-through of the relevant sketches becomes imperative. The 'Ballad of Nigerian Philosophy—I' makes a cynical remark of the style, the life fashion, of the period as one of acquisitiveness and unbridled ambition, of egoistic megalomania and of scandal in high places. It presents how one man could belong to the then existing six political parties as symbolized by the Cock, the Palm (tree), the Baby, the Hand, the Chair and the Hoe in order to be rich:

> When I'm done with the Cock, I'll turn to the Palm
> When I've done that awhile I'll sign on the Baby
> And after the Baby I'll join with the Hand
> So after the Hand I shall try out the Chair,
> and after the Chair I shall sample the Hoe
> Who doesn't join with the Hoe will end up a pauper... (p. 11).[4]

Thus, one man could be in possession of "six party cards" and because joining a party was primarily pursued for material acquisition, such a politician would end up getting something from each of the six parties. His possessions would be sextuplex: he will "build six mansions reaching to the sky," make himself "Chairman of six banks," keep "six concubines," "buy six motor cars as wide as they are long," "take six government loans," "take six titles," and of course, he will always have his "six cards" and be willing to "cross the carpet" for whoever "doesn't play cardmanship will not eat of the fat." Such a politician, to secure his gain, is willing to "take to thuggery" and "lick all ... arses" (pp. 9-11).

'In Carcarem Conicio' satirizes the "period of religious revival in the country [Nigeria] when politicians and laymen forgave their fellowmen to such an extent that convicted crooks or discredited public men were raised to the positions of trust, privilege and respect." Soyinka gives the example of a judge who swore into a "most dignified office of state a felon whom he had himself convicted." He points to this act as unparalleled in the "history of forgiveness anywhere in the world." Using Martin Luther, Pope and Cleric as characters in this sale of "State Pardons" and "indulgences for bankrupt bankers, defecting directors, for doctors of doctored doctorates" and "for the most topical scandals at the time..," Soyinka points out the irony that a few men still remained "unconverted to this new faith." For such people, "monasteries [a metaphor for imprisonment] were created where they would contemplate in solitude..." (pp. 12-14).

'For Better For Worse' looks at what Soyinka calls the "1963/65 dissolution spree by two famous politicians and their henchmen." At the height of "that period in politics, a poultry could be ordered dissolved for not laying eggs ready stamped with the symbol of their party." Like 'In Carcarem Conicio,' this sketch has its own irony, for "the one thing they wouldn't dissolve was what the people wanted most— the House of Assembly" (p. 22). The House was kept there as a figure of democracy to the outside world even if things done in it were undemocratic.

In 'Symbolic Peace, Symbolic Gifts', Soyinka looks at the political tours of the period:

> Showing the flag, demonstration of strength, family reunion, proofs of popularity, etc., etc., etc.—those tours went under all sorts of names and the tourists under all sorts of guises. Sometimes the published photographs of the rallies did not match the locale. And they all had the same finale—a presentation of symbolic gifts. (p. 25)

The rush to acquire things for themselves made the political elites forget their duty to the electorate, especially as it relates to the social life of the people. 'Obstacle Race' concentrates its effort on exposing highway conditions—the road-signs are hidden at dangerous corners and are overgrown by bushes, police checkpoints are right in the middle of the road and at road bends too, the drivers blare their horn when they are happy, pillars are erected right in the middle of a sharp curve to divide the road, the roads are "severely pot-holed" and the bridges are washed off. To cross from one side of the bridge to another, then, one goes, not by boat, but on the shoulders of a "flood-lift" man. The sketch shows total neglect of the maintenance of facilities.

There was a period in which politicians greatly interfered in the organization and affairs of educational institutions. On one occasion, a "university professor was dismissed from his post for allegedly being 'rude' to a government official serving on the University Council. This led to resignations from other lecturers and the attendant degeneration of the institution" (p. 38). Soyinka pursues this relationship between politics and academics through the story of a family disrupted by a politician and his thugs in 'Death Before Discourtesy.'

In 'Go North Old Man' the relationship between the news media and a ruling political party is examined. The political leader rebukes the boss of a supposedly "'independent' medium of public information and objective reporting–the N.B.C.[Nigerian Broadcasting Corporation]"[5] for reporting a strike by workers against his government, for not pronouncing the party's name correctly during broadcast, for quoting from the Bible only, instead of quoting "from the Bible and the Koran in the same sentence," and for general bias against his party. The boss of the Broadcasting Corporation betrayed his profession by accepting all that the political leader said instead of arguing for objectivity and autonomy. This was a factual occurrence in 1964. References to the "Golden Voice" and the "Northern Nightingale" show the political leader involved in this gagging of a news medium (p. 52).

The rise and fall of politicians, Obas (kings), party stalwarts, thugs and bodyguards between 1962 and 1965, especially after the Federal Elections of 1964, are succinctly graphed in 'Nigerian National Mart.' Obas suffered untold hardships as it became a "pastime of the politicians to reduce the salaries of 'difficult' Obas to one penny a year" (p. 56).

'Press Conference' satirizes the method the government conducted its press conferences, especially after a rigged election that brought "the regular shysters .... back in the saddle." In this particular press conference, a member of the cabinet, "caught out nakedly on a shady land deal, took to the time-honored method of brazening it out with irrelevances" (p. 70).

What Soyinka leaves out of treatment in these sketches, he summarizes, in a poetic manner in the 'Ballad of Nigerian Philosophy—II', from which I quote relevant stanzas. The speaker is a political Oba:

When Africa was the whiteman's grave
And none but fools came hither
I sold my subjects old or brave
For beads and ostrich feather
Impressed all treaties with my thumb
In blood—at my suggestion
And here I stay till kingdom come
A king beyond all question.

Chorus   And this is the law I do maintain
            Till death, and so would you sir
            That whatsoever Big Noise may reign
            I'll be the Ogbugbu of Gbu, sir.
    ....

The day the Union Jack came down
I burnt my royal photos
I drove white traders out of town
Defiled the Catholic grottos
I summoned the D.O. to my court
Abused his great grandmother
Nationalism became a royal sport
Without the sweat and bother

    ....

Elections brought reverses grim
I wept, but crossed the carpet
There's harvest ripe and rich for him
Who's wise and waits to reap it
From third to first, my chieftain grade
Was boosted and gazetted
For kings are no longer born but made
And much to man indebted

    ....

A Minister of State who was no Chief

Came once to an Oba's conference
Some chiefs would, like a common thief
Eject him from our presence
But I proposed we waive the law
And offered him my cushion
Prostrated full-length on the floor
I pledged my life devotion.

....

Make a confess, I sabbe shout
When palava dey for matter
Principle na good word for mout'
But compromise dey much better
That golden slice of national cake
E sweet pass any woman
Na donkey go work for monkey sake?
My friends I'm only human[6]

....

Nkrumah was a case in point
The judges said 'Not Guilty'
He sacked the lot and did appoint
New judges sworn to fealty
The men were doomed from the very start
The judges lost their position
So why should I blow a judicial fart
When they rape our constitution.

....

These trying times demand much care
With crises, plots and tension
From six hundred quid to penny a year
Is that a decent pension?
What matters if I sell my friends
And lick some ass's arse-hole
The new generation will make amends
I'll stay on the government pay-roll.
(pp. 73-75)

What we see then is that *Before the Blackout* hammers at the evils that plagued Nigerian politics and society before the cataclysm that ended Nigeria's first life. In the same breath as it exposes these dark deeds, it also turns its search light on the nature of the politics of the time.

Nigerian politics of the First Republic, according to M. R. Ofoegbu, lacked program orientation, or, if it had one, did not execute it. Perhaps this was because there was no past experience to serve as a reference point. The country had become a Federal Republic, thereby accepting the federation it implies. Unfortunately, the deep meaning of federalism seemed not to have been explored so that the functions, duties and relationships between the regional and central governments did not reflect the intended goal of a federal republic. Perhaps more significant was the fact that the governments failed to relate directly to modernization and development. The immediate danger was the loss of bearing and an ignominious surrender to the pressure of religious and ethnic pluralism, as we see in 'Go North Old Man' and 'Symbolic Peace, Symbolic Gifts', whereas what Nigeria desperately needed to survive as a nation was the formation of a powerful loyalty in its citizens to transcend religious, linguistic and tribal consciousness. Because Nigeria preoccupied itself with ethnic pluralism, it overlooked "the forces of social change (i.e., the dynamics of planning and development, education and growing urbanization and industrialization), which will, for the rest of the century and after, influence Nigeria's evolution."[7] Leaders were concerned with political parties and personalities.

This was the general nature of the politics of the First Republic. A closer look at events is imperative. The dramatic sketch 'Nigerian National Mart,' gives an outline of the event of the period—"the events of 1962/65 and especially the 1964 Federal Elections"—as they relate to "thugs, party stalwarts and bodyguards incorporated," "Obas, Chiefs and Sons Limited" and "Politicians unlimited" (pp. 54-56). It was a period of the country's bitterest elections as the three bodies—thugs, traditional rulers and politicians—fought against and among themselves.

We understand from 'Nigerian National Mart' and from Nigeria's political history that electioneering in 1964 was painful.[8]   Thuggery and organized violence reigned supreme. Long before anyone could really think seriously of an impending election, the Action Group, a political party that had been banned at this time, had alleged that there were plans to rig elections in the country. The party had alleged that ballot papers for this purpose were being printed in Western Germany and that the Chief Officer of the Ministry of Information, Western Region, was deeply involved in the German affair. The Chief Electoral Commissioner heeded the allegation but firmly established the impossibility of any party or candidate rigging the elections. The elections, he asserted, would be conducted in a free and fair manner.

But the mere mention of rigging the elections triggered the emotions of party fanatics. Already petty squabbles existing between these fanatics had begun to simmer and the rigging affair brought them to a seething point, giving the party bigots abundant grounds for antagonistic pursuits. Violence erupted and disturbances spread everywhere the political leaders went. It was one long period of unrest in which many heads, both innocent and criminal, rolled.

It was the Western Region of Nigeria that was the hottest spot of political turmoil. The Premier of that region, Chief S. L. Akintola, and his deputy had gone on a political tour to a part of his region; there he was confronted by a group of students who jeered at him. Then at the city hall where he was addressing the audience, someone had thrown a stone at him from the gallery. This act quickly ignited a fight between the thugs of the rival parties. Bottles, cutlasses, axes, stones and sticks were freely used. Many people were injured, some so seriously that they were rushed to the hospitals. Elsewhere the entourage of the Premier also met with hostilities, with party thugs breaking into the house of the vice-principal of a college while the latter had gone with his students to welcome the Premier.

The disturbances were widespread, that the President of the nation, Dr. Nnamdi Azikiwe,had to call for sanity and for respect to the Premiers as heads of their respective regional governments. The warning was not heeded, and the ill-timed visit of Dr. Michael Okpara, Premier of the Eastern Region and leader of a rival party, to the Western Region exacerbated passions. It was a time for the major political bodies to test their strength and exhibit their gallantry.

The escalation of violence brought in the police force and while its degree of effectiveness was commendable, it was accused of partisanship. Soyinka seems to share the same view, or at least to report it, when he writes in the sketch 'Nigerian National Mart' that the "thugs, party stalwarts and bodyguards incorporated turned out to be little more than a merger-plan with the Local Government Police" (p. 55).

By June 30, 1964, about four hundred anti-riot policemen had been drafted to Ibadan to bring peace to that turbulent region. Yet the police could not effectively stem the incessant violent attacks which had begun to increase; the situation continued to defy the police force. Neither human life nor possession was safe. Therefore, "everything," according to the play, "rose sharply in the insurance business—premiums .... nervous breakdowns and incidence of heart attack. It [was] understood that a desperate though abortive attempt was made to suspend all policies on motor vehicles" (p. 56).

There was a swift reaction to these events. The Prime Minister of Nigeria announced that he would do all in his might to combat thuggery and hooliganism. And the *Daily Times* editorial dwelt heavily on this serious situation when it stated, inter alia, that:

> The major trouble is that politicians and the political parties are allowed to run their private armies. Anyone who says that the attacks and reprisals that have marked the political scene in the West are spontaneous is lying with a wicked tongue. This is organized violence ... The police are helpless.
>
> Secondly, and even more important is the truth that the police know where to find the cells where thugs are kept, but have done nothing ...

> Damn it! How long will this murderous situation continue unchecked? This is a challenge to law and order, a challenge to established authority ...[9]

Political animosity continued but it took a new dimension with the formation of the Nigerian National Alliance (NNA) in the North and the United Progressive Grand Alliance (UPGA) in the South. Both groups preached sermons of hate and were avowedly contemptuous of each other. With every passing day during the countdown to the Federal elections, tempers ran high everywhere. Politics became extremely dangerous and people connected with political parties in all parts of the country could not talk optimistically of seeing the sun rise the next day.

It is in the relationship between supporters and party candidates that an interesting connection between traditional rulers—Obas, chiefs, and elders—and politicians becomes apparent. In politics—local or national—it was, and still is, important for the political candidate to buy over the chiefs and elders. As leaders of a large illiterate population, these traditional rulers exert a lot of influence and pressure on the people. They can intimidate people, especially their vocal opponents with curses and threats of disaster. Their anger and curses are particularly feared by their illiterate and traditional-minded subjects because they are said to be efficacious; they (the elders and rulers) have the backing of the gods and the ancestors. In Zulu Sofola's play, for example, a learned aspiring candidate for a political office comes from the city to his home in the village and tries to kick out the influence wielded by traditional rulers because "men out there in the world don't look into the future backwards. They do not allow thin webs of anachronistic tradition to blind them to truth. This country [Nigeria] is on the upsurge for modernity, progress and civilization, not interested in how to greet senile men." Because of this attitude he loses his village supporters to his opponents who are crafty enough to buy the elders over.[10]

The traditional rulers had become so potent in swaying political votes that during the elections of 1964, the Premier of the Eastern Region had warned the Obas to steer clear of politics. And commenting on the same issue, another political figure, Alhaji Dauda Adegbenro, had likened politics to a game of football (soccer) and said it would be the fault of any Oba who allowed himself to be kicked.[11] Some Obas did get kicked in the aftermath of electioneering, their salaries being slashed and their status down-graded. Soyinka explains in a footnote to the 'Nigerian National Mart' that it was a "pastime of the politicians to reduce the salaries of 'difficult' Obas to one penny a year" (p. 56). The "wise" Obas—those who supported the political party in power in a particular region—had their "chieftain grade ... boosted and gazetted, for Kings are no longer born but made, And much to man indebted" (p. 74).

In close connection with this was the limit forcefully placed on politicians in the area in which they could peacefully campaign. Political opponents were detained arbitrarily if they campaigned outside their dominant regional group. *Before the Blackout* refers to this type of politics as "regionalized." Any politician who left his region to campaign in another region or who tried to establish a wing of another party in his "home" region was bound to be intimidated. Soyinka dramatizes in the sketch 'Symbolic Peace, Symbolic Gifts' two "'regionalized' leaders ... dodging missiles" as an "Away Politician" dares to tour the region of a "Home Politician" (p. 25). And in a dialogue between two relatives, Zulu Sofola shows how Western democratic process has been misinterpreted and misapplied by native politicians:

> OWEZIE.   We had thought Okolo was in the same group with our son.
> EGO.   Don't you know that this new way of ruling people is supposed to turn friends into enemies?
> OWEZIE.   Is that so?
> EGO.   You people walk about like blindmen. Haven't you noticed that it was since this new system that brothers began to kill each other and friends began to roast and eat each other for supper?
> OWEZIE.   So whitemen eat each other?

EGO.   Where else did our people learn to do these new
    things? Ask those who go to Church if they don't eat the flesh
    and drink the blood of that man they call Jesu every Sunday.
OWEZIE.   But they killed him years ago.
EGO.   Yes, but have you not heard them say that his meat
    was so good, his blood was so tasty that each Sunday for these
    many years they would perform a rite to call him up from his
    grave so that they could eat him all over again.   This time
    they eat him raw because there is no time to cook him.
OWEZIE.   Mkpitime bless us!
EGO.   Now they have brought that same thing to us so that
    we can start killing and eating each other.   They call it
    Opposition Party.[12]

What is interesting in this outlook is the underlying
meaning that two cornerstones of Western civilization have
been grossly misunderstood and misused: Christianity and
Democracy.   Essentially, their concepts are one of peace,
love and healthy co-existence.   In Nigeria, these concepts
have turned the opposite as violence, hate and intolerance of
opposition mark its movement of time.

In the light of all the restlessness and political
malpractices, the Nigerian President, Dr. Nnamdi Azikiwe,
did make a national broadcast to warn the politicians against
"the way and manner electioneering campaign is being
conducted:"

It is no exaggeration to say that with regularity, I have been
receiving correspondence complaining of victimization, privation,
false imprisonment, malicious persecution, denial of bail for
trifling offences, refusal of permits to hold meetings, beating of
political opponents, etc.

In a Republic like ours which professes liberal democracy as a
way of life, these allegations, if true, are shameful and
embarrassing ...

Repeated reports from various sources indicate that a wave of
lawlessness is gradually engulfing certain parts of our beloved
nation ...

Whether our beloved Nigeria will continue to remain united as
one country or will become disintegrated into minute principalities
depends now upon two factors: whether our politicians would desist
from inciting our communities to liquidate themselves; and

whether our politicians would cooperate so that the law abiding elements in this colossus of Africa will experience a free and fair election ...

I have only one request to make from our politicians, and in this I hope I have the support of the other leaders of this nation: if this embryo Republic must disintegrate, then, in the name of God, let the operation be a short and painless one ...

If they have decided to destroy our national unity, then they should summon a round-table conference to decide how our national assets should be divided before they seal their doom by satisfying their lust for office ...

Should the politicians fail to heed this warning then I will venture the prediction that the experience of the Democratic Republic of the Congo will be child's play if it ever comes to our turn to play such a tragic role ...[13]

In spite of all the fighting and acrimony, the Federal Elections were held as scheduled on December 30, 1964. Polling ended at midnight after a mixed response throughout the country. But the polling did not end without gruesome incidents in some places. In Shagamu, a returning officer did report that persons disguised in police outfits, vanished with ballot papers. And in Egba East, the aftermath of a raid by a mobile armed gang left two dead.

The results of the elections were released in early January with an overwhelming majority vote for the NNA. But the question of calling the NNA to form the government almost brought a civil war. Some solution was arrived at eventually and Sir Abubakar Tafawa Balewa was invited to form the new government.[14]

So when Soyinka, in the satiric sketches in *Before the Blackout*, talks of "cross[ing] carpet," of taking "six [party] cards," of "the Cock," "the Palm," "the Baby," "the Hand," "the Chair," and "the Hoe"—all symbols of the various political parties—, when his ballads sing of thuggery, of cars perishing in political rallies, of chiefs downgraded and up-graded, of "crises, plots and tension," the above analysis is his preoccupation.

Looking through the microscope that *Before the Blackout* has put at our disposal, one can, in retrospect, make bold to isolate three forces as responsible for the impropriety, violence, and chaos of the politics of the era. There could be more.[15]

The first force was the resistance to modernization in the post-independence political period by many Nigerians. Traditional rulers who had played a key role in British indirect rule wanted to keep their sphere of influence with the "new masters," the emergent political leaders. They sought by all means possible to keep the politicians and the electorates under their sway, especially by employing fearful means of divine and ancestral vengeance if they, who were often acclaimed as deputy to the gods, were disobeyed. These traditional leaders, through their control of a large mass of illiterate subjects, resisted modernizing tendencies.

Urban growth has always been a modernizing factor and the development of cities was welcomed by the progressive elements in Nigeria. While the traditionalists opposed it because it liberated from their influence the young who fled to the cities for jobs, the progressives wholeheartedly embraced it as it created new reference groups and new associations. Urbanization was one great factor that held out prospects for evolving detribalized Nigerians. Detribalizing Nigerians meant an encroachment into the loyalties the traditional tribal rulers held of the people. Therefore, the rulers and the conservatives found a way to stop the integrative functions of urbanization. This was through the formation of tribal unions and clan improvement associations which, under the pretense of preserving cultural autonomy, became a reactionary force against the innovative detribalizing quality of urbanization. Such tribal unions and clan associations became essentially a revitalization of the tribe and the clan as "rival reference groups to the cosmopolitan nationalism of the cities and urban areas."[16]

The immediate consequence of this was the polarization of urban politics between the urban, detribalized group and the tribal and clan-oriented groups. Major Nigerian cities, especially in the more literate southern areas of Nigeria, were rocked with clashes between the protagonists of urbanization and clansmen.

In some parts of Nigeria, especially in the North, education—Western education, another agent of modernization— was hindered by some powerful Northerners who in a fervent religious pursuit directed their subjects towards Islamic and Arabic studies. Western education was seen as tied to an opposing religion, Christianity. So why embrace Western education? Indeed, Wole Soyinka satirizes this sort of mentality when in 'Go North Old Man' the boss of an independent broadcasting station draws the anger of His Highness for not quoting "from the Bible and the Koran in the same sentence" (p. 52).

Education has always been a revolutionary instrument and no matter how conservative and biased its content may be, it eventually removes mental shackles and pushes the recipient towards developmental action. It inculcates new ideas, whether dreamy or pragmatic, and prepares one's mind sufficiently enough either to challenge or uphold antiquated beliefs and assumptions. Some people resisted education, and by so doing, prevented themselves and others from seeing beyond their nose.

Industrialization, another agent of modernization, was inhibited in terms of labor demands of industries. As an integrative phenomenon in a multi-national country, it provides class and professional groups and associations that cut across tribes and nations and represent higher reference groups. It aids urbanization and urban integration. It creates new relationships between the urban areas and the nearby rural communities. During this period, the irresistible integrative functions of industrialization were inhibited and, therefore, some incalculable harm was done to the cause of political[17] integration.

A second counter-force had to do with party politics itself. Nigerian political parties were confronted with many things. There was the problem of social justice, of democratic values, of freedom and authority, and of social change. These issues are thematic in *Before the Blackout*, especially in such sketches as 'In Carcarem Conicio,' 'For

Better For Worse,' 'Death Before Discourtesy,' 'Press Conference' and 'Go North Old Man.' On these issues rested hopes for political stability and the evolution of a durable multi-party parliamentary system of which Chief Dennis Osadebey, the Midwest Premier during these rancorous years, advocated.[18]

The intra-party and inter-party conflicts in Nigeria in this period were so intense and so bitter that they proved destabilizing. The NPC (Northern People's Congress) was weakly articulated and was avowedly ethnocentric. The AG (Action Group) was split, disorganized, poverty-stricken and deprived of its articulate leadership. The NNDP (Nigeria National Democratic Party) was repressive and wasteful; it lacked a leadership that was genuine and substantial and was so much propelled by fear and love of political office as to be intolerant of political opposition. The NCNC (National Council of Nigerian Citizens) was apparently incapable of rising above the inherent contradictions in its comprehensiveness. Its medley of opposites—socialists and capitalists, modernists and traditionalists—portrayed a lack of foresight and originality, and gave room to incurable party rifts and organizational weaknesses. Things were not better with the political parties merger system. The two major alliances that were formed out of these mergers proved to be very defective at birth and grew up to prove a colossal failure in bringing stability to the political system and in realigning political parties on the basis of ideology and programs. Both the UPGA (United Progressive Grand Alliance) and the NNA (Nigerian National Alliance) failed to correct the ills of the multi-party system. Each deepened tension in the nation, whetting the tools of conflict. It was from these unstable party politics that arose the Ministers, a group of card carrying careerist politicians. This class of Ministers heightened the instability in the political system because ideology and program meant little or nothing to it as it acquiesced in "crossing the carpet" provided this ensured retention of ministerial appointments.[19] Really the fracas between the alliances was "who should disburse the wealth of the nation" and not "who has the best plans for increasing the wealth of the nation and ensuring justice and fair-play in its disbursement."[20] This is what the 'Ballad of Nigerian Philosophy—II' refers to when it sings:

Principle na good word for mout'
But compromise deh much better
That golden slice of national cake
'E sweet pass any woman
Na donkey go work for monkey sake?
My friends I'm only human (p. 74).[21]

One could say, therefore, that instability originated from sterile party politics, because the political order and shady deals could not evolve a conflict-free satisfactory system. It was the same story that ranged from the emergency declaration in the West through the census controversies of 1963 to the elections of 1964—a sad story of the instability of the parties, and thereby, of the political set-up. This instability generated leadership failure and produced a stifled judiciary and a parliamentary decline. It was a season of anomy—to borrow Soyinka's phraseology.

A third contributing force to the political violence and malpractices of the era was the general failure of men, ideas, and institutions in Nigeria. Institutions were misused and lofty ideas were played with. The Senate and the House of Representatives did not meet regularly, and parliament declined. Instability brought, first, non-violent civil disobedience, which later developed into violent civil uprisings against unpopular governments and politicians. The press complained of being gagged, the judiciary lost some of its independence to the Executive, judicial rulings on constitutional matters were muffled by legislative processes, and the Director of Public Prosecutions was brought under the firm supervision of the Minister of Justice. The trade unions lacked unity and organization. The general failure was that of men, of ideas, and of institutions.

An obvious failure was one of intellectuals. The satiric sketch 'Death Before Discourtesy,' for example, takes a look at the intellectuals in the politics of this era. Since Independence in 1960, the political involvement of intellectuals had become a feature of Nigerian politics. Their activities reached a high-water mark during the Action Group schism of 1962. But anticipating this was the very fact that Nigerian nationalism was created by early intellectuals.

However, as Independence drew nearer, constitutional changes brought more political and occupational opportunities. Conflicts were engendered and intellectuals exploited ethnic differences in order to gain advantages. Conflicts had progressed unabated and Nigerian intellectuals, instead of forming a breakwater of opposition against the evils of the time, largely took sides on tribal and selfish lines. National issues became important to them only to the extent that those enhanced their personal interests. Even in university campuses, issues were no longer fought on grounds of principle and respect to one's vocation. Says Tayo Akpata:

> Having got to the top so quickly with little or no competition due to the urge for Nigerianization, devoted to academic life only as a job and with no new empires to conquer, they tended to turn to the political sphere. To convince the politicians that they belong, the intellectuals became more narrow-minded and Machiavellian than the politicians.[22]

A satiric image of these intellectuals is drawn in 'Death Before Discourtesy.' Because of transient advantages, some intellectuals took to licking "some ass's arse-hole," kneeling down to kiss a Minister's hand, and closing their eyes when a Minister poached on their daughters' favor, and putting their families at the use of what Mini calls "dirty old [men]" making "improper advances." Yet all the while these intellectuals maintained that they did not want to put themselves at the same level—low level—as their neighbors, and that to keep their status untarnished before public eyes the best thing to do when a Minister assaulted the privacy of one's home was for the entire family to present itself as "one peace-loving family and appeal to his [Minister's] sense of justice," and, of course, pray (pp. 38-49). All these were done by the intellectuals to achieve their political ambition. By such deeds, they contributed to the political malpractices of the era that followed independence and therefore failed the nation. Like other political opportunists, they abandoned principles for compromise. Soyinka has nothing but anger for these intellectuals, fellows of his, who have helped to wreck the Nigerian political arena.

Whatever joy one derives from the satires in *Before the Blackout* is not one of hearty laughter and broad smiles but of a grin. It is understandable why Soyinka has taken the position of striking at the conscience of the nation. In his speech at the 1967 Writers' Conference in Stockholm, he gave what he thinks an artist should be to his society:

> When the writer in his own society can no longer function as conscience, he must recognize that his choice lies between denying himself totally or withdrawing to the position of chronicler and postmortem surgeon. But there can be no further distractions with universal concerns whose balm is spread on abstract wounds, not on the gaping yaws of black inhumanity. The artist has always functioned in African society as the record of the mores and experience of his society and as the voice of vision in his own time. It is time for him to respond to this essence of himself.[23]

This is what he does in *Before the Blackout*.

For all the brave rhetorics, wild hopes and feverish negotiations, the political factories before the blackout, that is before the military coup d'etat that ended the First Republic, failed to reach a satisfactory compromise. The political tastes of the period rattled allies and angered adversaries, and the scenarios for disaster they presented were very alarming. *Before the Blackout* shows no optimism. Rather, it presents the last twitches of a "civilization" in its terminal frenzy.

Having some bearing on what Soyinka writes about in *Before the Blackout* is Peter Enahoro's *How to be a Nigerian*. Although the work is not a play but a short work of prose, a novelette, it is good to examine it here briefly as a pointer to a parallel thinking in another art form, even if no other art form developed a socio-political concern as did drama during this period.

Published in 1966, *How to be a Nigerian* might have been written at about the time the satirical sketches in *Before the Blackout* were first produced. I have surveyed relevant portions from the book to reinforce the thoughts already expressed in earlier portions of this chapter. What Soyinka refers to in the 'Ballad of Nigerian Philosophy-I' as "That's the style, that's the fashion" (p. 10), could very well be what Peter Enahoro sees as the emergence of the "Nigerian" personality:

> It just struck me one day that with all the political acrimony that gripped the country, and in spite of the diversity of the country, a personality that was distinctly "Nigerian" had emerged, but few Nigerians realized it.[24]

To this emergent Nigerian, the tribe assumed an all pervasive importance. It became a fashion when looking for employment or when engaged in any important undertaking to state the tribe. Such statement about one's tribe became an "identikit," an identification kit that was ensured to give recognition and success to the bearer. All members of a tribe were brothers.[25]

In large urban areas and population centers, tribal unions were formed. These unions became terrors to politicians. The politician who wanted to be successful and to be free from intimidation had to court their support. It became the custom in the First Republic to recite the slogan, "Our unity is in our diversity." It was a vote-catching device said repeatedly, nevertheless drawing cheers from the crowds always. Even when a politician said nothing more but this slogan for the duration of his electioneering campaigns, his patriotism, keen foresight and sharp intellect were praised.

What were regarded as radical political parties were a compromise between trumpeted socialism and actual conservatism. Still other political parties became a compromise between strictly business ventures and group political interests. When they were parties, they were not political, and vice versa.

It was also the politics of grumbling. If a politician did not want to jeopardize his political future, he would grumble about things not being established in his constituency, no matter how unpragmatic for the moment such establishments would be:

> Once in the House of Representatives, an M.P. read out 48 postal agencies, four post offices, and one public library which he thought could be built for his people. He bought several dozen copies of Hansard and shipped them home. He was reelected. Not one of them was built.[26]

In the same vein, Ime Ikiddeh's short play, *Blind Cyclop*, shows a politician who goes to any length for money. He pursues his private work at the expense of government work. He uses his office as chairman of the Housing Committee to acquire lands and buildings which he rents out at extortionate costs to his tenants. Moreover, he receives bribes before allocating lands to, and approving houses for, people. His total life is one of debauchery. To him the employment of magical powers and money is an inevitable ideal towards successful electioneering. He is a man whose rhetorics is antithetical to his life:

> Now the time of reckoning has come, and I am appealing to you to judge each man according to his record (roar of applause). The burden of my speech is: Respect for Human Divinity (greater applause). Gone are the days when our illustrious town, and indeed the entire country and continent suffered under the insidious yoke of economic, social, and moral strangulation at the hand of the imperialistic ... (even greater applause). My party is committed to the total eradication of the exploitation of man by man (roar). To this end, and having the interest of our people at heart, we have set up a high-power committee to work towards better housing conditions, a strict control of rents, and the greater happiness of all ... (deafening roar and fade out).[27]

What this politician says is exactly the opposite of what he does.

An equally dismal picture of the politician and his malpractices is painted in *Shadows in the Horizon*. In this play, Kole Omotoso depicts a politician who is also a full-time merchant and trader and whose love of power and of money makes him treat his servants like dogs. He refuses to develop his area, moving his property and family from his birthland to Ikoyi because the area is "dirty," the people are "animals" and thieves, and he cannot bring up his children in such conditions. He does not see it as his responsibility to lead the people to a better life.[28] He condemns a fellow business competitor to death, without allowing him a hearing because the latter had tampered with his great possession. Of course, he is found wanting in leadership qualities and when there is a change of government, he is probed, found to have swindled the country of a huge amount of money, and executed.

And in Bode Sowande's *Farewell to Babylon*, there is a sub-plot of a political swaggerer who thinks because he is a veteran in politics, he is always right and can never say wrong things. Such a man has a propensity towards dictatorship and it is little wonder then that he is a friend to the tyrant President of Babylon, Field Marshal. He is an ex-convict, having been put in gaol once by his political enemies. It is an irony in life that this politician who now regards his people as "bushmen" and bloody illiterates, and who realizes that their backwardness is a corollary of illiteracy but does nothing to educate them and improve their lot was once a mere ticket collector.[29]

Portrayed in drama as cold and reserved to the commonality, selfish, acquisitive and megalomaniacal, obstinate and narrow-minded, incapable of inspiring the affection of their subjects and fellow citizens, licentious, prurient and corrupt, extravagant and pleasure loving, and exhibiting a gallantry that is only superficial, the politicians of this era could be said to be bad men and bad leaders. Presented as men of double-tongues and sweet lips, their rhetoric and their lives are antithetical. The plays show a perilous state of affairs. And in reality, things were so bad as to lead to a bloody coup d'etat by a group of military men that ushered in the death of the First Republic, 1966. Similar occurrences were to end the Second Republic of President Shagari in 1983, except that this time there was no bloodbath. But the military itself is gradually becoming a part of the problem of cyclic instability and gross corruption. It hands power back to democratic rule in 1992 without correcting the socio-political malaise that arguably first made it seize political power by might.

THE QUEST
FOR
LEADERSHIP

•4•

The artist or redeemer may torment the world—his ideas may bring about revolutions; subsequent generations may esteem the sterling quality of his work—but as far as his person or life is concerned there is no redemption, for this is what he has to sacrifice in order to achieve his end. He loses his soul in order to save others. This is the image of the true messiah and it is this element which makes Eman so much like the conventional Christ.

Oyin Ogunba

When Ukwu, a character in the play, *The Old Masters*, cries out in anguish "What we need is a leader," Sonny Oti is only giving voice to one of the themes that some Nigerian dramatists have tried to explore in their works—the question of leadership. Ukwu's cry comes in the wake of a deep, revolutionary social change as the new Christian teaching and colonial administration challenge traditional social and cultural institutions. Ukwu needed a powerful leader in these new circumstances.

Ukwu's cry has also become the cry of many playwrights in the face of a new socio-political change— self-government. It had dawned on many Nigerians that independence meant more than flag-waving patriotism; it meant more than the intoxicating idea that Nigerians were governing Nigerians. There was a realization that it was one thing for a people to govern themselves and another to have the right leadership that the trying times called for. Political impropriety, violence and ethnic bickerings had shown that the right leadership was absent. Playwrights, especially Wole Soyinka, Femi Osofisan, Gordon Tialobi, Kole

Omotoso, Bode Sowande and Zulu Sofola became conscious of this absence of leadership, and in some of their plays gave an over-riding importance to the examination of leadership quality. Indeed, to some of these playwrights, the quest for true political leadership becomes a near obsession. Although there is the tendency often times to make politics, the art of government, synonymous with leadership rather than service, the probings of these dramatists tend to show that the idea of service is inherent in leadership and that good government is remote where leadership and service are divorced. To these dramatists then, leadership includes service and the question to which they seek an answer is who can give the true leadership. Towards an answer, the following classes of people are examined: the traditional ruler, the priestly class, the peasant class, the intellectual, the armed forces, and the artist. I have left the professional politician out of consideration here because his treatment in the previous chapter is enough evidence that he is not yet the right leader. The armed forces will be treated separately.

1.   The Traditional Ruler

In the pre-Independence Nigeria, traditional rulers— Obas, chiefs, emirs, and a council of elders—in cooperation with the colonial masters, had provided the leadership on which that era had survived.   In spite of all their shortcomings they had ruled that period, and their subjects had survived, even if their lives were of servitude and had been made to swear the oath of fealty to their rulers.   The authority of these rulers was based on the concept of the ruler as representative of the gods. But Independence meant freedom, freedom not only from colonial authority but from the bondage of those who claimed to rule the people in obedience to a higher authority. Independence meant a new age and a new nation. It meant that the old order must change to yield place to the new for the gods who had in earlier times made traditional rulers their deputies had then decided to "fulfill themselves in different ways." New and radical structures of judgement had to be erected. Would the obas and chiefs be able to provide such leadership? Would they who rode on the shoulders of their subjects, wiped their hands on the heads of their servants after meals and used their people as personal properties be able to sit on the same table with these lowly creatures as the new age demanded without being schizophrenic?

The Lion and the Jewel (1963) subtly looks at the traditional ruler in confrontation with the first harmless sparks of the new era. Baroka, the 'Bale' of Ilujinle, rules his people with an iron hand. Not only is he self-centered and pervert, he is the antithesis of progress, an embodiment of deceit, and, therefore, an obstacle to the demands of the new age. He cannot guarantee efficient and effective administration. Baroka does not possess the requirements for leadership in the new era but he clings to it tenaciously. He is rapacious and voluptuous, and the tensions of the new age that is displacing him have made him a destroyer. Not only is he "the hindquarters of a lion" out to destroy Sidi, "the twinkle of a jewel" in what might be looked at as a confrontation between old age and youth; he is bent on thwarting the ambition of Lakunle, the school teacher, in what might be seen as a struggle between arch conservatism and progress. Definitely, one does not give a "jewel," symbol of a new age, to a "lion," symbol of unmitigated autocracy. The latter would see the former as an infringement on his cherished power and would do everything possible to destroy it.[2]

What Soyinka seems to be saying is that the traditional ruler, as represented by Baroka, the ruler of Ilujinle, cannot be the desired leader of the new age for the following reasons:

Baroka indulges in corrupt practices and bribery. In order to foil the attempt by the Public Works Department to build a railway through the empire he has carved for himself—the railway would have brought some modernizing influence and outside progress to Ilujinle, and thereby challenge to some extent the conservative authority of the

Bale—Baroka resorts to bribery. Lakunle tells the story
how Baroka did it:

> LAKUNLE: They (surveyor, foreman, prisoners) marked the route
> with stakes, ate through the jungle and began the tracks.
> Trade, progress, adventure, success, civilization, fame,
> International conspicuousity ... it was all within the grasp of
> Ilujinle ... (The wrestler enters, stands horrified at the sight and
> flees. Returns later with the Bale himself who soon assesses
> the situation. They disappear. The work continues, the
> surveyor occupies himself with the fly-whisk and whisky.
> Shortly after, a bull-roarer is heard. The prisoners falter a
> little, pick up again. The bull-roarer continues on its way,
> nearer and farther, moving in circles, so that it appears to come
> from all round them. The foreman is the first to break and
> then the rest is chaos. Sole survivor of the rout is the
> surveyor who is too surprised to move.
> Baroka enters a few minutes later accompanied by some
> attendants and preceded by a young girl bearing a calabash
> bowl. The surveyor, angry and threatening, is prevailed upon
> to open his gift. From it he reveals a wad of pound notes and
> kola nuts. Mutual understanding is established. The surveyor
> frowns heavily, rubs his chin, and consults his map. Re-
> examines contents of the bowl, shakes his head. Baroka adds
> more money, and a coop of hens. A goat follows, and more
> money. This time 'truth' dawns on him at last, he has made a
> mistake. The track really should go the other way. What an
> unfortunate error, discovered just in time! No, no, no
> possibility of a mistake this time, the track should be much
> further away. In fact (scooping up the soil) the earth is most
> unsuitable, couldn't possibly support the weight of a railway
> engine. A gourd of palm wine is brought to seal the
> agreement and a cola-nut is broken. Baroka's men help the
> surveyor pack and they leave with their arms round each other
> followed by the surveyor s booty.) (pp. 23-24)

The Bale is also lewd and deceitful. Having been
dazzled by glitters from Sidi, the jewel of Ilujinle, his erotic
passion is inflamed. He must marry Sidi, one of his
subjects, but he cannot get her to yield to marriage the
normal way. So he hatches a plan that he is impotent and
deceives his people into believing it. Sidi, unaware of the

plan, goes to him, to mock the man who had wanted to force her into matrimony, and she is entrapped. Baroka makes love to her and Sidi becomes his wife; just another wife, the current favorite whose juice must be sapped and who must be squeezed dry and pushed to the sides, like Sadiku, the Bale's first wife.

Surely, a traditional ruler who goes about bribing people so as to get his way, and who is deceitful, progress-thwarting and conservative might not be able to offer the effective leadership that is required. Elsewhere, Soyinka has disapproved of a traditional ruler because of the ruler's Machiavellian pursuits. He sings:

> These trying times demand much care
> With crises, plots and tension
> From six hundred quid to penny a year
> Is that a decent pension?
> What matters if I sell my friends
> And lick some ass's arse-hole
> The new generation will make amends
> I'll stay on the government payroll.[3]

James Ene Henshaw's *This is Our Chance* further disqualifies traditional leadership in the emerging nation. Like Baroka in *The Lion and the Jewel*, Damba, the traditional ruler of Koloro, is anti-progress, anti-education. To him, education—Western education—is corrosive to tradition, and the sanity of a people depends upon tradition! He sees himself not only as the executor of tradition but as the embodiment of tradition itself. He is tradition personified. For those of the new age who want to pervert his kingdom "with new and heretical ideas likely to upset the whole tradition, peace, and dignity," Chief Damba has this to say:

> Tradition is sacred. Custom is above all. To question Tradition is sacrilege. If men do not respect Tradition how can our Society stand? How can we be proud of our fore-fathers and pass on our pride to our children? What would happen if you or I were allowed to change our ancient practices as we like? For us Tradition is not

a passing thing. It is the earth on which we live and the air which we breathe....[4]

Note the emphasis placed on tradition with a capital T. Tradition has become a person whose virginity must not be violated. But to Bambulu, the radical who represents the dawning era with all its turbulence and iconoclasm, the die is cast. He is the apostle of the new age, the new man who is liberated by independence and cannot be confined to the old, servile ways. He must incessantly assault the ears of Tradition with what it does not want to hear:

> Though the world outside is active, moving and progressing, people are questioning and debating, here in this place, this prison called a village, where silence is the most golden and the most abundant of virtues, we move like sheep from day to day, from year to year, doing nothing, but worshipping Tradition and splitting hate against our so-called enemies. In this prison called Koloro you may be a heretic; there have been many before you, but only on trivial matters such as the method of planting or reaping, or even on market prices and women's dresses, but never on the rocks of traditional marriage. At any rate, I have stepped into the ring. The die is cast. (p. 21)

Among other things, Bambulu is stepping into the ring to fight the ruler's belief in vendetta and the taboo placed on marrying outside one's tribe. He is fighting for education in modern affairs and outlook and fighting against the traditional ruler, Damba, for succumbing to the whims and caprices of a fortune-teller. He is saying that the leadership required by the times would have to trace events to pragmatic economic causes, political exigencies and the national social structures—ideas which are well beyond the guess-work, narrow interpretations and predictions of the fortune-teller and oracle-dependent leader.

In Zulu Sofola's *Old Wines are Tasty*, there is some understanding that the traditional rulers never really understood the concepts of colonialism and independence in the first place, and therefore, have no equipment for fostering the leadership independence requires.

AKUAGWU: I am here gaping like an ass because the itch has reached home. Our forefathers were all in their beds when the new system of ruling people was fashioned and forced down their throats. They fought and lost. So one day we were told that a place called Nigeria is now our country and that our king now lives in a place called Lagos. They also told us that the whiteman brought these new ways on us because they could not understand our ways. So their wings grew over the land of our forefathers. We prayed and waited for those bad visitors to return to their homes... [5]

The same frame of thought is continued by another elderly man:

ODOGWU ... These intruders returned to their countries at last; but before that they made sure they chose some-bastard blackmen to carry on from where they left. That shocked us because we did not think such blackmen existed; but we did not shed tears over it because it never reached Olona until a few months ago when a strange thing happened. We made some sacrifice to our goddess to drive away evil from amongst us. But a week ago we heard something that would make a chicken bury its head in the sand. We heard that Okebuno, the son of Mukolu, was coming down from Lagos in a big car with orders which we must obey. (p. 34)

What we hear is the voice of "a bunch of dangerous senile illiterates and myopic half-wits" (p. 43), who want to protect the land they rule first from colonial rule, and after independence, from other Nigerians ruling over them. They are tribal or ethnic conscious, and they do not see beyond their "homeland." That concept of Nigeria as a union of many tribes is out of their frame of reference. They, therefore, cannot rule Nigeria as an Independent nation. They must oppose Okebuno fiercely because he speaks the language of progress and tries to initiate a civilization which they do not understand:

This is a modern age when people fly to the moon. This world is on the move and Nigeria refuses to be left behind. The stars are in the palm of our hands. The unknown is being explored. Progress is everywhere. No one wants to be left behind. It was the quest

for better life for my people that made me come to this dark jungle
with light. I came down from Lagos because I had dreams of the
day when Olona sons and daughters will walk high among their
peers in the world and take our country to places. But alas. Olona
is still in a deep coma. (p. 43)

He sees no attunement to new ways in the "bunch of
feathered idiots clinging on to some stupid tradition" (p. 44),
and the traditional rulers totally reject Okebuno's novel idea
of leadership by telling him that "it is old wines that are
tasty, not the new" (p. 44).

There are other numerous examples of the attitudes of
traditional rulers to the wind of change that could be drawn
from Nigerian drama. From Soyinka's Oba Danlola in
Kongi's Harvest, through Sofola's Emene in *King Emene* to
Femi Osofisan's Alafin Abiodun in *The Chattering and the
Song*, it is the same story—the story of power-drunk, bribe-
offering,   self-important,   progress-thwarting,   diehard
traditionalists and arch-conservatives who view the new era
and its products with suspect and do all in their might to
stifle any opposition and extinguish the new light that has
been brought.   The thinking seems to be that such
voluptuous and lascivious rulers cannot offer the much
needed leadership. The leadership the dramas look forward
to must be progressive and disinterested. Having been much
acquainted with the "use" of their subjects as personal
possessions, regarded as semi-divine ("second to the
gods"), and having wielded an authority that no one dared
challenge   before   the   advent   of   colonialism   and
independence, the traditional rulers found it difficult to
reconcile themselves to the ideas about democracy ushered in
by the new period. So the traditional rulers cannot offer the
leadership needed by the Independent Nigeria. They would,
as much as possible, draw the hands of the clock back, or
they and the nation might move at cross purposes.   The
dramas seem to look elsewhere for the messiah.

2.   The Priestly Class

The history of Nigeria abounds with the activities of priests and priestesses who gave some form of leadership to their people. In some cases, the traditional ruler was also the chief priest, therefore combining in himself secular and religious powers. If contemporary examples could be drawn, one might talk of the Pope as the religious head of Roman Catholicism and as the secular head of the Vatican. But it is really to Iran we must look where the late Ayatollah Khomeini wielded an awesome political and religious power. The "priest-kings" of traditional Nigeria were awful in power display. One easily recalls the history of King Jaja of Opobo, the greatest political figure in the Bights of Benin and Biafra during the colonial era. Not only was he a political leader and a powerful merchant, he was also the high priest of "ikuba," a grotesque tribal temple in which the bones of human victims of war were carefully arranged and which held the iguana as the animal totem of his kingdom. He warded off missionary influence as one would evade the plague, and not even an illness that almost claimed his life would make him consider missionary teaching. Indeed, the claim by the missionaries that he was visited with a terrible sickness because of his sins made him more steadfast in his belief so that "sleeping under three chickens suspended from the roof with heads downwards, four of his lieutenants propitiated the gods by sacrificing human beings, goats and fowls."[6] He was determined on preserving indigenous religion and institutions at all costs.   Convinced that indigenous religion was the cement of African society, he stuck to it and was thus, in Opobo, both the spiritual and secular head of state. To create awe in people, he always wore a smoking cap on his head.

The traditional rulers were also religious leaders because they were aware that religion was central to the men they ruled since there were no scientific explanations to natural occurrences. Events were interpreted in accordance to god's pleasure or displeasure; since the king was regarded as "God's Deputy," he only knew the mind of the gods. Therefore, religion hedged the king with divinity and awe, permeated the life of the individual from birth to death,

subjected the low-born to their superiors, the serfs to their
overlords, and more than anything else, formed the basis of
secular authority because it instilled fear and respect.
Religion was so important that removed from the traditional
society in Africa, the moral and political systems would
collapse.

Though religion was so important to the traditional
African, the "priest-kings" did oppose missionary
enterprises. Apart from the fact that Christianity created
priests that had no secular powers, there was the fact that
Christianity created new references so that those converts
who renounced their tribal religions also discarded the
restraints that went with them. They entered into new
obligations which were not really binding, and found that
they could flout the authority of the kings with impunity.

Quite a good number of traditional rulers in Nigerian
drama behaved like King Jaja of Opobo. In Zulu Sofola's
King Emene, the King carries on the religious activities of
Peace Week in disregard to popular feelings but it is in Wale
Ogunyemi's *Ijaye War* and Ola Rotimi's *Kurunmi*—both
deal on the same subject—that one sees an awesome display
of both religious and secular authorities. The chief
character, Kurunmi, a true historical figure in these historical
plays, was the Are-ona-kakanfo[7] and had established a
personal ascendancy in Ijaye. He was a worshipper of
Sango, the god of thunder and of lightning. Not satisfied
with this, he is reputed to have usurped the headship of the
various cults, and was feared more than the gods. He is
quoted to have said, "If Sango does not kill you, I myself
will," and in anger at his oracle man he said, "If the Are
[Kurunmi] calls and you say you are busy consulting the
oracle, what if the oracle says well and the Are says ill?"[8]

What seems to be the message of these three plays,
especially the latter two, is that leadership by "priest-kings"
is not ideal for Nigeria. Such rulers are too power-drunk to
give effective leadership. At the end of the plays, there is a
new order that takes over the government following the
defeat of the "priest-kings."

However, there were men who concerned themselves with religious leadership only. They were the spiritual overlords, but if they are different from those discussed above, it is because they lacked the political and secular control. However, their spiritual authority is overwhelming. With the granting of independence in 1960, plays did focus on the activities of these men who "speak with the voice of gods" to see if they could offer the right leadership to the country.

In Wole Soyinka's *The Swamp Dwellers*, we are invited to witness the life-pattern of a priest of the traditional religion to see if he could be the messiah. Everywhere he goes, "Our holy man, the Servant and Priest of the Serpent of the Swamp," Kadiye, is heralded by drums:

> The drummer is the first to enter. He bows in backwards, drumming praises of the Kadiye. Next comes the Kadiye himself, a big, voluminous creature of about fifty, smooth-faced except for little tufts of beard around his chin. His head is shaved clean. He wears a kind of loin-cloth, white, which comes down to below his knees and a flap of which hangs over his left arm. He is bare above the waist. At least half of the Kadiye's fingers are ringed. He is followed by a servant, who brushes the flies off him with a horse-tail flick.[9]

He goes into a house and the family head reverently bows with arms across the chest to welcome him; the wife of the house quickly rushes in and kneels before him to receive a blessing from Kadiye. He is well entertained with wine. Nothing seems strange in all this till we realize that action takes place in a swamp and that there is famine caused by floods, and that where everyone is poor and barely surviving, Kadiye lives well, very well. His skin is tender, smooth and well-preserved; he is fat, rolling "himself like a fat and greasy porpoise," his "thighs ... like skinfuls of palm oil ..." (pp. 101-102). Kadiye is a selfish, careless fellow, who acting on behalf of the Serpent, his god, and not on behalf of humanity, his clients, not only fails to serve as a useful intermediary between god and men but sets the bounds of human conduct and swallows their offerings with

little or no regard to their fates. Such a man lacks the ability
to lead a people to survival and so has no leadership role in
the new nation.

The Swamp Dwellers seems to be saying too that the
new nation cannot be led on the traditional African
philosophy of sacrifice. Igwezu tries to probe into the
meaning of offering, of sacrifice, whether sacrifice has any
supernatural relevance or whether everything comes by
chance and by nature merely fulfilling its course. Sacrifices,
as the Kadiye's utterances portray, become a sort of fee to
the Serpent to give the things asked for. But when the latter
fails to fulfil its part of the deal, the-people have a right to
question priestly authority as Igwezu does in this interesting
dialogue:

> IGWEZU: Who must appease the Serpent of the Swamps?
> KADIYE: The Kadiye.
> IGWEZU (His speech is increasing in speed and intensity):   On
>   whom does the land depend for the benevolence of the reptile?
> KADIYE: Kadiye.
>
> ....
>
> IGWEZU: And so that the Serpent might not vomit at the wrong
>   season and drown the land, so that He might not swallow at
>   the wrong moment and gulp down the unwary traveller, do I
>   not offer my goats to the priest?
> KADIYE: Yes.
>
> ....
>
> IGWEZU: And did he offer them in turn to the Serpent?
> KADIYE: He did.
> IGWEZU: Everything which he received, from the grain to the
>   bull?
> KADIYE: Everything.
> IGWEZU: The goat and the white cockerel which I gave before I
>   left?
> KADIYE: Every hair and feather of them.
> IGWEZU: And he made it clear—that the offering was from me?
>   That I demanded the protection of the heavens on me and my

house, on my father and my mother, on my wife, land and chattels?

KADIYE: All the prayers were repeated.

IGWEZU: And ever since I began to till the soil, did I not give the soil his due? Did I not bring the first of the lentils to the shrine, and pour the first oil upon the altar?

KADIYE: Regularly.

IGWEZU: And when the Kadiye blessed my marriage, and tied the heaven-made knot, did he not promise a long life? Did he not promise children? Did he not promise happiness?

(Igwezu has shaved off all [Kadiye's beard] except a last smear of lather. He remains standing with one hand around the Kadiye's jowl, the other retaining an indifferent hold on the razor, on the other side of his face.)

KADIYE (Does not reply this time.)

IGWEZU (slowly and disgustedly.): Why are you so fat, Kadiye? (The drummer stares, hesitates, and runs out. The servant moves nearer the door.)

....

IGWEZU: You lie upon the land, Kadiye, and choke it in the folds of a serpent.

....

IGWEZU: If I slew the fatted calf, Kadiye, do you think the land might breathe again? If I slew all the cattle in the land and sacrificed every measure of goodness, would it make any difference to our lives, Kadiye? Would it make any difference to our fates?

(The servant runs out also.)

KADIYE (in a choking voice.): Makuri, speak to your son...

BEGGAR: Master ... master (Igwezu suddenly shaves off the final smear of lather with a rapid stroke which makes the Kadiye flinch. Releases him and throws the razor on the table. Kadiye scrambles up at once, tearing the cloth from his neck. Makes for the door.)

KADIYE (panting): You shall pay for this ...

IGWEZU: Go quickly, Kadiye ... And the next time that you wish to celebrate the stopping of the rains, do not choose a barber whose harvest rots beneath the mire. (pp. 108-110)

The images conveyed by the setting of this piece of dialogue—a barber, a razor, a hand around the jowl of the man being shaved, the standing posture of the barber as contrasted to the sitting, hemmed in posture to the man being shaved, the indifferent hold on the razor and the antagonistic tone of the barber—seem to point to the doom of the priest and all he stands for. One, including Kadiye himself when he calls on Makuri to speak to his son and the priest's followers when they fled, has the feeling that Kadiye's neck might be sliced open by Igwezu. It seems Soyinka is almost saying that the priest himself be sacrificed to the serpent whom he had used to deceive the people and enrich himself, and that he be made to undergo such a harrowing life experience that he never try to dupe the people any more. Definitely, there is a rejection of priestly leadership here.

A priest of the Kadiye type cannot initiate any useful leadership in the post-independence Nigeria because he perpetuates a system which makes possible the inequality between the affluent priestly class and the indigent ordinary people. Says Oyin Ogunba:

The Kadiye, deeply sunk in avarice and gluttony, is the kind of spiritual leader who enjoys the perquisites of office to the fullest. He himself observes that whether it rains all the year round or not, people still die and give birth to children. Since he performs burial and circumcision rites (for fees) for members of the community, this means he will always be able to live far above the level of the masses, and keep exploiting them.

Kadiye, the ghoul preying on these swamp dwellers, does not possess messianic qualities. He would lead the people to disaster.

Nor can the lecherous charlatan of a prophet, Jeroboam, in *The Trials of Brother Jero*, be a true leader. He is just one of the many deceitful prophets that made the beach their prophetic grounds. In their competition to acquire certain portions of the beaches far their "spiritual" work and to put some fellow prophets out of business, "some prophets ... gained their ... beaches by getting women penitents to shake their bosoms in spiritual ecstasy. This prejudiced the councillors who came to divide the beach ..." among them.[11]

According to Jeroboam, even such initial division of the beach did not stop the prophets' ambition to out-do each other. The Town Council came to the beach to settle the "Prophets' territorial warfare once and for all:"

> My [Jeroboam's] master, the same one who brought me up in prophetic ways staked his claim and won a grant of land ... I helped him, with a campaign led by six dancing girls from the French territory, all dressed as Jehovah's witnesses. What my old Master did not realize was that I was really helping myself ... (p. 145)

He had used foul means to snatch the land from his master and put him out of a job.

Jeroboam is a man with two faces. While in his private life he is a debtor, a self-confessed rogue and a follower of the "Daughters of Eve" and "Daughters of Discord," he is in public appearances the holy of holies, donning a "white flowing gown and a very fine velvet cape, white also" and standing "upright, divine rod in hand" (p. 152). Because of his outward posturing, people think of his "goodness" and begin to call him "the Velvet-hearted Jeroboam ... Immaculate Jero, Articulate Hero of Christ's Crusade ..." (p. 153). Jeroboam is also the chief engineer of the structure of dominance and dependence, and he regards his relationship to the worshippers not as that of a shepherd to his sheep but as a shopkeeper to his customers:

> JERO: ... I am glad I got here before any customers—I mean worshippers—well, customers if you like. I always get that feeling every morning that I am a shopkeeper waiting for customers. The regular ones come at definite times. Strange, dissatisfied people. I know they are dissatisfied because I keep them dissatisfied. Once they are full, they won't come again. Like my good apprentice, Brother Chume. He wants to beat

his wife, but I won't let him. If I do, he will become contented, and then that's another of my flock gone for ever. As long as he doesn't beat her, he comes here feeling helpless, and so there is no chance of his rebelling against me. Everything, in fact, is planned. (p. 153)

Indeed, everything is planned by Jeroboam to perpetuate his dominance over his dependents. To one of his ardent followers, he prophesies that the man would be made a chief in his home town some day; to another he heightens the belief that he would be the first Prime Minister of a new state that would be created. Yet another worshipper wants children and even though she is aware that often times Jeroboam's "mind is not on the service," she still seeks Jeroboam's solution to her "sad case" (p. 157). Jeroboam keeps all of them hoping, and he realizes that as long as he keeps them hoping he can keep them utterly dependent on him. He allows Chume, finally, to beat his wife because he is in financial debt to Amope, Chume's wife, and the latter has begun to make life unbearable for him. But he realizes that by allowing Chume to beat his wife and therefore satisfy his emotion, he has "lost him as the one who was most dependent" on him. But "It was a good price to pay for getting rid of [his] creditor..." (p. 168). And when he wins the conversion of the Member of Parliament, a conversion so fraudulently executed that the man calls Jeroboam "Master!", Prophet Jeroboam is near the zenith of his power. He now has political influence which would allow him to pervert justice as he wishes. Power now collaborates with dupery and roguery, so that when Chume comes charging at him with a cutlass on suspecting some dealing going on between his wife and Jeroboam, Jeroboam makes no secret of his intention to use the Member of Parliament as an instrument to certify Chume mad and to put him away for a year in a lunatic asylum. The people look towards Jeroboam to give the necessary leadership but he beguiles them offering them deceit. With him as a leader, his prophecy that he "saw this country plunged into strife" could be true.

In *Jero's Metamorphosis*, a continuation of the story of Brother Jeroboam, the prophet has now settled down to prophecy as a lucrative business. He has become anything but spiritual and religious. He seems to have understood the dialectics of materialism so well that he transacts his "spiritual" business with more confidence and precision than we have seen in his earlier appearance in *The Trials of Brother Jero*. We are also made to see the inner lives of his fellow prophets. All of them are putrid inside though sparkling white outside: Ananaias is an ex-convict, and has recently committed "crimes of arson, unlawful wounding, attempted murder" and has become a thug for a certain businessman. The police are looking for him.[12] At the gathering of the prophets in Jeroboam's place, Ananaias attempts stealing a fellow prophet's wallet. Caleb is a drunkard. Matthew, now on parole, is a fornicator and a sex maniac, while Isaac is a drunkard, a con-man and a forger (pp. 198-9). And all of them, in the lust for worldly power and color, take to military ranks. Shadrach calls all of them thieves, robbers, rapists, and cut-throats (p. 210).

These plays seem to point out that men of this calibre cannot lead the nation. The priestly class lacks a proper orientation and a deep understanding of its own calling to be able to lead. It must heal itself of many gaping, mortal wounds. It is only when it survives its own self that it can have time to think of others. But the sad story presented by these dramas would prevent any nation that wants to survive from giving the helm to the priestly class. So the quest for leadership continues.

3.   The Peasant Class.

Nigerian drama has not really given much thought to the peasant class as a power source for political leadership. There seems to be a pervasive understanding by the playwrights that the time is yet to come when a farmer could be considered fit to offer leadership to the nation.

In *The Swamp Dwellers* and *Death and the King's Horseman* Wole Soyinka presents farmers who are so tied to

the belief in destiny and the supernatural that they could be
easily deceived. They do not see why things should change.
Their importance in these plays does not derive from their
occupation but from their relationships to the protagonists.

The first writer to attach some political importance to
farming as an occupation is Femi Osofisan, in his play *The
Chattering and the Song*. But Osofisan's work does not
really portray the farmer as a leader; rather, it sees the
occupation as a leveller. It is a socialist idea which seems to
exclude leadership. There is belief in equality, and in this
work this equality can only be achieved when everyone is a
farmer:

1.   When everyone's a farmer
              We'll grow enough food
              In the land
              No insurrection
              When all are fed
              Less Exploitation
              You eat all you need

              ....

2.   When everyone's a farmer
              We'll wipe out the pests
              In the land
              No more injustice
              Labour's for all
              No more oppression
              All hands to hoe

              ....

3.   When everyone's a farmer
              We'll burn out the weeds
              In our lives
              No alienation
              Working on the farm
              But brothers and sisters
              Sharing everything.[13]

It seems *The Chattering and the Song* does not believe
in the leadership of one man. It seems to advocate
leadership by the masses. Moreover, the fact that it sees

farming just as a leveller indicates it does not see the farmer
as possibly leading but as showing a way of life to the
society. But the idea in the above verses is myopic. Its
failure to recall the essence of the division of labor and of
professionalism raises grave concern. A one-profession
nation bears inherent disintegration. It must be reiterated that
the greater corpus of dramatic works appears not to have
given any serious consideration to the farmer as a possible
leader of the nation, as of now. However, although Daodu
in Soyinka's *Kongi's Harvest* sees himself as "only a
farmer" who does not "run this place,"[14] his ability to
organize some formidable opposition to the ruling
dictatorship seems to point out that an era in which the
farmer is to be reckoned with as a socio-political force is
already dawning.

4.   The Intellectual

One would have thought that Nigerian playwrights
would put national leadership in the hands of the intellectual
class—teachers, professors, doctors, lawyers—but a study
of Nigerian drama points to the contrary. Zulu Sofola, Femi
Osofisan, Wole Soyinka, James Ene Henshaw, Kole
Omotoso and Bode Sowande all seem to indicate in their
plays that the intellectual would do a greater and much more
violent harm to the nation than would any other person. His
acquisition of knowledge makes him able to justify whatever
he does even if he knows he is guilty.

In James Ene Henshaw's *This is Our Chance* and in
Wole Soyinka's *The Lion and the Jewel*, the "intellectuals,"
Bambulu and Lakunle, not only create communication
barriers between them and the people; they have begun to
preach false values to them and have become egoistic. In his
village in which only he is literate, Bambulu astonishes
everyone by his display of learning. He wants to know
from an illiterate man, Ajugo, whether the composition of a
certain poison is "miotic, pyretic, caustic, mydriatic,
hypnotic, anaesthetic, or narcotic."[15] He is simply trying to
impress on the people how learned he is and to create around

him an aura of fear and respectability. He wants to show
how awesome he has become by being educated. But
Bambulu's approach is mild when compared to Lakunle's
pseudo-intellectualism. Lakunle's great fault is his
misconception of civilization, and is therefore capable of
disrupting true civilization at the birth of the new nation. His
bright idea of civilization for the emergent nation consists of
eating with knives and forks from breakable plates, walking
side by side and arms interlocked with his wife in the street,
high-heeled shoes for the lady, red paint on her lips with the
hair of her head stretched. He would also teach the wife to
dance the waltz and the fox-trot and to spend the week-ends
in night clubs in the cities.[16] He adds to this list elsewhere
when he says:

> Within a year or two, I swear,
> This town shall see a transformation
> Bride-price will be a thing forgotten
> And wives shall take their place by men
> A motor road will pass this spot
> And bring the city ways to us.
> We'll buy saucepans for all the women
> Clay pots are crude and unhygienic
> No man shall take more wives than one
> That's why they're impotent too soon.
> The ruler shall ride cars, not horses
> Or a bicycle at the very least.
> We'll burn the forest, cut the trees
> Then plant a modern park for lovers
> We'll print newspapers every day
> With pictures of seductive girls.
> The world will judge our progress by
> The girls that win beauty contests ...
> Where is our school of ballroom dancing?
> Who here can throw a cocktail party?
> We must be modern with the rest
> Or live forgotten by the world
> We must reject the palm wine habit
> And take to tea, with milk and sugar... (p. 34)

The main fault with Lakunle's approach is one of priorities. Beauty contests, parks for lovers, pictures of seductive girls—these are truly good offspring of civilization; they are not the essence of civilization, nor what qualifies a leader. To reject cool palm wine for hot tea in a land whose climate is hot for most of the year is a misunderstanding of civilization, for above all, true civilization is a perfect adjustment of the individual within his particular social framework. Lakunle, the intellectual, lacks this adjustment. Having tasted of a foreign culture, he would bring it to his land without adapting it. Instead of initiating smooth cultural transition, he would bring violent cultural clashes because he misunderstands what true progress is.

How capable are the professors from the universities in leading the nation? This seems to be the concern of Femi Osofisan's *Kolera Kolej* (as adapted from the novel), Kole Omotoso's *Shadows in the Horizon*, Zulu Sofola's *The Sweet Trap*, Bode Sowande's *The Night Before* and Wole Soyinka's *The Road*.

Kolera Kolej presents professors who are not beyond petty squabbles and intrigues. They pour invectives on each other without qualms. They even fight, as Osofisan cleverly satirizes when Dr. (Mrs.) Abeke Paramole, Head of Mass Communications, fights it out with the Head of Defence, in which the latter has his head scalded with hot food and the former prevents people from coming to his aid as she screams and swings a pestle at them.[17] Not only do these professors use blackmail to acquire positions of authority but also employ their personal "babalawos"[18] for full service. While the country is in dire need of practical solutions to problems, the professors invent idealistic slogans to confound the people. At the same time, the Vice-Chancellor is fighting seriously that his post be left for him for life. More than this, Femi Osofisan thinks they are incapable of giving effective leadership because they never condemn any bad regime; rather they support it with theories garnered from different sources.

As if to continue the line of thinking in Osofisan's *Kolera Kolej*, Kole Omotoso's *Shadows in the Horizon* shows professors who have abandoned reading and writing and intellectual engagement so that they can pursue private businesses. They are so taken up with materialism that they are willing to use any means to acquire immediate wealth. Says Prof. Kofo Orimoogunje, a character in *Shadows in the Horizon*:

> As soon as those people come, I'm going to shoot them and all this will belong to me, everything here, the houses, the taxis, everything will be mine. Very simple. Just pull the trigger, like this. But the report of the gun? What about the noise of the gun? That would bring witnesses. And anyway, while I'm busy shooting Atewolara, that cunning business man would go behind me and do something foul. Or if it is the merchant I decide to shoot first, the retired security man is going to recall all his wartime experience and save himself, and then kill me. No. I must think of something else. Something quiet. Something deadly. Poison.[19]

There is no doubt that Orimoogunje is still creative, but his creativity is geared in one direction now—how to make creative means of destroying anyone who crosses his path of material acquisition. He is an angry man, angry at the rich people who have made it in life, angry at his salary which he thinks inadequate for a professor and angry at his fellow professors "who take all [one's] ideas, ... go and write a paper, or an essay or even a whole book with [one's] ideas and then they don't even acknowledge [the person's] existence" (p. 18). He is prepared to destroy professors and businessmen all should they dare form any opposition to his yearning. Unfortunately, for him, he gets killed before he can kill others.

There is also a feeling that professors pursue only abstract notions and do not help find practical solutions to pragmatic occurrences. The professor in Wole Soyinka's *The Road* is so obsessed with the idea of death that he uses Murano, "the dramatic embodiment of [the] suspension" of death as an experiment.[20] Murano has crawled "out of the darkness, from the last suck of the throat of death;" he has "the spirit of a god in him" and by keeping Murano in his power "it came to the same thing, that [he] held a god captive" (p. 223). When he puts the "egungun" mask on Murano, the Professor comes in very close contact with death, for the egungun is an ancestral mask of the dead and it is believed that when worn the dead rises to assume life in it once again. The tragedy of his research is that he does not live to find the answer, or if he found it he did not live to communicate it for the moment of the egungun/ Murano metamorphosis was also his moment of death (p. 228). It seems it is Soyinka's way of saying that anyone who discovers the essence of death must die, and that death and its essence cannot be separated in the same way as the essence of life is discoverable in living and not in death. It seems also a way of saying that the Professor in the play would have led the nation better if he had faced unemployment, thuggery and road accidents that sought urgent solution instead of pursuing the unplumbable essence of death.

And in *The Night Before*, Bode Sowande seems to present a picture of professors who cannot face real life situations. The play represents a grim situation in which the Vice-Chancellor and his Senate of professors are unable to settle a small problem in the campus and have to call in anti-riot policemen who out of nervousness maul the students instead of firing into the air to scare them. And even on some occasions, like the situation presented in Zulu Sofola's *The Sweet Trap*, these intellectuals deteriorate to such pettiness as to invite thugs to disrupt the social life of their fellowmen who disagree with them.

Again, the intellectual is seen in some drama as a class that has abandoned its rightful role of speaking the truth. Those in the class either condone injustice and corruption in silence or, when they are vocal, they rationalize them away. *A Dance of the Forests* gives such an instance. At the Court of Mata Kharibu, there is trouble as the Warrior refuses to go to war to recover the Queen's clothes from the husband she has deserted because he—the Warrior—feels that it is an

unjust war and cannot lead his men to battle merely to
recover the trousseau of some woman. Mata Kharibu's
intellectual, the Court Historian, rationalizes and justifies the
war:

> (Enter the Historian (Adenebi) with scrolls.)
> HISTORIAN: Don't flatter yourself. Every blade of grass that has
> allowed its own contamination can be burnt out. This thing
> cannot last. It is unheard of. In a thousand years it will be
> unheard of. Nations live by strength; nothing else has
> meaning. You only throw your life away uselessly.
> MATA KHARIBU (apprehensive): Did you find anything?
> HISTORIAN: There is no precedent, your Highness.
> MATA KHARIBU: You have looked thoroughly?
> HISTORIAN: It is unheard of. War is the only consistency that
> past ages afford us. It is the legacy which new nations seek to
> perpetuate. Patriots are grateful for wars. Soldiers have never
> questioned bloodshed. The cause is always the accident your
> Majesty, and war is the Destiny. This man is a traitor. He
> must be in the enemy's pay.
> MATA KHARIBU: He has taken sixty of my best soldiers with
> him.
> HISTORIAN: Your Highness has been too lenient. Is the nation
> to ignore the challenge of greatness because of the petty-
> mindedness of a few cowards and traitors[?]
> WARRIOR: I am no traitor!
> HISTORIAN: Be quiet Soldier! I have here the whole history of
> Troy. If you were not the swillage of pigs and could read the
> writings of wiser men, I would show you the magnificence of
> the destruction of a beautiful city. I would reveal to you the
> attainments of men which lifted mankind to the ranks of gods
> and demigods. And who was the inspiration of this divine
> carnage? Helen of Troy, a woman whose honor became as rare
> a conception as her beauty. Would Troy, if it were standing
> today lay claim to preservation in the annals of history if
> thousand valiant Greeks had not been slaughtered before its
> gates, and a hundred thousand Trojans within her walls?   Do
> you, a mere cog in the wheel of Destiny, cover your face and
> whine like a thing that is unfit to lick a soldier's boots, you, a
> Captain ... Your Majesty, I am only the Court historian and I
> crave your august indulgence for any excess of zeal.   But
> history has always revealed that the soldier who will not fight

has the blood of slaves in him. For the sake of your humble
subjects, this renegade must be treated as a slave.
MATA KHARIBU: Not only he. Every one who thinks like him,
be he soldier or merchant. I will have no moral termites a
thousand miles within my domain. Mata Kharibu is not the
idle eye that watches contemptible insects eat away the
strength of his kingdom.[21]

Because of the sophistic rationalism of the Court
Historian, the Warrior and his men are sold into slavery,
with the Court Historian making some profitable deal with
the slaver.

Equally incapable of rationally humane behavior is Dr.
Bero in *Madmen and Specialists*. In his actual taste of
human flesh, in his psychical maiming of the mendicants, in
the shooting to death of his father, Dr. Bero is a bizarre
image of the inhumanity perpetuated by an intellectual. He is
the embodiment of intellectualism exposed in all its fragility,
criminal leaning and cannibalistic tendency. His
combination of medical training and military undertaking as a
secret intelligence agent is destructive to man. His mind is
one of violent opposite struggles—the will to save life
(medicine) and the will to destroy life (military secret
intelligence). In these violent struggles man simply becomes
an experiment.[22]

If Nigerian drama does not trust leadership by teachers,
professors and doctors, equally distrustful is its look at
intellectuals engaged in legal services. It sees most of those
in the legal profession as men who do things contrary to
their vocation—they pervert justice. This is obviously the
view in *The Wizard of Law* in which Zulu Sofola dramatizes
Ramoni, a legal practitioner who goes out to dupe merchants
of their wealth and protects himself with the alibi of insanity.
More awesome is the picture of Yajin's father, a judge,
presented in Osofisan's *The Chattering and the Song*. Says
Sontri to Funlola, who cringes from him:

Her father is a judge, you know, if you haven't heard of him then
you haven't been breathing. An eminent judge, known and
respected from Lagos to Kaura Namoda! Esungboro! The Fearful

Spirit who deals out death penalties with the same ease as a wealthy man deals out fart into the air! Forty-six years on the bench! Dear father did so well, killing off the nation's bad children that, to reward him, they're going to put him on the Armed Robbery Tribunal![23]

These awesome judges can also pass and revoke sentences at will.

The picture of the intellectuals painted in Nigerian drama then is that of men who cannot be trusted with the leadership of a nation. To these intellectuals nothing is sacred. Life and property are unsafe, concrete problems are abandoned for abstract ones, and idealism replaces reality. They cannot even lead satisfactorily the little group entrusted to their care. And for a people who cannot take care of little things, it would be a most fatal error to entrust a whole nation to their care. Bearers of light, they ought to show the way to others to follow but because of selfishness, wickedness and intentional myopia, they trim the light to the extent that it shines for themselves only and are thereby able to fool and mislead those who have not seen the light but who put their trust in them. It seems to me that a nation led by such men exists precariously.

5.   The Artist[24]

It is possible that a particular class, in setting out the guidelines for leadership, might itself prove to be the messiah it proclaims. This seems to be the case of the artist in Nigerian drama that concerns itself with socio-political affairs. The artist, in his possession of a peculiar intellectual and emotional sensitiveness to life and to situations and in his creativeness, could very well be the leader he is looking for. This is the idea one could get from the treatment of Eman in Wole Soyinka's *The Strong Breed*. Eman, the teacher and healer, possesses the artist's quality; so also is Onita in *The Night Before* by Bode Sowande.

It seems imperative from Nigerian drama that the artist, or any person who must lead the nation, must be Christlike in his humanity. Eman, apart from the fact that the name could be the short form of Emanuel —"god-with-us" —and therefore another name for Christ, answers Girl's question whether he is the "carrier" positively—the carrier or scapegoat on whose head is piled the sins of the world, and who by destroying himself gives life to others. Says Girl, "Do you mean my carrier? I am unwell you know. My mother says it will take away my sickness with the old year."[25]

Eman believes that the Messiah must come from within the people, not from outside intervention. He tells the people that "a village which cannot produce its own carrier contains no men" (p. 129). Because he "continue[s] to stay where nobody wants [him]" (p. 120), he must be ready to suffer for his ideas, especially as he gives expression to the evils plaguing the society.

Eman, like his archetypal scapegoat Christ, is betrayed by the very people he is helping because they do not want him. They do not want him because he is difficult for them to understand, and he is difficult for them to understand because he is a creator, an artist, trying to put in form those things that are often times verbally ineffable. The difficulty in comprehending his moves and ideas makes him become a stranger in the society. Indeed to the people Eman is out of his mind. But then, according to Eldred D. Jones, such is a martyr and "because his conduct is inexplicable in terms of a selfish rat race in which each man fends for himself,"[26] and because his ideas are revolutionary, he must be annihilated. He becomes an embodiment of an ethics of a higher order, of a transcendental nature—a morality so powerful that it shatters all social boundaries. And because Eman is all these, his leadership would be through suffering, a rare leadership that demands self immolation as the ultimate sacrifice. It is by offering his life that Eman is able to penetrate the consciousness of the various kinds of people who make up the society. Oyin Ogunba puts it succinctly when he writes that:

> The artist or redeemer may torment the world—his ideas may bring
> about revolutions; subsequent generations may esteem the sterling
> quality of his work—but as far as his person or life is concerned
> there is no redemption, for this is what he has to sacrifice in order
> to achieve his end. He loses his soul in order to save others. This
> is the image of the true messiah and it is this element which makes
> Eman so much like the conventional Christ.[27]

Eman is sacrificed as a carrier, but the martyr's blood
has begun to change the life of the society even as he dies.
The people for whom he is sacrificed shamefully creep
away; "Not one could raise a curse." Words had dried in
their throats and they had fled, leaving the high-priests who
performed the sacrifice—Oroge and Jaguna—unattended (p.
146). Things would never be the same again.

In *A Dance of the Forests*, written for the Nigerian
Independence celebrations in 1960, Soyinka first toys with
the idea of the artist as possessing the qualities of leadership
necessary for the nascent Nigeria. Demoke, the artist in that
play, unleashes his creative energies to serve, but because he
becomes selfish, jealous and intolerant of possible rivalry in
Oremole, his apprentice, whom he casts down to death,
Soyinka seems to have abandoned the idea of a redeemer
artist. In *The Strong Breed*, he finds the time ripe to come
back to the topic and probe into what a true leader should be.
He becomes convinced that it is the artist who possesses
those qualities. Discarding the selfishness of Demoke, he
lifts the selflessness of the Court Poet—one of the few
people in *A Dance of the Forests* who dare raise voice
against Mata Kharibu and his wife whenever they over-reach
themselves—and builds up Eman in *The Strong Breed* as the
conscience of the nation, and who, because his quality defies
the mundane comprehension of the generality becomes a
stranger to the people: "Let me continue a stranger ... Those
who have much to give fulfil themselves only in total
loneliness" (p. 125).

Nigeria has had a troubled political past. Since the
departure of the British colonial masters and the attainment
of nationhood in 1960, the quest for the right leadership has
been one of futility. Those who rushed to fill the vacant

posts saw themselves as masters and equated leadership with what suited their interests. Even the soldiers who have unconstitutionally taken over the government on several occasions have not fared better than the politicians. It is at this juncture one should study *The Strong Breed* and *The Night Before* meditatively. What *The Night Before* expects of the artist of the "rebirth" is worthy of note:

> You leaders of tomorrow you must be grateful for your new baptism. By the honor of your nation you rank among men of the world. You must face life with the vigor of the reborn. You are the privileged ones. You are the chosen few. Go out and minister unto your nation, the virile and tender plant of today, the strong and mighty Baobab of tomorrow. Turn the old hut into a skyscraper, the lake into a dam. Build a straight road from a footpath and lead mankind to progress, because progress is the watchword of today.[28]

These are echoes of Christ advising his disciples before sending them out to create a new world. The task before the true leader in Nigeria is not dissimilar to the task that faced the early disciples of Christ.

THE ARMED FORCES
AND
THE NIGERIAN CIVIL WAR

•5•

The Ibo soldier became a spokesman of the East, and in a sense, of the NCNC; the Yoruba, of the Action Group (the Military Governor of the West was seemingly identified with the Action Group) and the Northerner, of the NPC.

O.D.

In "The African Writer and the Biafran Cause," a paper read at a seminar on political science at the Makerere University, Kampala, Uganda, Chinua Achebe, one of Nigeria's and Africa's foremost writers stated that:

> ... an African creative writer who tries to avoid the big social and political issues of contemporary Africa will end up being completely irrelevant—like that absurd man in the proverb who leaves his burning house to pursue a rat fleeing from the flames ...
>
> If an artist is anything he is a human being with heightened sensitivities; he must be aware of the faintest nuances of injustice in human relations. The African writer cannot therefore be unaware of, or indifferent to, the monumental injustice which his people suffer.[1]

This seems an echo of what another writer, Wole Soyinka, had said in Stockholm during a Writers' Conference in 1967—that when the writer can no longer function as a societal conscience, "he must recognize that his choice lies between denying himself totally or withdrawing to the position of chronicler and postmortem surgeon." The artist, he said, must cease to distract himself with "universal concerns whose balm is spread on abstract wounds, not on the gaping yaws of black inhumanity." He calls on the artist to respond to his essence "as the record of the mores and experience of his society and as the voice of vision in his own time."[2]

With such philosophy constantly in mind, one can see why some Nigerian playwrights have devoted time to treating the Nigerian armed forces, especially through the perspectives of the Nigerian Civil War (1967-70). For over two decades (1966-1979), (1983-1992 projected), the Nigerian armed forces have been involved in politics as they toppled the elected civilian governments, staged coup d'etats and counter coups among themselves, fought a secessionist movement and handed back the government to a democratically elected government.[3] Having occupied such a position in the socio-political affairs of the nation, it becomes imperative that the leadership by the armed forces as seen by dramatists be examined.

What, in the first case, are the factors influencing the armed forces to seize the government of a country like Nigeria? Claude E. Welch, Jr., in his book *Soldier and State in Africa*, gives about eight factors that affect domestic military interventions—the declining prestige of the major political party, schism among prominent politicians that tends to weaken the broadly based nationalistic movement that hastened the departure of the colonial power, lessened likelihood of external military intervention in the event of a military uprising, contagion from seizures of control by the military in other African countries, domestic social antagonism in ethnic terms, economic malaise, corruption and inefficiency of government and party officials, and the heightened awareness within the army of its power to influence or displace political leaders.[4] It is true that all these factors, especially those of tribal antagonism, corruption and inefficiency of government and political parties existed, as we have seen in previous chapters, in Nigeria. But were the armed forces of the period impeccably clean? Were they above corruption and inefficiency, and were they capable of correcting the existing evils and offering the leadership that was desperately needed?

The Nigerian armed forces, like modern armed forces in general, have, among other characteristics, the centralization of command and the rule of obedience and discipline. These characteristics are supposed to unite members of the armed forces and to keep them well above tribal or ethnic considerations. Favored by these qualities, the military in Nigeria seems to be in a unique position to offer good leadership. However, these claims seem questionable in the Nigerian situation, for the successful military disturbances that have rocked the nation five times (twice in 1966, once in 1975, 1983 and 1985) have indicated that far from being detribalized, the military has shown itself to be as susceptible to the claims of the lineage, clan or ethnic group as the mass of Nigerians. After the January 1966 coup d'etat by the Nigerian military, for instance, "a number of Ibo men who had joined the army under fictitious Hausa names and who were regarded as Hausa, quickly reverted to their original Ibo names,"5 and after the July coup of the same year, the Hausas showed they were Northerners first before anything else.

What we find of the Nigerian armed forces, at least of the military that ruled Nigeria from 1966-79, is that the military training did not form the members into cohesive entities with strong national consciousness, and that their barracks were not melting pots in which they could lose some of their ethnic, tribal or regional blood. The two bloody coup d'etats of 1966 give a strong support to this. One of the charismatic leaders of the first military seizure of government in Nigeria, the late Major Chukwuma Kaduna Nzeogwu, did point out "that in the South, the coup seems to have been tribally oriented."6 But so also was the July reaction: thenceforth, the Ibo soldier became a spokesman of the Eastern Region and the Hausa, of the Northern Region. Writes a certain O. D. in "The Military and Politics":

> In Nigeria it can be argued that the July reaction to the January coup was related to the suspicion that the latter incident was not

unconnected with party politics. Perhaps a better example would be the reaction of the members of the Military in October 1966 after the killings in the North.   The Ibo soldier became a spokesman of the East, and in a sense, of the NCNC; the Yoruba, of the Action Group (the Military Governor of the West was seemingly identified with the Action Group) and the Northerner, of NPC.[7] The officer corps of the armed forces had kept in reasonably close contact with the friends they had made at secondary school, many of whom had gone into the Universities and the civil services, and that they tended to take their political cues from their civilian counterparts. (One might add here that the case for the secession of the Eastern 'region' was drawn up by dons at the University of Ibadan, many of whom were educated either at Government College, Umuahia, or at Christ the King's College, Onitsha, the two schools which provided not less than two-thirds of the Army officers of Eastern origin.)[8]

The image of men of the armed forces whether as corrupt or honest, capable or incapable of leadership, can only be fully explored in the context of the Nigerian civil war (1967-70), for most of the plays treat the qualities of the armed men in this context. In Gordon Tialobi's *Full-Cycle*, Elechi Amadi's *The Road to Ibadan*, Wole Soyinka's *Madmen and Specialists*, Uwa Udensi's *Monkey on the Tree* and Rasheed Gbadamosi's *Echoes from the Lagoon*, we are made to face the grim realities that the armed forces are not as detribalized and nationally conscious as one would think, and that like the professional politicians they ousted from government, the armed forces also get caught up in the cross-currents of personal, lineage, clan and ethnic loyalties and sentiments. Some of these plays see the disaster these men pose to the nation because they are educationally deficient. They have little brains in very strong physiques. Apart from their overwhelming superiority in matters of force and violence and a special skill in the destructive use of arms, the armed forces have very little or nothing to offer. The leadership of a nation relies mostly on the strength of the brain.

This is the view one gets in *The Road to Ibadan*. Amadi's play depicts the war in a fierceful rage in which civilians, running helter-skelter as they are caught in between the belligerents, have no hope of witnessing the dawning of another day. The situation is one of deep concern because the soldiers shoot at the fleeing refugees without first finding out whether they are enemy soldiers or not. Moreover, there is a difficult communication barrier created between the soldiers and the civilian refugees as the former claim superiority over the latter. It is in this state of affairs that an Army Commander, Captain Koko, who claims not to be educated and makes fun of "'bukuru' people"[9]—educated men—nevertheless makes some confession truer and more important than he might have thought when he says that armed men and women fight because they are "animals" and "the fact that we [fighters] can think makes very little difference to our animal behavior." They do things "exactly like animals" (pp. 115-116). Earlier on, in commending the student nurse who had come to help the soldiers because the war has made it impossible for her to continue her studies, Captain Koko had confided that before Wigo came he was "managing and damaging" (p. 97).

Captain Koko does not even fight his war thoroughly as he allows the love of a woman to interfere with his duty, thereby endangering the lives of the soldiers under his command:

> CAPT. KOKO: ... No one can fight two wars at the same time—an external physical enemy and an internal emotional conflict.
> WIGO: But Captain, you've made no mistakes so far. You have fought very bravely.
> CAPT. KOKO: So you see it, but you are wrong. For instance I ought to have posted sentries at that crossing in the river. I failed to do so because I was not reappraising my situation with sufficient frequency. If the enemy had had a little more courage they could have sacked my headquarters during the last attack. (p. 129)

The Road to Ibadan then seems to give some strong reasons why the military should not lead. Not only do soldiers behave like animals, refuse to think, are ill-educated and do not even perform their military task effectively, they

"damage" even as they try to "manage" affairs of
responsibility. If politics is the art of governing, of
governing human beings by human beings, and if human
beings are highly characterized by thinking, the repudiation
of thinking by soldiers makes them animals, the main
differentiation of a human being from an animal being in the
rational processes, and thereby disqualifies them from giving
any effective leadership or government. History has no
record of any nation that was purposefully led by irrational
beings. Even in the chaotic origins of the world as depicted
in *Genesis*, the Creator had put the irrational beings under
the rational ones.

Gordon Tialobi, in his play *Full-Cycle*, also uses the
civil war as an approach to the treatment of the military in
politics. In this dream play, General Maga is brought before
the Supreme Court to be tried for war crimes. Under his
leadership, murders, rapes, lootings, and many other crimes
were committed while the civil war raged. The court, in
which the Judge refers to Maga as a "criminal" even before
he is tried, is anything but a place for justice. The Judge is a
puppet type and has "not much power over [the] Court or its
happenings."[10] It is not surprising then that he is coerced
into allowing Sergeant-Major Bondo be the usher, the
accuser, and the major witness.

Sergeant-Major Bondo, formerly of the 7th Paratroop
Brigade, tells the court how he had been commanded, during
the civil war that had ended, to take paratroop action against
an enemy enclave. The Sergeant-Major had duly briefed his
men of the operation but while they were airborne they had
forgotten which area of the "demilitarized zone" they were
told to act against. He had previously destroyed all
documents pertinent to the action because of the military
tactics that says, "read and destroy." Thus disoriented and
without any frame of reference as to whether the action was
to be "north-northeast or north-north-west" of the
demilitarized zone, he had decided to end the dilemma by a
toss of the coin. The coin came up tails, and that was what
he had chosen for north-north-west. The result was
calamitous. Thirty-five miles north-north-west of the

demilitarized zone led straight to his own village. They
descended on the village and in their savage rage and
genocidal propensity they "wiped out everybody, everything
that moved, that flew, that swam ...," including his mother
and his "favorite goat!" (pp. 151-152). What is surprising is
that General Maga, now out of office and perhaps has been
toppled from government by a more radical group of soldiers
of Sergeant-Major Bondo's temperament, is being
prosecuted for the irresponsible acts of the latter while
Bondo goes free.

What *Full-Cycle* seems to be criticizing is not only the
appointment of Judges that serve the mind of the military
rulers but other more touching issues like military coup
d'etats and genocidal warfare. Throughout the Nigerian civil
war, the secessionist soldiers of Eastern Nigeria (Biafra) had
claimed strongly that the Federal soldiers were waging a
genocidal war against the entire people of Biafra—soldiers
and civilians alike. The soldiers were also accused of
murders, rape and looting.

Other ills exposed in the play include the demobilization
of the soldiers who fought the war without adequate
planning, facing the firing squad and bribing one's way
through to get a job. Perhaps no other person would have
been in a better position to point an accusing finger on the
military regime than the Usher, himself an ex-soldier, when
he says:

> You see, during the war, I wiped out my entire village. Never
> mind if it was my fault or not. The fact is that I did it for the war.
> And why? Because you people said it was to free us from political
> oppressors and tyrants, corruption and bribery, tribalism,
> nepotism—name it, you said it. And what happens after the war?
> Whereas I could have had this job for fifty pounds and my
> seventeen-year-old daughter thrown in, in fact, now I have to add
> my thirteen-year-old girl as well ... (p. 155)

What *Full-Cycle* does here is that while accepting that
the civilian government of professional politicians was bad,
the very ills in the society against which the armed forces
had staged a coup d'etat and which they had promised to

eradicate are still being perpetrated, only this time on a larger, more heinous scale, by the military administration. Gordon Tialobi, therefore, seems to ask if there was any rationale for seizing power from the civilians and leading the nation into a war that was bloody and massively destructive. There is the contention whether these men who violate young girls, pervert justice, are unable to arrest crimes and force the nation into a war can be the messiah that Nigeria is looking for. The structure of the play in the manner of dream, waking reality, dream, seems to point out Tialobi's feeling that events as shown in the play should only occur in dreams, in fiction, yet by inserting a waking reality in between these dreams he seems to affirm that seemingly impossible as these things are, they do occur in the reality that is Nigerian.

Uwa Udensi, in her play *Monkey on the Tree*, also looks at the military through the perspectives of the Nigerian civil war. In her production comments she says that the realization that the "play [is] about actual people, in a war which actually took place, and reflecting another potential and real war situation" is important towards producing the play.[11] The other "potential and real war situation" Udensi refers to has to do with South Africa. Indeed, most of the mercenaries in the play are given South African names, and the two situations (in Nigeria and South Africa) are brought together in the statement that even "God has become a mercenary" (p. 28). Here is a subtle attack on the role played by church representatives in trying to calm down people from violent revolt against oppressive regimes. By not opposing such authorities because of fear of the reaction of the governments, the church only protects its own interests and makes God a mercenary while the people suffer. It is the realization of this that makes Nkomo, a black South African mercenary fighting in Nigeria, cry out to the priest:

> Yes God's. He made me and nailed me down ... Tell Him [God] to go back to South Africa and take His crow-bars with Him, or perhaps He will carry a gun like me. Tell Him to go down into the crypts of any church in Johannesburg and blow open the crypts,

blow up the coffins and there, retrieve His cross before the scars of
diamonds and gold burn forever deep into it. So deep that one of
these days He will come back crying for vengeance, for destruction,
crying for blood and hate!

Yes, in the crypts, under the streets, below the asphalt, the
pavements, the gutters, lies the cross smothered in diamonds, in
gold and here [Nigeria] in oil. God has become a mercenary! (he
breaks the cross to pieces and drops them in a heap). (pp. 27-28)

The problem that Udensi tries to confront here is larger
than at first understood. It is the problem of evil. Why does
God allow evil—in terms of suffering, hardship,
oppression, poverty... —in the world? Is it not possible that
God, if he be all-loving and omnipotent, could create a
world in which everything is in its right place—a problem-
free world? Why do those who speak for God, like Father
Man in the play, put the blame on the "sins" in "our hearts"
and pray to God to "protect us from ourselves, from
destroying one another through hatred, pride and greed"
when in the first place he (God) could have created a perfect
man? All these questions are at Udensi's heart and she
creates an outlet for her frustration over them by making
Nkomo the soldier defy God:

I want to tell God that my heart is full of hate. I want him to
know that I hate you [Father Man and Humanity]. I want him to
know that I shall kill and kill and kill, again and again and again
and again, and nobody is going to stop me. I want him to witness
my killings as he did my days in the ghettos. I would like him to
see that it is the same me but that now, I am master ... (p. 27)

Implicit in this angry declaration is the question of
leadership. Can soldiers give the right leadership? From the
image of all the soldiers given in *Monkey on the Tree*, the
military is not carved out for political leadership. The true
leader is not the master, but the soldier claims to be the
master. He is ready to kill again and again, not only soldiers
but in the case of Mosis, a regular soldier in the Nigerian
Army, hard-working civilians like Mr. Joseph Mark, a
Shell-BP oil prospector. After killing the man, Mosis had
also shot Mark's wife and only son and had attempted to

rape Jane, Mark's daughter. Other soldiers had looted the belongings of Mr. Mark's family (p. 11).

Udensi also sees the soldier as a man who cares little about life and who goes out "seeking death." To him death "is all beauty and happiness" and shooting "a man or a woman ... brings pleasure" (p. 19). Ultimately, the soldier is to be judged by the fact that "destruction [to him] ... is production" (p. 21).

Though *Monkey on the Tree* takes a dismal look at the military and its operations, the play is by no means pessimistic. Indeed, amidst the deaths and fury of war, there is an optimistic note that "things will be better after the war" (p. 31). The mention of children who are "very nice" and who "should be seen some day" suggests the continuity of life, of a better life when the war is over and the soldiers gone.

Like *Monkey on the Tree*, Rasheed Gbadamosi's *Echoes from the Lagoon* deals with Nigeria at war. It examines the relationship between the military and the civilians, the poor and the rich during the war and the issue of patriotism.

In setting a background to the events of war, the play begins in an optimistic manner by recalling efforts at "Peace Talks." Ten-Ten, the newspaper vendor, advertises his newspaper by paraphrasing the headlines of the news, "Peace in our time! See the warm handshake!" People are happy because the military leaders have "finished talk in Ghana" and hopes for averting a war are aroused.[12] However, the informed audience knows that this hope is a false one, for the decisions of the historic meeting that was held at Aburi, Ghana, in January, 1967, were unanimously accepted but differently interpreted by the military leaders that represented the Nigerian Federal Government and the Eastern Nigerian Government. Because the most touching issues of the nine-point agreement—the Northern Nigerian riots in which many Easterners were killed, the resultant refugee problem created by the Easterners who returned to their region, and the nature of a new constitutional system that Nigeria would adopt as a nation—were differently interpreted and defended by the spokesmen of the two governments,antagonistic feelings were heightened. The optimism generated by the smiles and warm handshakes with which the play begins then quickly gives way to the reality of a civil war and its accompanying pessimism.

Important in the treatment of *Echoes from the Lagoon* is the meaning of war. To Erinla, the business magnate of a transport company, who "wishes the government all the good luck in its endeavor to preserve the unity and territorial integrity of the country" (p. 36) war is a means to enhance name and wealth. He does not go to war but he loves the war to continue and he sends his emotionally weak son, Dele, to join the Air Force so that when the boy retires as a Colonel he would hand over the business management to him. Why? Simply because the name sounds good: "Colonel Dele Erinla of the Air Force, retired, Managing Director of Erinla Transport Ltd." (p. 65). But there is more to this as we see in Erinla's dream:

> I had a vision ... I was hoping I would be smiling up in heaven watching Dele fill the skies with aeroplanes. Not motor vehicles. Aeroplanes! I had big plans. I had thought Erinla Transport would grow bigger and bigger, expand into commercial airlines business, the biggest private airlines in Africa ... (p. 65)

To Tanko the poor boy who later becomes a soldier, war is a means of going to a "better," "more peaceful" life "somewhere beyond the skies" when "life in this world has hardly been worth it." Moreover, when one joins the armed forces "there'll be food and shelter and a sense of belonging to something meaningful" (p. 53). Erinla puts Tanko's thoughts better when he says, "Take any jobless man. Or take a young man on a ten-pound-a-month job and pay him nineteen pounds ten and you've got thousands of volunteers [for war]" (p. 43).

Contrasted to Tanko the survivalist soldier is Dele, a soldier with a conscience. A B-26 plane bombs an airport for civil aviation, killing Dele's European friends. Shocked by such killing of civilians, he deserts the force. While Tanko is the image of the mindless soldier and Dele that of a conscientious one, thus pointing to the possibility of finding good and bad soldiers in the military, it seems possible to argue that the military is mostly made up of the latter because at the moment Dele becomes conscientious he ceases to be a soldier; he deserts the force with "no trace of him."

Gbadamosi seems to argue in the play that if "peace talks" fail there is another alternative means by which peace could be achieved—by desertion. If all men were to desert the armed forces, which is similar to saying if all were to refuse to go to war or fight a war, would there be war? This seems to be Gbadamosi's sympathetic treatment of the emotionally wounded Dele, but he also realizes that in practical life there are war fanatics, business men (Erinla) who must make money out of war and the wretched of the earth (Tanko) who must fight a war so that they can survive. The latter case is one of irony, as some people can only live (have food, money, shelter) only by seeking death (in war and armed rebellion).

While Erinla and Tanko are both odious individuals who have warmongering in common, Tanko seems to present himself as the more patriotic of the two. He presents himself as a "loyal citizen of [his] fatherland" and a "loyal federal soldier" and castigates Erinla for his unpatriotic behavior:

> Your type owns everything; you split up the goodies of this country and in your greediness you led us to war. We the younger generation are now putting it right, dying on the battlefields. And how do you reward us? You stab us in the back! (p. 88)

While Erinla does not pretend to be patriotic, he is equally aware that in Nigeria it is difficult, if not impossible, to find a patriot, and obviously the survivalist soldier cannot be patriotic:

> Show me a soul in this country who's doing something for nothing, and I'll show you a saint. There are no Nigerian saints, are there? (p. 43)

Definitely, Tanko who himself confesses he had no choice but to join the army in order to live is not a saint.

There are other issues raised in *Echoes from the Lagoon*, like the question of Allah's (God's) existence and the lot of man on earth, and the effects of war, but the most provocative one seems to be the analogy between war and abnormality. Erinla's wife was abnormal at the time of their marriage "in 1940 when the whole world was at war" and Dele, Erinla's son, experiences a state of mental abnormality during the civil war. Is there a parallel between war and insanity or is the playwright simply saying that war is an abnormal affair and that the people, place and time that are caught up in it are abnormal?

Finally, when Tanko says, "I'm a Nigerian soldier. I fought in the 16th Brigade at Owerri, sir. And I'm proud I belong to the army of unity and I'm a loyal citizen of my fatherland!" (p. 85), is there an intended satire by the dramatist? Is there a realization that disunity—violent disunity, to be precise—was begun by members of the Nigerian armed forces and that Tanko, like most soldiers, did not fight out of patriotism?

In *Madmen and Specialists*, one comes to the darkest of the dramas that deal with the armed forces and war. Written after the Nigerian Civil War (1967-1970), the play is unrelentingly pessimistic as it shows the erosion of humanity and civilization to blatant, contaminative, militaristic inhumanity. There are two main issues concerning war that the play devotes much attention to: war as cannibalism and those involved in it as cannibals, and the physical and intellectual maiming that war brings on men.

In the dialogue between Priest and Bero, we are invited into the horrors of cannibalism:

PRIEST: Strange man, your father, very strange ... I'm really
   anxious to know if he still intends to legalize cannibalism.
BERO: He does.
PRIEST: I knew it. A stubborn man, once he gets hold of an
   idea. You won't believe it but he actually said to me, I'm
   going to try and persuade those fools not to waste all that
   meat. Mind you he never could stand wastage, could he? I

remember, he used to wade into you both if he caught you wasting anything. But human flesh, why, that's another matter altogether.

BERO: But why Pastor. It's quite delicious you know.

PRIEST: Just what I say. It's ... what did you say?

BERO: (reaches out and pulls out the Priest's cheek):   This. Delicious.

PRIEST (struggles free): You're joking, of course.

BERO: No. Your friend will confirm it when he comes.

PRIEST (increasingly horrified): You mean he ...

BERO: No, not him. He never meant anything. At least, not that way. But we found it delicious just the same.

PRIEST: You?

BERO: I give you the personal word of a scientist. Human flesh is delicious. Of course, not all parts of the body. I prefer the balls myself.

PRIEST (vehemently): I don't believe you.

BERO: You don't? Well, then, why don't you stay to dinner?

PRIEST: Dinner? (Cheering up.) Of course,. I see all you want is an argument like your old man. Delighted, of course. Only too delighted to oblige ... (He is stricken by a sudden doubt). Er ... dinner ... did you say dinner?

BERO: Dinner. I came well-laden with supplies. (The Priest glances at Bero's bulging briefcase lying near by, gulps.)

PRIEST: I ... er ... I am wondering if I haven't got a little christening to attend to. I ... er ... couldn't simply come for drinks afterwards?

BERO: A christening so late in the evening?

PRIEST: Well, you know, the blessing at home and all that. The christening was this morning. (He is already retreating.) God bless you, my children both. I shall hurry back as soon as it's all over. Can't get rid of these extra parish duties ... welcome back once again, my boy ...

(They watch him take flight.)[13]

The case here is one of actual cannibalism.   Some soldiers who fought in the civil war did claim to have tasted human blood.   Whether such claims were true or were simply made to instill fear in the civilian population is beyond the scope of this chapter. But beyond this aspect of real cannibalism extends that of metaphorical or philosophical cannibalism.   War is a period in which man unleashes his animalistic behavior and preys, as it were, upon his fellow man. Animals kill each other for food. If man has decided to kill his fellow man, he could very well eat him also to satisfy the beast in him. War brings man to those pre-civilized days in which, as Hobbes says, man to man was a wolf. War breaks down civilization and returns man to those barbaric days before men chose to forego some rights and put issues at some arbitration for the sake of peace.

Those who survive man's cannibalistic tendency in war enter into the world of the handicap. The deformity could be physical or mental; in the case of *Madmen and Specialists* it is both. Says Bero, of his father, to his sister concerning the Mendicants—Aafaa, Blindman, Goyi, Cripple:

> Father's assignment was to help the wounded readjust to the pieces and remnants of their bodies. Physically. Teach them to make baskets if they still had fingers. To use their mouths to ply needles if they had none, or use it to sing if their vocal chords had not been shot away. Teach them to amuse themselves, make something of themselves. Instead he began to teach them to think, think, THINK! Can you picture a more treacherous deed than to place a working mind in a mangled body? (p. 242)

The "thinking" here refers to the philosophy of "As "—an incomprehensible concept used by the mentally deranged that could mean anything. The issue here is one of an unsound mind in an unsound body. A worse devolution of man is unthinkable.

Madmen and Specialists takes a pessimistic view of a military regime, especially the one that precipitates a civil war. There is a presentation of how the humanity of civilians is contaminated by the inhumanity of the soldiers. Dr. Bero, formerly a surgeon who saw that life was renewed in sick men, after joining the Intelligence Service during the war, turns his theatre into a butcher house. He becomes one with the soldiers, thereby losing his humanity. In his newly acquired inhuman touch, he first certifies his father insane and then shoots him dead. Here again is that image of the soldier as the harbinger of death we have seen in the other plays discussed in this chapter. Indeed, there is a pervasive feeling in the play that anyone who comes in touch with the armed forces does lose some humanity. Old Man Bero himself, since he begins to work for the army, becomes a true cannibal, persuading "those fools [soldiers] not to waste all that meat [human flesh of those killed at war]" (p. 240). The beggars themselves, now only half-humans, are also victims of military action. These men have been reduced to their present state of handicap because the military has used them: first, they are conscripted into the army to fight a war and their bodies have been shattered. Then comes Old Man, who in his own way of rehabilitating the handicapped, leads the beggars to mental imbalance. So these beggars, who, before the intervention of the military were whole and human, are given a devastating twist to the opposite, and have now become ugly shadows of their former selves.

Madmen and Specialists also makes some further criticism of the megalomania and hypocrisy involved in the rule by the armed forces. Says Aafaa, in mockery of the military rulers:

> In a way you may call us [soldiers] vultures. We clean up the mess made by others. The populace should be grateful for our presence. (He turns slowly round.) If there is anyone here who does not approve us, just say so and we quit. (His hand makes the motion of half-drawing out a gun.) I mean, we are not here because we like it. We stay at immense sacrifice to ourselves, our leisure, our desires, vocation, specialization, et cetera, et cetera. The moment you say, Go, we ... (He gives another inspection all round, smiles broadly, and turns to the others.) They insist we stay. (pp. 220-221)

The love of power and the insincerity in the speech are obvious. He has his hand on a gun to blast the brains out of anyone who will dare tell the military to leave its position of political leadership. Moreover, it was not necessary asking the people to tell the soldiers to quit because the populace did not invite them in the first instance to take over leadership. They are not elected leaders; the populace knows the means to remove its elected officials from government.

There is also a depiction of contrastive life-styles between the man who declares the war and the people who actually fight the war. In a scene Aafaa calls the "Visit of the First Lady to the Home of the de-balled," the Head of State comes "smelling of wine and roses" with his wife clinging to his arm. His "corpulent First Lady" passes some imported cigarettes round to the inmates (p. 258). The agonizing realization here is that the true heroes (and the victims too!) of the war are "de-balled," that is, their scrotal bags have been shattered by bullets and are therefore incapable of consummating any sexual yearning whereas the author of the war lives in complete sexual capability as he demonstrates by paying a visit to the disabled with his wife clinging to his arm. He lives well—he smells of wine and roses—and his wife is corpulent whereas the "disgusted," "disappointed" and "crucified" mendicants are only too happy to struggle for the imported cigarettes brought by the First Lady.

Bode Sowande's *The Night Before* also looks at the armed forces, but it does this outside the war context. The play reveals a burning anger welling up in people against the waste of human resources, the very hope of a possible better day, carried out by the armed forces. In a bold Author's Note to the play, Sowande tells us that:

> While the search for 'alternatives' continues among conscious progressives, 'accidents' and repressions occur against the struggle, often with methodic planning. It is for this reason that I dedicate this play to the 'unknown students' lying in some graves, or lunatic asylums or prison cells of those dictators who litter what they call the 'Free World'.[14]

It is a very bold comment because it openly advocates a search for leadership ("alternatives"), and therefore, a change of government, of a government of "dictators"— dictators, because, among other things, armed forces rule by decrees. In the course to effect a possible change "accidents ... with methodic planning"—therefore, they are no longer accidents but stratagems—occur among the irrepressible, boisterous students. In Nigeria, students are very important in galvanizing support or opposition to the ruling government, whether civilian or military.

The chord Sowande is strumming at is clear when he dedicates the play to students either dead or imprisoned. In 1971, during a struggle between students and the military government of General Yakubu Gowon over the National Youth Service Corps, Kunle Adepeju, an undergraduate of the University of Ibadan, was shot dead. Then during the 1977/78 academic year, Segun Okeowo, the Students' Union Leader of the University of Lagos and the President of the National Union of Nigerian Students (NUNS), was rusticated for his stand on some national issues in which nine people, most of them ranging from the primary school to the University, from Lagos in the South to Zaria in the North, were shot dead by a squad of the Nigerian armed forces.

Says Nibidi in *The Night Before*, "the anti-riot squad were the crack-shots of counter-insurgency—and they did their job well... They marched on in formation" against students, poised to strike! (p. 38). This is the height of sarcasm. In Nigeria, students as well as civilians are not allowed to possess and carry arms. Permission has to be obtained even before fireworks can be used to celebrate events. For crack-shots to march in formation and shoot at these unarmed students show an inexplicable disregard for human lives by the armed forces. Using the "Biafran" secession of July 1967 as a direct point of reference, these same "crack-shots of counterinsurgency" used over two and a half years to achieve victory over an armed rebellion.

There is an acute perception in *The Night Before* that the presence of the armed forces in politics is a sordid situation which cannot be changed by physical action alone because the oppressor is physically stronger than the oppressed. To confront military leadership physically is to betray the cause through a suicidal undertaking, for those who allow their bodies to be mangled by the bullets of the armed forces become useless to the cause. Whoever wants to effect a leadership change must strive to keep body and soul together. To this end, *The Night Before* seems to advocate that physical action must be backed by a spiritual attitude and prayer:

> Oh Lord fight this oppression,
> Oh Lord build up this nation,
> Oh Lord burn this Babylon
> Why don't you deliver us! (p. 39)

As we shall see in another of his plays in the next chapter, the call here is not for a deus-ex-machina to "fight," "build" and "deliver" but for the man who wants a change of leadership to realize that he has a sense of a sacred mission. He must see himself as an instrument of divine powers to make things what they should be in his nation. Goaded by such a perception, he cannot fail.

DICTATORSHIP

•6•

"God created man in his own image."
Is the dictator also an image of God?

Although Nigeria has never really experienced a totalitarian government, it has not totally escaped "redemptionist" or "revolutionary" regimes which are evolving in the Third World countries of Asia, Africa and Latin America. It has experienced a series of military regimes in which the entire constitution, or parts of it, is suspended and power is concentrated in the hands of soldiers who rule by decree. The rule by decree thus concentrates authority in the hands of the military elite, thereby making it a form of authoritarian rule. In Africa, countries like Ghana, Central Africa Republic, Equatorial Guinea and Uganda have proved susceptible to dictatorship when they gave birth to such men as Kwame Nkrumah, Jean-Bedel Bokassa, Marcias Nguema and Idi Amin. And without exception, all the African nations which have non-elected military leaders—Nigeria, Republic of Benin, Zaire, Togo, Sudan, Somalia, Niger, Ethiopia, Liberia, Mali, Burkina Faso, Mozambique,...— with a little twist, could become a dictatorship. The inclination of these countries towards "strong-man" regimes has been traced to the feudalistic background of African traditional institutions and to the fact that colonialism did not actually cancel this form of rule but strengthened it as the colonial powers, especially in British territories, ruled "indirectly" through the African chiefs. It has also been said that at independence, only a negligible minority of native intellectuals capable of political thought and action emerged and that the strong belief of these intellectuals in rapid progress—urbanization, industrialization, education, welfare state—could only be brought to accomplishment through dictatorship. There is much to be argued for and against these claims but such an undertaking is not of immediate concern to this study. Dictatorship will only be examined here through the eyes of drama.

Two Nigerian playwrights have been most vocal in their treatment of dictatorship. They are Bode Sowande and Wole Soyinka. Though their plays are different in structure, there are similarities in their treatment of dictatorship. *Farewell to Babylon,* [1] *Kongi's Harvest,* [2] and *Opera Wonyosi* [3] indicate that in dictatorship, every activity in the life of the Individual—his religious beliefs, his culture, his domestic expenditure, his occupations, and even his most intimate relations with his family—is brought under a scrutiny. People are made to live in fear of sudden, secret penalties for violations of decreed norms.

The plays show the concentration of power in the hands of an individual or of a group. Legitimate socio-political groups and institutions deemed non-conformist to the totalitarian aspirations are suppressed, if not totally eliminated. There is no allowance for a group or an individual to compete with governmental interests. The constitution is suspended and the dictator unleashes laws that are perpetually changed at will. The dictator may choose a puppet law enforcement agency and judiciary to give the impression that he is fair in dealing with the citizens. Civil liberties are highly restricted, if not completely eliminated, as such liberties are viewed as a fertile background towards questioning the legitimacy of the dictatorship. The dictator or the authoritarian ruling elite chooses an ideology that purports to make him or the government the Messiah that has come "in the fulness of time" to redeem the people. As a "redemptive council," a ground-plan is laid for an aggressive foreign and domestic policy which is aimed at transforming and disciplining humanity and at giving the people "a new lease of life." Voluntary labor and undertaking which the citizens have always executed in joy before the arrival of the dictatorship now give way to obligatory mass labor and services. The dictator is clever to give it the stamp of popular approval. And, of course, the dictator controls the socio-political sphere by employing despotic methods which range from propaganda and intimidation to terror.

The plays also show that a dictatorship usually provokes some unrest within the legitimate geographical boundaries of the country. It employs a number of means to crack-down on such unrests—secret service agents, highly disciplined, robot-like soldiers and police, the gagging of the press and the suppression of free expression, an active propaganda aimed at the ignorant masses and the tightening of international borders. The dictatorship could also use some diversionary methods; it could provoke some diplomatic aggression on the international scene, thereby furnishing the people with something to keep them occupied. In such a situation the dictatorship assumes the posture of the defender of the dear masses against an enemy outside its country.

Finally, all the plays depict the natural tendency for clandestine groups to arise in strong opposition to the totalitarian regime. Such groups could be those who have been displaced by the unilateral seizure of absolute power by the ruling dictatorship; they may be lovers of true democratic processes, those who have been hurt by the activities of the dictatorship and now seek unmitigated vengeance, or they may simply be another group of power lovers who, out of envy, wants to unseat the government and set up its own dictatorship. The success of these groups, whatever their intentions, hinges on the indispensable conditions that there is a reasonable hope and a plausible chance of being able to overthrow the regime, and that there is mass support given by a large percentage of the citizens who consider the dictatorship intolerable and sincerely desire a change. These two conditions—mass support and the ability to overthrow the government—are not mutually exclusive. They go together to ensure success: the masses will support clandestine attempts to usher in a change only if they perceive a real possibility of the success of such an undertaking.

Bode Sowande's *Farewell to Babylon* is a "testimony of the lives of those who live under the dictatorships that grow like Hydra—especially in the Third World—and other parts of the world." Says the playwright:

> The play witnesses a triumphant thrust within 'Babylon', expressing the groans and pains of those who fight to say 'Farewell to Babylon', showing the price they pay. As they succeed, their euphoria is muted by their experience, but we recognize the common bond of humanity. We realize the urgency of the need to strive for an alternative society. (p. 55)

The title of the play is at first confusing. Babylon, an ancient city of South-West Asia and capital of Babylonia, and later of the Chaldean Empire, was famous, not only for being the largest city in the world during the reign of Nebuchadnezzar but for its culture and magnificence. Indeed, Herodotus, the historian, saw it as the world's city of ultimate splendor. The city had the great temple of the god Marduk with its associated ziggurat that was popularly referred to as the Tower of Babel. Its "Hanging Gardens" were one of the "Seven Wonders of the World."

The society of Babylon was quasi-feudal. It was divided into classes: on the upper layer were the priests, wealthy land owners and propertied men, and merchants. On the middle level were the peasants, the less wealthy merchants and artisans. Slaves formed the lowest class. Babylon had an ugly side to its luxurious existence when in 648 B.C., Ashurbanipal laid siege on it and in the resultant famine, the inhabitants were driven to cannibalism.

In the Bible, Babylon looms large with the rise of the Neo-Babylonian Empire, and several oracles and prophets predict its doom because of its wickedness and hostility toward the Jews. Among the Greeks and the Hebrews who suffered captivity and deportation, the city was famed for its sensual living, wickedness and heathenism. Down the ages, however, Babylon has come to mean any rich and magnificent city or state which is believed to be a hot bed of luxury and wickedness.[4]

"Farewell to Babylon" could very well be the adieu to a place that was once orderly, magnificent, beautiful and luxurious when it was under a good ruler, but which has begun to deteriorate and suffer reverses because of the wickedness and mismanagement perpetrated by dictatorship. Because of the disintegrative tendencies in which it is engulfed, its inevitable doom is being predicted. "Farewell" could be the death pangs of the once happy land or the final twitches, groans and exit of the dictator who has made himself synonymous with the state. At the end of the play, Babylon the state survives Babylon the dictator.

The use of "Babylon" also universalizes the intention of the play. It agrees with the playwright's concern that dictatorship is not confined to any one nation but a world-wide phenomenon, "especially in the Third World—and other parts of the world." The immediate concern, however, seems to be Africa, because there are images in the play which point to some African dictators in all but name. There seems to be some concern too that the playwright's country, which, at the time he wrote, was under a military regime might deteriorate to dictatorship, but this fear is a muffled one in the play.

In *Farewell to Babylon*, Bode Sowande tries to tell the sordid story of a totalitarian regime in a background setting. The huge backdrop is "illustrated with tortured human faces peeping through barbed-wire fences, iron-bar windows and such testimonies of dictatorship." Then, in what seems to be a vision akin to what George Orwell's 1984 saw in Big Brother, the play tells us that "High above in bold relief is the portrait of an Eagle looking to the left, surmounted on a wreath of barbed wire, fiercely dominating the whole playing area" (p. 53). The whole playing area is the world of Babylon. The playwright's choice of "left"—the Eagle looking to the left—is a powerful image, especially in a culture that associates left with evil, sinister, or things that never go the right, orderly way.

The dictator in *Babylon* is Field Marshal, a personification of evil who has acquired titles as he wishes. He is a Soldier, President, Supreme Eagle of the Realm and Alhaji. There are echoes of two of Africa's former dictators—Idi Amin of Uganda and Jean-Bedel Bokassa of the then Central African Empire—who had a mania for bedecking themselves with titles at will. One made himself a Field Marshal without ever going to war; the other an Emperor of a country that is only about 241,000 square miles. Field Marshal has all the gadgets of dictatorship—torture chambers, spies and security agents. Moniran of *The Night Before*, another play by the author of *Farewell to Babylon*, having been relieved of his fiancee, Ibilola, by a fellow graduate, on the night before their convocation, has, after years of diplomatic careering become the Head of the State's Security, "The Octopus." Indeed, just as Field Marshal has become synonymous with wickedness in *Babylon*, so has Moniran become synonymous with the Octopus, "the faceless man" people "dread so much."

The octopus, a sea animal without a shell, is equipped with eight dangerous, powerful, muscular tentacles and a pair of highly developed and sensitive eyes. It hunts for under-water preys which it seizes with its sucker-bearing arms. The power grip paralyses the victim and by the secretion of a poisonous salivary substance, the octopus partially digests its prey to be ultimately chewed by its horny, beak-like jaws and tooth-ribbon. A clever animal, the octopus sometimes barricades itself with large stones, secretes a dark, ink-like fluid from its ink sac or hides in a rocky crevice at the approach of danger. It even possesses a chameleon-like quality in that it can change color, usually from pinkish to brown, according to mood and environment.

Like the octopus, "The Octopus" has many arms and highly developed eyes with which espionage is carried out. With these organs it has partially paralyzed Babylon and half digested it for the easy consumption of the beak of the

"Supreme Eagle of the Realm", Field Marshal. And because it is engaged in torture and spy-work, it hides itself, like the octopus, in areas it cannot be visible, barricading all easy access to it and changing color to be able to adapt to its espionage profession successfully. Since no one sees it and yet one feels its dangerous operation, "The Octopus" has become faceless and dreaded (p. 66).

Revolution is also possible within a dictatorship itself, among the apparently strong members of the government. This is what we find in Moniran, the boss of "The Octopus." He has not been totally, irredeemably corrupted by the dictator. Somewhere deep in his heart there is still left a touch of humanity. It is this humanity in him mixed with his will to survive that make him live a dangerous existence, apparently a foe to his fellow citizens because he is the principal agent and the strongest backbone of the dictator but inwardly an agonizing young man sympathetic to the plight of his people and waiting for an opportunity to change the order. It is because of this drop of humanity, the great resistance of his conscience from being stifled that Moniran finally becomes the chief executor of the coup d'etat that brings Field Marshal's dictatorship in Babylon to an end. But before this occurs, Moniran must live a dangerous existence:

> What would you do, should you dream of an illumination? A bright lamp that you held in your dream from youth and now you find your feet lead you to the gates of hell. Would you say to the Devil, I came to fetch embers to burn Babylon? You would be a fool if you did. So you keep sealed lips, and live a dangerous existence. (p. 65)

What is required then is patience for things to sort themselves out. It is in this line we can explain the tag 'Patience' which Sowande gives to the first part of *Farewell to Babylon*. Already there are anarchists, dissidents and ideologues abroad, some groups are revolting, people are tortured, "the prison is congested, bursting with new arrests" (p. 68), and business tycoons like Majidun are feeding fat on the poor people, but there must be patience.

The dictatorial government has the means of torture, of oppression and of immediate annihilation. Hence the need for patience and the fact that it is the patient and calculative Moniran who is able to initiate a change of government and rid Babylon of its dictator.

While men wait patiently, singing the song of the hope of overcoming the foe some day, they must also capture the rhythm of the time in prayer. The prayer is not that of waiting for a divine, supreme being to come down from its lofty, invincible, celestial fortress to execute some program for a humanity that lies doggo. No. Prayer, in Sowande, is a spiritual act, a mental undertaking, a kind of meditation and philosophical enquiry by which man reorientates himself for his life's fulfillment, to prepare him to accomplish successfully the great task ahead. Such work, though frightful and immense, in which man could use the help of a god, must be done by man alone, man as man, and not by a deus-ex-machina.

Part Two of *Farewell to Babylon* is subtitled "Countdown." It is the countdown to the coup that topples Field Marshal's dictatorship. The dictator goes to an important meeting of the Organization of African Brotherhood and Kasa, a Major in the Army of Babylon, decides that "He [Field Marshal] will not come back" (p. 116). Without violence, without shedding blood, a new government headed by Major Kasa comes into power giving an unconditional pardon to the farmers and people in revolt and inviting them for a dialogue with the government. Moniran, his humanity fully restored, would go back to being a career diplomat, but his help is needed in the next two years to take the country back to parliamentary democracy. The government will be that of the people.

The dictator in *Farewell to Babylon* seems to have been drawn after President Idi Amin, the Ugandan strongman, who was toppled by a Tanzanian-backed force of Ugandan exiles and dissidents in April, 1979. Like Idi Amin who took delight in the acquisition of titles—he never seemed to have enough—and like Bokassa too, the dictator of Babylon is a Field Marshal, an Alhaji, and, of course, a clown. And this dictator attends an important meeting of the Organization of African Brotherhood! Organization of African Brotherhood seems to be a dramatic version of the O.A.U. (Organization of African Unity) of which Idi Amin was not only a member but its Chairman in 1975, a year before Sowande wrote the play in Sheffield, England. The coup, however, that topples Field Marshal in the play, seems modelled after the one that threw General Yakubu Gowon of Nigeria out of government. By a masterstroke Sowande brings the events in Uganda and Nigeria together in the play, for it was at a meeting of the Organization of African Unity in Kampala, Uganda, under the chairmanship of Idi Amin that Yakubu Gowon heard the news of his dethronement.

Some ideas come to mind in the linking of a dictator to the Organization of African Unity, that is, if, as I strongly believe the Organization of African Brotherhood is accepted as its dramatic equivalent. There is the idea that Sowande is questioning the rationale or judging the morality of allowing a dictator to be a member of such an organization. It seems that by allowing a dictator to be a member, and attend a meeting of that "Brotherhood", there are connotations that other members are brother dictators by design. Or it could be by default—by their refusal to expel the dictator from membership.

Farewell to Babylon is an indictment of dictatorship, even if the coup d'etat that shatters the dictatorship looks too easy and even if an aspect of the play seems at first inconsistent with the overall purpose of the play. Somewhere in the play, Onita, the meditative irrepressible Doctor of Philosophy, having tasted of the wrath of Field Marshal for being an agitator of the down-trodden, sets man to think when he parrots the Bible, "So God created man in his own image" (p. 80). The argument, pursued to its ultimate conclusion, could refer to the dictator being an image of God also. Both the sufferer of dictatorship (Onita) and the author of this suffering (Field Marshal) are both "moved movers" in their relationship to God, the Unmoved Mover and the First Principle of Causality. Onita and Field Marshal are therefore images of the incomprehensible God, and each one of them as dictator or sufferer only fulfills the image of God. This would exculpate Field Marshal and so raises the question of the problem of evil.

However, there is a cause to say that the dictator is not Sowande's image of God. If he were, the playwright would have concluded the play in a stalemate, but as it is, the dictator is defeated and a better regime comes into power. One of the consistent attributes of God is his persistent goodness. The dictator is presented as bad, as evil; and evil as the antithesis of good makes the dictator the antithesis of God, and therefore, a devil, the source of evil in the socio-political set up who must be eliminated for the society to regain its pristine wholesomeness.

Like Bode Sowande, Wole Soyinka is attracted to the theme of dictatorship. His first indication of interest in it is in *Before the Blackout* where Babuzu Lion-Heart, the President Leader, the Indestructible One, the Immortal Lion of Africa, the Resurrected, rules with terror and makes everyone tremble before him. The first version of the sketch had Asa-gbe-fo—probably Osagyefo (the Saviour) Kwame Nkrumah of Ghana. Having lost his throne, Soyinka found him not as relevant as the inimitable Babuzu, Lion of Malladi, "an aberration without one redeeming quality." Just as Asa-gbe-fo seems a parody of Osagyefo, so does Babuzu of Malladi parody Kamuzu of Malawi.[6]

In presenting Babuzu as indestructible, immortal and resurrected, Soyinka seems to have perceived dictatorship in Africa as indestructible, and even as a phenomenon that cannot be opposed. It is, perhaps, to correct this notion that he comes back to treat dictatorship in *Kongi's Harvest* and *Opera Wonyosi*.

Kongi's Harvest is stethoscopic of a dictatorship and its opposing powers. From the beginning of the play, we are acquainted with indications of some challenge to the tyrannical regime. There is a strained relationship between the traditional ruler and the government of Kongi, but the opposition is more than a struggle for power by two people. In reality, "three citadels of power" can be isolated in the play: Kongi's, Danlola's and Daodu-Segi's.[7] The latter groups are in a bitter opposition to Kongi's dictatorship.

Kongi's citadel of power consists of his agents of tyranny—the Superintendent, the Organizing Secretary, Right and Left Ears of State, the Carpenters' Brigade and the Reformed Aweri Fraternity. Of these, two groups are worth mentioning as they represent the physical and mental powers of the dictator, Kongi.

The Carpenters' Brigade is a body of robot-like human beings who execute with utmost fidelity Kongi's physical works, mostly works of destruction, force, and propaganda:

> (the Carpenters' Brigade march in, uniformed, heavy mallets swinging from their waists. They clear the stage and reset it for the harvest scene—decorated dais, buntings, flags, etc. On a huge cyclorama which completely dominates the stage, pictures are projected of various buildings, factories, dams, etc., all clearly titled Kongi Terminus, Kongi University, Kongi Dam, Kongi Refineries, Kongi Airport, etc. Finally, of course, a monster photo of the great man himself...) (P. 115)[8]

The awesome power and the pathetic situation of these men are brought out in some of the verses of the anthem they sing:

> Men of peace and honor
> Are the Carpenters' Brigade
> But primed for fight or action
> To defend our motherland
> We spread the creed of Kongism
> To every son and daughter
> And heads too slow to learn it
> Will feel our mallets' weight.
>
> Our hands are like sandpaper
> Our fingernails are chipped
> Our lungs are filled with sawdust
> But our anthem still we sing
> We sweat in honest labour
> From sunrise unto dawn
> For the dignity of labour

And the progress of our land.

For Kongi is our father
And Kongi is our man
Kongi is our mother
Kongi is our man
And Kongi is our Saviour
Redeemer, prince of power
For Isma and for Kongi
We're proud to live or die! (pp. 115-116)

What we see in these men who give "the Nazi salute" is
the success of the dictator Kongi in totally wrecking their
minds and turning them into beings beyond redemption.
Only those like them can possibly survive in Kongi's
dictatorship. Those who cannot forget their humanity must
be in opposition to Kongi and must, therefore, ally with the
other two citadels in opposition of Kongi, or flee the
country.

The Reformed Aweri Fraternity—"a big name for little
heads"—does the brain work for Kongi, although the latter
reserves the right to give impulsive orders. The group
engages in writing Kongi's books and in philosophical
disputations. Often times, they arrive at things which can
neither be understood, explained nor remembered:

> FIFTH [AWERI]: ... Nor proverbs nor verse, only ideograms in
> algebraic quantums. If the square of SQY (2bc) equals QA
> into the square root of X, then the progressive forces must
> prevail over the reactionary in the span of .32 of a single
> generation.
> FOURTH: I trust you understood that as well as you remember it.
> FIFTH: No. As well as *you* understand it.
> FOURTH: I've had enough of your negative attitude... (p. 72)

The megalomania of Kongi the dictator is beyond
approach by an ordinary human being. Not only has he
named every good thing after him, he has become "the Spirit
of Planting, the Spirit of Harvest, the Spirit of Inevitable
History and Victory" and "every Ismite" (pp. 129-130).
According to the Organizing Secretary, who maintains a link

between Kongi and his distanced citizens, Kongi is also "the
Giver of Life" (p. 93). The calendar would also be affected
by Kongi's lust for power: "everything shall date" from
"K.H.," "the year of Kongi 's Harvest" or "B.K.H., Before
Kongi 's Harvest" (p. 92).

While the physical opposition posed by the Danlola
citadel of power is not very strong, that of the Daodu-Segi
citadel is very strong, and though it cannot match the
madness of Kongi's, it is this group of drunkards, farmers
and prostitutes that may be effective in revolting against the
dictatorship. If Kongi's physical power lies, as he claims,
on the mallet-wielding Carpenters' Brigade (p. 91), Daodu's
men who wield hoes and cutlasses like "metallic lunatics" (p.
121), could provide a formidable confrontation. It must also
be noted that in any crude warfare that could develop, the
mortar and pestle, and the cooking utensils carried by Segi's
Women's Corps are possible weapons. But in terms of
mental power, the Danlola citadel poses the greater threat to
Kongi. Danlola has tradition and the Old Aweris in his
camp. There is a spiritual superiority here. For Kongi to
survive, Danlola must be destroyed.

The position of powers is not clear at the end of
Kongi's Harvest. The head of an old man, possibly the
severed head of Segi's father, is like the head of John the
Baptist, served in a copper salver to Kongi. There is an
ensuing scramble but it is not certain if Kongi got killed
thereby ending his reign of terror or whether he mastered the
situation and got Daodu and Segi eliminated. It is also
possible that everything ended in a stalemate, Kongi going to
his retreat to continue his tyranny and Daodu and Segi
retreating to their stronghold or to a neighboring country
where they would continue their struggle against Kongi's
dictatorship. The mixture of royal music and anthem which
rises loudly at the end of the play seems to suggest the
raging confrontation between the Danlola-Daodu-Segi forces
and those of Kongi. For awhile, the battle is indecisive,
neither lost nor won, but then comes an "abrupt halt as the
iron grating descends and hits the ground with a loud, final
clang" (p. 138). There is a note of finality here but it is an

ambiguous one as to the victor. It could be the fall of the
iron man, Kongi, from his high position, and therefore, the
end of his reign of dictatorship or it could be the fall of the
iron hand on his enemies. If the latter is the case, it means
Kongi has succeeded in mastering the situation, bringing
with it more tyranny. One thing, however, is certain: the
seed of open revolt has been planted and things can never be
the same again. Daodu and Segi, Kongi's implacable
antagonists, might be killed or kept in detention, but they
have struck a disturbing note in the relationship between the
oppressor and the oppressed, between Kongi and the
citizens of Isma.[9]

Some critics have identified Kongi as Kwame
Nkrumah, Ghana's first president, who was entitled the
"Osagyefo" (the Saviour), and often posed as a Messiah, as
Kongi does in the play, not only to Ghana but to Africa.
Like Kongi, he had the habit of retiring to seclusions. The
first dictator of an independent African country, he brought
the two-party rule to subjugation, indoctrinated the youth
and promulgated a detention act. Other critics have identified
Kongi as Kamuzu Banda of Malawi, because some of the
statements in *Kongi's Harvest* are attributed to him.[10]

Though there are resemblances to political figures living
or dead, it could be argued that *Kongi's Harvest* is not about
the dictator Kongi, and, therefore, not about Nkrumah or
Banda, but about "Kongism" or totalitarianism wherever it
rears its head in the continent of Africa. The same is
applicable to Bode Sowande's *Farewell to Babylon*, that it is
not specifically about Idi Amin but about any tyrannical
government in Africa that is Idi Amin-like. For a relatively
very brief period of Independence, Africa has teemed with
too many dictators and potential dictators, as to go
unnoticed: Kwame Nkrumah of Ghana, Jean-Bedel Bokassa
of the short-lived Central African Empire,[11] Idi Amin of
Uganda, Marcias Nguema of Equatorial Guinea, Mobutu
Sese Sekou of Zaire, Sekou Toure of Guinea, Mohammad
Ahidjou of the Cameroon.

But if *Kongi's Harvest* fails to mention actual names
and places, not so is *Opera Wonyosi*.[12] Though modelled

after John Gay's *The Beggar's Opera* and Bertolt Brecht's *The Threepenny Opera*, *Opera Wonyosi* is thoroughly grounded on the Nigerian-African socio-political environment. The "Foreword" to the play is important for its mentioning of the names of "singularly repellent and vicious dictators who feature in the play: 'President-for-Life' Idi Amin... 'Emperor-for-Life' Jean-Bedel Bokassa ... and 'President-for-Keeps' Marcias Nguema..." (p. i). 1979 was an "unprecedented Year of the Purge" for these dictators.

Soyinka's fundamental question is how dictators succeed in retaining power so long. He has numerous answers. First, is the "active connivance and mutual protection" by other dictators and rulers in Africa. Secondly, international ignorance is carefully nurtured by the diplomatic representatives in various nations. Thirdly, there are false reports given by "expatriate elites" in order to protect their self-interest. Fourth, there is the existence of "moulders of 'informed' public opinion," who, pampered by a deceptive "privileged" reception by the dictator and his agents fail to see that such is not the lot of the masses. Finally, there is the presence of "'dispassionate' observers of society" who are not even vocally committed towards the eradication of dictatorship.

Though the Central African Republic, on the eve of its being renamed the Central African Empire, is central to the play, two other countries are linked to it. They are Nigeria, whose Civil War exiles have become a formidable force in Central African Republic, and which exports horrible security experts to help perpetuate the reign of Boky's dictatorship, and Uganda, whose dictator, Idi Amin, is a personal friend of Emperor Boky. While, on the apparent level, the link between these three countries is one of social decadence, there is the bond of dictatorship that exists among the three on a subtle level.[13]

But it is on the relationship between Idi Amin and Emperor Boky that the play dwells at some length. Both of them are murderers. They know how to silence the voice they do not want to hear and how to kill—for pleasure. They bedeck themselves in fashionable medals and try to outdo each other in titles. The competition for title and supremacy between the two "friends" reaches such a height that Boky wants to win and end it once and for all:

> Amin forced on me my coming elevation you know. He'd become a gross caricature of everything I represent, so the only choice left was to aim far above his horizon—nothing less than a black Napoleon. Now you must admit that was original thinking—that was really outclassing that nigger—I mean, how do you top the Imperial crown? No way baby, no way ... After the imperial crowning, protocol will be so strictly observed that only God will be granted the occasional interview—and even then, strictly by appointment. (p. 26)

There was, indeed, an actual coronation ceremony of President Bokassa, represented by Emperor Boky in the play, in which Bokassa changed his title from President to Emperor, and the name of his country from Central African Republic to Central African Empire. His crown and throne were made of gold, and the entire resources of an impoverished, land-locked nation were said to have gone toward that coronation. *Opera Wonyosi* ties this up with the wedding ceremony of the former Head of State of Nigeria, General Yakubu Gowon, when Boky says, "Even during your Civil War in Nigeria, your Chief had a wedding that was, from accounts right princely. Straight out of the Arabian Nights..." (p. 29). Not only was that wedding performed with pomp and pageantry, but, according to the "Textual Notes" to the play, "commemoratory stamps were printed and launched throughout Nigerian embassies while this then Head of State claimed the (late) capture of a Biafran stronghold as his wedding present" (p. 85). Boky argues that if the Nigerian populace did not riot over Gowon's extravagance at a time its sons and daughters were killing themselves at a war that could have been avoided, then there should be no riots by the hungry people of Central African Republic over his own extravagance. This is Soyinka's way of attacking not only the dictators but those "'dispassionate' observers of society" who in their indolence maintain dictatorship, by default.

Soyinka shows what apathy towards a dictatorship can lead to by bringing another historical fact into the play;the massacre of schoolchildren by Bokassa's agents, after they had been rounded up, at the command of the Emperor himself. In carrying out this affair, Boky compares himself to King Herod whose "right" and "worthy example" is worthy of emulation, and then goes on to exhort the squad he has brought in to carry out his heinous crime that, but for Herod, could have been unique:

> Those [schoolchildren] are ingrates at your feet. Juvenile delinquents. Future criminals. Little ingrates! Putative parricides! Pulp me their little brains! Wastrels! Prodigal sons! Future beggars! Suspects! Vagabonds! Rascals. Unemployed. Subversives. Bohemians. Liberals. Daily paid labour. Social menaces. Habeas corpusites. Democrats. Emotional parasites. Human Rightist Vagabonds. Society is well rid of them. They disgrace Imperial dignity. Louts. Layabouts. Now their heads are under your feet. Your chance to clean up the nation once for all. Protect property. Protect decency. Protect dignity. Scum. Parasites. What do you do with parasites? What do you do with fleas? Bugs! Leeches! Even a dog is useful. But leeches on a dog? Ticks? Lice! Lice! Lice! Crab-louse! Stomp! Imperial Stomp! Studs-In. Grind! Pre-frontal lobotomy—the Imperial way! Give your Emperor a clean empire. Sanitate. Fumigate. Renovate. (He clubs the squad right and left to give them encouragement, decimating them until the very last one keels over. Finally realizes he's alone.) Hey, what's this? A mutiny? (pp. 28-29)

This speech is important not only for the massacre but also for its depiction of the effects of dictatorship. Where one man takes decisions and controls affairs, the limited vision would give rise to social defects: beggars, criminals, vagabonds and social menaces. The good aspect of the speech is in the mentioning of subversives, bohemians, human rightists and liberals who must necessarily pose a challenge to the dictator. But then there is the sad realization that in decimating children, the Emperor has gone to the ultimate in protecting his dictatorship, for the killing of the young means the destruction of future leaders and hope. There is the feeling that Boky's empire will be without people. Hence the important stage direction which tells us that finally, Boky "realizes he's alone." So it must be, for the dictator, by dealing out death and stifling liberty, excludes himself from the province of free man.

Though *Opera Wonyosi* parades social stock characters and their sin—collaborative cannibalism—what gives the play force is the evil of dictatorship and the realization that all excesses in social and political life occur because of "power." It is on this note that the play ends—that "Power is delicious" (p. 83), especially to a dictator and his associates.

It seems to me that by exposing the inhumanity in a dictatorship, *Opera Wonyosi*, *Kongi's Harvest* and *Farewell to Babylon* not only reject the evil by condemning it in revolting images but encourage all Africans to fight against it wherever it rears its head. This is why, though actual names of some dictators are mentioned, it is not the names that matter but the phenomenon of dictatorship itself. There could be a message particularly for the Nigerian audience: never to allow any dictatorial government to survive, and to be wary of one. It is in this light that Bode Sowande's "Prayer in a Dictatorship" becomes important:

> If it be a government
> of the people
> for the people
> by the people
> Pray let it be.
>
> If it be a conscious step
> to the rule
> by the law
> that is just
> pray let it be
>
> But ...
>
> If it be an iron grip
> of one man, or many
> In a clique, centreheld,
> In a web strong as steel,

Pray rise Judas and resurrect in this rank
perform a duty,
for once,
a wholesome duty;
Be Brutus to their Nero,
Forsake this dictator, his retainers; dislodge them!
Their conscience poured into fire,
to yield its lava or cast of Gold divine—
Before damnation day—Before D. Day.
And Earth and Heaven will say, Amen for ever.[14]

THE
NATIONALIST STRUGGLE
IN
AFRICA

•7•

The age of miracle has passed, my dear friend. If you believe things will change without some hard thinking and work, you're mistaken. Freedom's not given out like a present. You've got to fight and shed some blood. Some may die—.

The Cassava Ghost

There is a dearth of dramatic writing on the struggle for independence in Africa in Nigerian drama. The pre-Independence nationalist plays written by Hubert Ogunde, are not really dramas of nationalist struggle but those that simply reflect the socio-political atmosphere of the British administration of Nigeria. They are not openly geared towards decolonization, and they do not advocate the violent expulsion of the colonizer. Perhaps the scarcity of dramatic material on violent decolonization is due to the fact that in the Nigerian experience, the movement from colonialism to independence was relatively peaceful; no armed struggle was required to achieve self-governing status.

But if Nigeria has had a peaceful nationalism towards independence, the same cannot be said of other countries in Africa, especially in the East and South. Those countries, especially Tanzania, Kenya and South Africa, have expressed their socio-political concerns in such revolutionary masterpieces as *Kinjeketile, The Trial of Dedan Kimathi*, and *Sizwe Bansi is Dead.*[2] In Nigeria, only one playwright worthy of note has consciously employed a Nigerian colonial situation to reflect the nationalist struggle in Africa in a play, *The Cassava Ghost*. The play is unique in the sense that it seems to put the theories concerning the relationship between the colonized and the colonizer, especially those expressed by Jean-Paul Sartre, Frantz Fanon and Paulo Freire,[3] in dramatic terms.

The theme of a violent struggle is set by the playwright, Ezenta Eze, at the beginning of the play by giving the subtitle, "I'll fight for you" to Act One. And to make clear the point that he is using a Nigerian situation to speak about his overall concern, Africa, the playwright introduces "a large map of Africa which hangs on the center of a wall" (p. 3)[4] The meaning is that it is Africa that is being fought for. We know who the belligerents are from the dialogue between Tunde and Tina:

> TUNDE
> Ma! Don't worry. God will help you. When I grow, I'll fight for you ... kill Doctor Akri and all the white people.
> TINA
> That'll not be necessary when you grow up, dear.
> TUNDE
> They killed Master Kosoko ... a good man like that.
> TINA
> But they thought he was bad because he spoke up against them.
> (p. 5)

The fight is against the colonial masters—"the white people" —and their collaborative native—Dr. Akri—by the nationalist fighters Tunde and Tina. The animosity that now exacerbates to murderous tendency is generated from the attempt to muffle the voices of otherwise "good" men like Kosoko whose weakness in life is their excessive extrovert nature that is misinterpreted as a form of agitation.

The confrontation is a complicated one for it is not simply that of the natives united against a common foe, the colonialist, but on a more profound level, that of the native against the native. At first, this latter level of confrontation is difficult to explain till one finds what seems to be an answer in Jean-Paul Sartre's Preface to *The Wretched of the*

Earth. Sartre points out that when "colonial aggression turns inward in a current of terror among the natives," there ensues some disillusionment in the natives and in this "period of ... helplessness, their mad impulse to murder is the expression of the natives' collective unconscious." He states further that ...

> If this suppressed fury fails to find an outlet, it turns in a vacuum and devastates the oppressed creatures themselves. In order to free themselves they even massacre each other, ... the man who raises his knife against his brother thinks that he has destroyed once and for all the detested image of their common degradation, even though these expiatory victims don't quench their thirst for blood.[5]

The natives kill themselves, just as Tunde intends to do to Dr. Akri. But that is not the end. It is only a stage in the movement toward the final confrontation between the natives and the colonial master. Toward this end, the metaphysical is even invoked by the natives. Says Tunde, "You know, ma, tomorrow all the school boys will go to Master Kosoko's grave and we'll sing for him" (p. 6).

What Eze puts in dramatic form here is the wide belief in the traditional African that the dead are not really dead; they do bite. Even men who are weaklings while they live assume an awe-inspiring status once they die. Death raises them to the level in which they dwell and communicate with spirits, and spirits are held to be more powerful than human beings. The dead live in the world of spirits but come to the mundane world to interfere with the acts of man as they are needed. It is this participation in the life of the living by the dead that Eze brings to play when the boys go to the grave of the dead Kosoko to "sing for him." By going to the grave, they are seeking inspiration and support from the dead. Kamanu, one of the leaders of an underground movement, puts this in words when he tells Tina that "Kosoko's blood is on our head. But his spirit lives in our hearts, constantly pushing us to do something" (p. 13).

A note of importance here too is the realization that it is schoolboys who go to the grave of Kosoko. It is a note of the inculcation of the spirit of revolt and nationalist struggle in children even before they know what the struggle is all about. In this way, the struggle is kept alive and is assured continuity till success is achieved. Because the commitment is total, "all decolonization," which calls for the "need of a complete calling in question of the colonial situation ... is successful."[6] The involvement of children imbues it with this total commitment. The attempt to give the struggle a death blow would mean the elimination of both the children who are taught to fight, and the adults, who teach the children to fight. The result of such an attempt would be genocide, since the old and the young would be decimated. And this is exactly what the colonial master will not do since the purpose of colonialism in the first place is to rule over a people. This is perhaps an extension of Frantz Fanon's meaning when he states that "all decolonization is successful."

Most nationalist struggles in Africa are secured with rites and religious ceremonies. The historical example is the 'Mau Mau' that occurred in Kenya during its fight for independence in the 1950's. It could very well be the first example in Africa in which nationalist fighters bound themselves to secret terrorism of their colonial overlords by oath-taking during a religious ceremony. The oath bound the members to a determined, forceful expulsion of their rulers, and to accept torment and death rather than divulge the secrets of membership and members. Jean-Paul Sartre has an inkling of this when he writes that the natives "will take the greatest precautions against their own kind by setting up supernatural barriers, at times reviving old and terrible myths, at others binding themselves by scrupulous rites."[7] However, he misinterprets these acts as means by which an "obsessed person flees from his deepest needs ..." and which simply keep the people busy, miming out, "secretly, often without their knowing, the refusal [of dehumanization] they cannot utter and the murders they dare not commit ..." They become "a weapon against humiliation and despair. Mumbo-jumbo and all the idols of the tribe come down among them, rule over their violence and waste it in trances until it is exhausted."[8]

Sartre's interpretation of the effects of these rites and ceremonies is not quite accurate. When the nationalist fighter goes through them, he, as it were, arrives at a higher state of being in which his determination to effect decolonization reaches a fever pitch. The trances, oftentimes hypnotic, put him in a state in which fears of pain and of death in the hands of the colonial soldiers are forgotten. In those moments, the only ideal before the nationalist fighter is to rush to achieve his goal, and all obstacles to it are seen as surmountable.   This is the principle behind Kimakaze (Japan), mass murder (Guyana's "Jonestown") or suicidal war and terrorism (Middle East and Persian Gulf) that the world knows so well.   The rites and ceremonies do not deaden the will to act; they heighten it.

In *The Cassava Ghost*, an indication of the existence of a secret oath is first given when "a voice signal is heard" in the form of "caw-caw-caw" (p. 6).   It is a code of identification of members of the underground movement that is fighting to unseat the colonial ruler. Later we know that people, including some children like Tunde, have really been made to take an oath whose violation means death (p. 43) and that members of the underground movement which include "clerks, laborers, servants, ex-servicemen, regular soldiers, police ... every one you can think of. Even night-soil men and prisoners..." have even permeated the offices of the colonial ruler. Says Kamanu:

> ... we have men all over—in the government houses, in the Churches and the firms. And no one would open his mouth to inform or betray, because we've sworn a sacred oath, with blood and the name of Kosoko. We're unknown, but, we're powerful to the point that we can terrorize and murder in the most unholy manner and no one will ever find out who did it. We're Kosoko, but a greater Kosoko—many but one with him ... (pp. 17-18)

And their secret oath on their blood (p. 15) and the blood and the name of Kosoko would be particularly effective in putting them in a trance-like state to fight their, and Kosoko's, cause because it is the eve of the anniversary of Kosoko's assassination:

Tomorrow, the third anniversary of our hero's death, the unknown
hound will be unleashed to pursue that wayward, bully, rooster.
Your [Tina's] job will be to block its escape. Provoke it, rout it
from all its hiding places and leave the hound to make the kill.   (p.
18)

In the impending great confrontation between the ruling
power and the nationalist fighters, one important fact
appears—that there are no neutrals. One must take sides
during these struggles, either for the ruling power or for the
nationalist fighters. But either choice carries a penalty from
the side one refuses to support.

The play also focuses some attention on the theme of
unity that nationalist fighters try to achieve among
themselves even as they fight a common enemy. Often times
there are various groups of nationalist fighters, each trying to
undo or outdo the other and be the one to take the reigns of
power from the colonial ruler. Let us listen to Kamanu:

I told you. Our main trouble is unity ... unity, madam. If there
can be unity in this country ... believe me, our condition will be
changed like that.
(Snaps his finger) There'll be nothing under the sun we can't do.
(p.8)

It is also Tina's concern as she leads a feminist faction:

All I care is that for the first time, there's some kind of unity in
this country. The North, South, East and West speak with one
voice now. We'll fight together, win together or die together...
(p.9)

The problem facing Tina and Kamanu is how to unite
their factions. While Tina leads a group of united women,
Kamanu leads that of men. The two groups—men and
women—are yet to be united in a concerted action against
their colonial ruler who is their common target.

The nationalist struggle in The Cassava Ghost has a
major distinguishing mark from other similar struggles.
This is the active presence of women in the fight. Indeed, it
is the women, in spite of men, who are leading the fight.

Tina believes that it is the men who have no power of endurance and who sit with their hands folded between their legs, "hoping that a dead man [Kosoko] will come to free [them]" while "the women are out fighting" (p. 9).

The use of women here is important if we consider woman in the African context of "motherhood" as a more aggressively protective and unifying factor than "fatherhood." It is believed that while the woman is more emotional and less intellectually-inclined when it comes to protecting her children, the men are more calm and intellectual in their approach. The essence is driven home in an analogous behavioral pattern of the hen and the cock. When a hen senses that there is a hawk in the vicinity, it protects its brood under its wings while the cock does nothing similar to it. If the hawk comes undetected and snatches one of the chickens, the hen takes to the air as far as its wings can carry it to fight with the hawk and creates a lot of disturbance by its cackling and raving movement in the neighborhood. The cock does nothing like that.

On another level, the mother is considered more protective and unifying because of her protective enclosure of the baby in the womb and because the umbilical cord makes mother and child one. But it is important that the intention of the playwright be not misunderstood. While debunking male chauvinism in Kamanu's statement that "the thing about women [is that they have]—no power of endurance" (p. 9), there is a fundamental assertion of man's heroic power. It is Kosoko, the charismatic husband of Tina, who had begun the nationalist struggle and who had infected Tina with his ideal. The anger Tina expresses is that other men have failed to follow the example of her assassinated husband to carry on the struggle, expecting Kosoko to come from the dead and fight their cause for them. Men's lethargic disposition has made the women active.

The play also addresses the question of what makes the revolutionary fighter carry on vis-a-vis the superior firepower of his antagonist. Here we are shown "women fighting with nothing but cassava sticks, beating down police, breaking steel doors, looting, crying, shouting" (p. 10). What sustains such a fighter is determination, or in the words of Kamanu, "courage ... unity ... determination." There is that firm purpose that action will never stop until all the demands are met or until everyone engaged in making the demands is wiped out (p. 11).

The nationalist fighter often bases his philosophy on the argument that he and his people are exploited and that "exploitation must end" (p. 13). Paulo Freire eloquently expresses this philosophy by pointing out that the "oppressed"—"any situation in which A objectively exploits B or hinders his pursuit of self-affirmation as a responsible person is one of oppression"—unveils the existence of oppression and commits himself to its transformation through praxis. He argues that the existence of a situation of exploitation, as Tina claims in the play, constitutes violence in itself "because it interferes with man's ontological and historical vocation to be more fully human." He says that with the establishment of this relationship of oppression, violence has already begun, and that never in history has violence been initiated by the oppressed. "How could they be the initiators, if they themselves are the product of violence?... Violence is initiated by those who oppress, who exploit, who fail to recognize others as people—not by those who are oppressed, exploited, and unrecognized..." Freire furthermore believes that there must be an act of rebellion by the oppressed, for only this rebellion can initiate love. For "it is only the oppressed who, by freeing themselves, can free their oppressors" and by that act restore humanity to both themselves and their oppressors.[9]

It is this sort of argument that is employed dramatically by Ezenta Eze, especially when Tina lists the things that the colonial ruler uses to dehumanize people and takes a stand that "this exploitation must end." She realizes that to initiate a change, philosophical argument must be supported by action:

The age of miracles has passed, my dear friend. If you believe things will change without some hard thinking and work, you're mistaken. Freedom's not given out like a present. You've got to fight and shed some blood. Some may die—. (p. 13)

But action for change is not guaranteed an immediate success. The reality is that those who begin the demand for change may not live to see what freedom they have fought for. They, like Kosoko, may die. But what keeps the struggle going is the apparent selflessness that the fathers of such fights show, although those who may inherit the struggle and carry it to success may allow personal aggrandizement and lust for power erode the vision of the forefathers.

Even as the various groups of nationalist fighters oppose a common enemy who must be dethroned for them to be free, they face one of the dilemmas of most revolutions—that the nationalist fighters, lacking a united front, fight against themselves. Such intranationalist fights are usually a background to destability or civil war after the colonial ruler is gone and the affairs of state in the hands of the natives. Such internal squabbling is shown in the opposition between the Women Improvement Union of Nagase, led by Tina, and Kamanu's Amalgamated Workers' Union, an underground movement:

KAMANU

Madam, please, listen to me. I was sent here to seek unity with you. Your business is our business. Your enemy is our enemy. What affects your destiny, affects our destiny as well. We're ready to join with you to fight the common enemy.

TINA

Never! (Short pause) You know what the natives say? A child once bitten by a snake fears to go near a worm. (p. 14)

The struggle between these two parties of fighters is more than the fact that at the beginning of the struggle "a handful of traitors" had assassinated the first nationalist leader, Kosoko, whose command is now assumed by Tina. The feud has taken on a more ominous and much larger dimension in that it has become a confrontation between men and women:

TINA

You're interested in freedom—for men, of course. And, you want to use women to get it. When you've gained your objective, you'll turn and use it against the women.

KAMANU

Freedom for our country is freedom for all.

TINA

That's good, but far-fetched. I'm interested in something much more realistic and of immediate importance. I'm at the present concerned about taxation without representation ... the inequality, disrespect and injustice to which the women of this country have been subjected.

KAMANU

Right! But, all I'm saying is that this is too much for you alone to handle. Men alone may not be able to do it, let alone women. It must be team work. How on earth can you expect to have equality, respect, justice and representation when this country is not free? Let's put first things first. When we've achieved freedom from colonialism, then individual freedom will follow. What do you say?

TINA

We don't need you. (p. 16)

The battle of the sexes is the one thing the nationalist fighters cannot afford if they are to be successful in dislodging their colonial rulers.

This feud between Tina's fighting women and Kamanu's underground men is not unprecedented. Indeed, the very beginning of the nationalist movement, also called Liberation Movement by Kamanu (p. 19), was marked by the rivalry and rift between the founding fathers—Kosoko and Dr. Akri. The animosity developed to such an extent that Dr. Akri decamped to the side of the colonial ruler they were opposing and betrayed Kosoko and the "ignorant natives" who had confided in Akri, and led them to their doom (p. 25).

Another dilemma faced by the nationalist fighters, as viewed by most Africans is their inability to get the support of otherwise sympathetic and benevolent Western nations who see all forms of populist nationalist agitation as "communist inspired." It is the fiery Tina who brings this to the fore in her hot argument with Dr. Akri:

DR. AKRI

Tina, the news has spread all over the world.

TINA

That the women's riot in Nagase is communist inspired. Isn't it?

DR. AKRI

The Governor General has been under fire from the colonial office.

TINA

Good! *Communist Inspired!* Ha-ha! Every demand for fair and decent treatment is communist inspired. I'm beginning to be jealous of the Communists. They get the credit for everything constructive. If you tell the truth, you're a Communist. If you demand justice, you're a Communist. If you ask for your rights, you're a Communist. Jesus too, must have been a Communist.

DR. AKRI

(Rises) Blasphemy!

TINA

Thank you for the information. I might as well begin to look into communism now, since it seems to be more democratic than "Democracy" itself. (p. 27)

But Eze's treatment of this dilemma is softened by his sympathetic realization that the use of Communism as an alibi for lack of Western support for nationalist struggles or for covet action against such struggles is the brainchild not of the Westerners themselves but of Africans who, in their bid to gain personal power over their rivals, misinform the world, as Dr. Akri does in the play:

GOVERNOR WEST

We understand you fired him [Kosoko] from your party later on.

ACTOR AKRI

Yes. Somehow, he was getting too radical.

GOVERNOR NORTH

Could he have been a communist agent?

DOCTOR AKRI

I'm sure he was. As I've said, our goals were primarily economic and social—not political. I'd rather become a perpetual slave under the Empire rule than live, even for one day, under the communists. (pp. 111-112)

Dr. Akri achieves the power he wants when he betrays his friends, misinforms the colonial rulers and makes friends with them. He suddenly becomes rich and "the one-time strong, outspoken nationalist capitulated and became a stooge" (p. 31); he becomes a knighted Commander of the Empire, Chief Medical Officer, Member of the Legislative Council and Member of the Distinguished Order of the Empire.

It is also pertinent to point out how Eze clearly ties education and the communist-inspired syndrome into another dilemma that the nationalist fighters, like Tina, face. Most of them are trained, like Dr. Akri and Tina, in the ways of the Western world. When they return to their native lands from these democratic countries, they try to put into practice the ideals they have learned, yet they are referred to by those who should encourage them and give them sympathy, as corrupters, communists and emancipationists (p. 29).

Occasionally, the revolutionary is seen as anti-Christianity. *The Cassava Ghost* shows the reason for this in the dialogue between Dr. Akri, a representative of the ruling establishment, and Tina, an iconoclast only concerned with the freedom of man. To Dr. Akri, the Christian religion is worthy of emulation for it is one of the few religions that "seem to understand the futility of the human efforts to oppose nature." To Tina, Christianity is not worth much for it is subjective, not practical and progressive (p. 33). Furthermore, Christianity is

> ... the religion of the wealthy ... The more pounds you put in the plate on Sunday, the more gifts to the priest, the better Christian you are. You get a special pew in the Church where you sit, hypnotized and fearful, while the preacher hammers into your head that you must be subject to the Higher Powers. He that defieth the powers, defieth the ordinance of God; and he that defieth God brings to himself damnation ... (p. 37)

The nationalist fighter must oppose the ruling powers whose authority has been sanctified by Christianity. Bowing to such precepts would deaden the will to act against and oppose the authority. And the nationalist fighter, if he must initiate change in the socio-political set up, must oppose the ruling powers and therefore run against the dictates of the Christian religion.

But if Christianity is rejected because it cannot provide the necessary stimulus for action, the nationalist fighter is not bereft of religion. He replaces Christianity with African traditional religion, a religion in which the gods and spirits can sanction anything and in which chants, charms and superstitious acts are believed to be effective and which can be used to boost the morale of the illiterate masses. For if the nationalist struggle must be successful, the support of the masses is indispensable, and their support must be hemmed in by African traditional religion:

DR. AKRI

(Stunned) Madness ... Sheer madness. Who do you think you are? Joan of Arc? You're simply going to bring destruction upon these illiterate and unprotected women. Are you going to fight armed soldiers and police with chants and charms?

TINA

(Moves swiftly, and picks up the cassava stick from under the bed.) You see this?

DR. AKRI

Yes. It's cassava stick.

TINA

It's weak and fragile, isn't it? But it's the most important plant in the country. It's the staple crop ... the live wire of the people. Take it away and they will die by the thousands.

DR. AKRI

So?

TINA

It's not just the cassava, you know. It's something greater than this. (Shows him the stick) Something greater than the roots of this stick. It's the life-giving element which the natives call the Cassava Ghost that is our weapon. It'll lead and guide these illiterate and unprotected women, you say, against the guns of your brave soldiers and police. Women are the cassava. And only if these soldiers and police have not tasted the cassava, will they overpower us.

DR. AKRI

Juju,[10] eh? You've gone superstitious too? (p. 36)

Eze's use of "women" in the play is worth commenting on. In its initial usage in the play, especially in the confrontation between Tina and Kamanu, the word refers to females as distinct from male. Later in the play, with the suggestive union of the nationalist factions, the term is still used but then it is in the larger, metaphoric sense as an oppressed majority. Nationalist fighters often claim to fight for the cessation of the oppression of the masses. The issues of undue taxation, of representation in the government and in the legislative council, of equal rights and privileges (pp. 28-29) are echoes of the demands of Africans where such are denied them in the continent. Settling these issues is not an easy one, for apart from the reluctance of the ruling power, there is the suspicion in the mind of the fighters that the ruler's only intention is to "trick ... [them] out to conference, arrest ... [them] and then stamp out all chances of resistance" (p. 30).

The Cassava Ghost also tries to point out why revolutionary action is usually slow and prolonged. Suspected members of the movement are often times incarcerated while the leaders, when not assassinated, might be exiled. But the most important factor is the amount of care taken by the leaders before they carry out any action, for once they miscalculate the hand of the clock is set back for many years. Says Tina:

> Make sure now. The plan sounds good, but if it miscarries, you know what will happen ... This country will be set back for another ten to twenty years. (p. 57)

We also know why the colonial government, in spite of its acquisition of weapons of war, finds it difficult, if not impossible, to crush a nationalist revolution once it begins. The underground movement is so organized that it takes a long time before the government knows of its existence. Even when it knows the movement exists, it is almost an impossible task for it to locate its members, some of whom might even be in government circles, carrying out an internal disintegration of the administration. Kamanu is right when he tells us that:

...the most dangerous enemy to fight is the one you don't know. Remember, the government knows nothing about the Movement. We've got them bound with iron strings, and like a worm, we've eaten up their inside. By the time they'll find out, we'll have dealt the fatal blow. (p. 57)

The Cassava Ghost also examines the great misunderstanding and ignorance between the colonized and the colonizers that prevent them from peaceful co-existence. To the colonial rulers, the colonized are "primitive people who know nothing about ... morality ... and who have no understanding." They are "creatures, ignorant, uncultured heathens" that cannot be reasoned with and whose intelligence is lower than a dog's (pp. 68-69). They are people who understand only the use of force, for force is the only thing they fear. Says Mrs. London, after the Governor General has told her he might negotiate with the colonized to give the "people a chance, discuss their problems and seek some compromise:"

> ... all the books I've read on colonial policies unanimously agree that in dealing with the uncivilized peoples, whether they are Chinese, Indians, Caribbeans or Africans, the official must bear in mind that he is not liked, but feared. Feared because of the force he commands. (p. 69)

Earlier, she has told the Governor General that trying to win the nationalist fighters through a soft approach is sheer stupidity.

The colonized people have their own misjudgment too. Because they have been maltreated by a few colonial masters, they conclude that all expatriates are the same; they fail to believe in the individual and they judge all men through the fault of a few. For example, a former governor, Mrs. London's father and the father-in-law of the present governor in the play, was "remarkable with the cruel massacre of the natives. Suppression, oppression, extortion. Everywhere he went he left the same legacies" (p.

62), and now Governor General tells us he inherits "the hatred he's left behind:"

> ... All the governors, the whole line of expatriates, all our citizens—the entire race, are all one and the same to these people. They call us by every imaginable name—some true, some not—imperialists, colonialists, exploiters, undemocratic democrats and so on. They make no exceptions, mind you. (p. 70)

Eze seems to point out that this is not the way things should be and depicts Governor General as a victim of actions he is not responsible for. There is a realization that not every man of law, not everyone who rules the colonial territory may be heartless. Underneath, the Governor General's rule is the heart of sympathy, especially as he realizes he has been used by his wife and her father. He seems to loathe himself for what they have made him:

> Governor General! The greatest man in the land. What a sham ... I was much happier as a Patrol Sergeant—poor but happy. I was alive ... with feeling and sympathy for people. It gave me a great deal of satisfaction to help people carry out the law. I was a human being. But now, that's all gone—a thing of the past. With you as wife, your great ambitions and this exalted Imperial Crown to uphold, I've become nothing but a heartless beast. (p. 61)

And even when the leader of the underground movement sends a letter of threat that if the imprisoned Madam Kosoko (Tina) is not released, the "forces of liberation" would carry out a "complete annihilation" of the imperial forces, and calls on Governor General to save himself, his country and the empire (p. 64), Mrs. London still goads her husband from negotiating with the movement. While Mrs. London and her father represent the bad side of colonialism and Governor General the good aspect, the unfortunate thing is that it is the force of the bad side that the natives feel and from it draw their conclusion that all expatriates "are all one and the same." And when actual violence ensues, the good are killed with the bad, as we see in the regrettable abduction and murder of Peterson, "a great friend, a brother. The one white man ... who loved the black man" (p. 100).

In the conflict between Mrs. London and Governor General, Eze tries to dramatize why the colonizers themselves have conflicting opinions on how to handle the colonized. A unanimous policy on tackling the problems of the colonized is impossible to reach because the views of those who are present at the colonial scene and carry out the administration, and those who are far away from the scene and yet try to influence decisions because they are of higher authority do not converge. Because the authorities at home dictate one thing and the administrator at the scene executes another, strife exists between the two, and so are incapable of taking a concerted action against the nationalist fighters. Governor General addresses this problem when he says:

> Our colonial policies compiled by those you call authorities have become ineffective. Might have worked in the past but not now ... You see, ... time changes and people change with it. This is a new class of people—trained in our institutions, understand our language, have been exposed to our most prized possessions—democracy and religion. (p. 71)

Since no unanimous line of action is taken, the colonizer enters his own dilemma, for he is "caught in a trap—a trap set long ago, and, by destiny" which he is to trigger off and then "there goes everything, tumbling, crumbling—crashing, ... enough to make one sick" (pp. 71-72), that trap "assembled when [they] set out to colonize—gingered by ... eminent authorities in colonial policies, [those] hard-boiled, iron-handed patriots..." (p. 72).

Colonization starts out as a good job to bring "democracy and religion" to people, to "civilize" the world but ends by breeding a "dangerous race war" (p. 75). When at this stage it becomes "obsolete" and "seemingly endless flares of nationalism" are evoked, the rulers are reluctant to grant independence to the natives for fear of vengeance. This is the concern of Governor General when he says:

> ... we can't live with old ideas forever... trampling on others' heads
> ... eliminating oppositions and enslaving the weaker ones? What,
> when the tide turns? The weak become the strong and the
> oppressed the oppressors? (p. 75)

Governor General's fears of such turn of events are not unfounded as Paulo Freire makes us aware in his research and philosophy in *Pedagogy of the Oppressed*. He points out that in the initial stages of the revolution, the oppressed themselves tend towards becoming oppressors or "'sub-oppressors'" instead of striving to eliminate the existence of the oppressed-oppressor relationship and thus to liberate everyone. The reason for this is that their frame of thought and reference has been conditioned by their "existential situation." "Their ideal is to be men; but for them, to be a 'man' is to be an oppressor. This is their model of humanity...; the one pole aspires not to liberation, but to identification, with its opposite pole."[11] This is the genuine fear of the Governor General—that the oppressed might turn the tables and become the oppressor. This is the vengeance the colonizers seem afraid of that they are reluctant to grant independence.

Paulo Freire points out however that this should not be, that the oppressed be not himself an oppressor when power comes to him:

> In order for this struggle to have meaning, the oppressed must not, in seeking to regain their humanity ..., become in turn oppressors of the [erstwhile] oppressors, but rather restorers of the humanity of both.
> This, then, is the great humanistic and historical task of the oppressed: to liberate themselves and their oppressors as well. The oppressors, who oppress, exploit, and rape by virtue of their power, cannot find in this power the strength to liberate either the oppressed or themselves. Only power that springs from the weakness of the oppressed will be sufficiently strong to free both.[12]

The Cassava Ghost seems objective in listing the good things colonization brings to the colonized—medical facilities, trade, cultivation of food crops, Christianity and education. It points out, however, that instances exist in which these benefits are used to serve the colonizer himself and to abuse the colonized. They are known to have been used to "blindfold and divide" the natives so that the colonizer "could better subjugate" them. Doctor Akri is pointed out as the ultimate example of such a success (pp. 126-127).

The Cassava Ghost also examines the fact that once a nationalist revolution begins, the sorrow that lies in its wake does not affect the colonizers only; the colonized also has his dues to pay. To both sides the innocent and the guilty, the passivist and the activist, the pacifist and the bellicose, the male and the female are swept in one massive, destructive avalanche. On the side of the colonizer, Peterson, "the one white man who loved the black man" is killed by terrorists; on the side of the colonized, Paul's three-month pregnant wife, is killed by the police.

Paul's lamentation of his wife's death is central, philosophically, to the play. In his feeling of being left alone in the world—previously he had lost his father and mother, his first wife is barren, and now the one who would have given him a child to inherit his name and belongings is killed—Paul questions God for hating him so much. In Peter's answer to Paul lies the theology of revolution: "Don't blame God. God didn't make some people to prosper and others to suffer. If so, he's not God" (p. 90). This theology hinges on the problem of evil, an existential one. It has driven people to outright atheism, to the God-is-dead philosophy or to the idea that the remote God or the slumbering Christ and his saints have no interest in the affairs of humanity. This problem has made man to redefine his relationship to God and to question whether the colonized and the colonizer have the same God even if they do attend the same Church.

Part of this revolutionary theology is that man now makes God in his (man's) own image. The voice of people, of the masses, now becomes the voice of God. No longer does God dictate to man; man tells God what he wants to do and goes on to do it without waiting for any formal answer from him. He knows God can no longer dissent; vox populi has become vox dei.

This theology challenges the idea that God made man in his (God's) own image because it contradicts the idea that God is perfect. If God is perfect and he makes man like himself, then man must be perfect. But this is not so for what is reflected in man is imperfection.

Orthodox theologians have explained away the problem of evil and man's imperfection with reference to man's free will. God made man perfect but also gave him a free will. It is his free will that propels him towards evil. And some people have always questioned why he could not make an evil-free free will. And the answer: it will not be free will for free will connotes total freedom. Because such questions and answers seem endless, revolutionary theology, in its concern for the liberation of man, has ceased to argue with theologians and philosophers of established religions whether man has a free will or not, and has totally excluded God from the problem of evil. Man faces a problem; it is he who has to solve it without reference to an external, all-powerful being called God. The means for oppression and the means for removing that oppression are within man himself. God will not come from his holy heights to fight for man; man must redeem himself. Says Peter, "As long as you live, you'll have troubles." And in contention with Paul who tells him evil should not come his way because he has never "troubled" anybody, Peter says:

> It makes no difference. You may be as holy as Joseph. You'll still have troubles. People will bother you—though you don't bother them. God didn't make it so. It's all our own fault. Man has brought troubles to the world. (p. 91)

The crowd of nationalist fighters in the play accepts this idea that the problem it faces is man-made and is ready to solve it its own way. Because the crowd is determined to solve it, the only alternative it leaves itself is death: (The crowd roars "Give us Freedom or Give us Death.") That voice of the crowd to put affairs in its own hands, is according to Kamanu "the voice of the people ... the voice of God." (p. 125).

The Cassava Ghost also shows the vivid reality of war, whether nationalist or otherwise. There are the countless dead, the mutilated bodies and the fact that often times those soldiers who survive the war are not better than the dead. There is the realization too that after the war, promises of a brighter future for which the war is fought remain a chimera (pp. 96-97). As for those who seek consolation in saying that it is an honor for one to die for his country, *The Cassava Ghost*, calls it "foolishness" and damns that idea of patriotism as "country, my yash" (pp. 91-92).[13] Paul, in an enlightenment, brought by sorrow for his wife, asks why those who praise the people that die for the country will not themselves go and die for the same country. The idea is that everyone wants to live and that the consolation of patriotism for the family of those who die is nothing.

The nationalist fighters, in the end, win independence for the country, but are they ready for it? Would Dr. Akri's idea that the people are "not ready for independence" yet prove true? Governor General tells those who have unseated him the challenge to come:

> It's your prerogative to be free. But the big question is not whether or not you're free, but what do you do with your freedom? Freedom can be very dangerous if you don't know how to handle it. (pp. 143-144)

Here is an echo of Jean-Paul Sartre's great idea that man is doomed to be free. Freedom is itself a challenge, not a bed of roses.

MAN
AND
THE MASSES

•8•

We therefore call on you comrade servants, dear and beloved comrade servants, to return to the path of rectitude and assume your responsibilities to us. Only then shall we be in a position to sit together in a comradely atmosphere, servants and masters all, to discuss what you call your grievances...

Shadows in the Horizon

What has become an interesting phenomenon in Nigeria's dramaturgy since the latter half of the seventies is the emergence of some plays that are for the most part preoccupied with interpreting socio-political situations in Marxist ideology. These plays are constructed in the perspectives of class antagonism or of the selfish, wealthy man, versus the exploited, poor masses. They portray the poor people in the nation, the ordinary people, as exploited and enslaved by the rich and look forward to a revolution that would alter things. Worthy of note in this category are the plays written by Kole Omotoso, Femi Osofisan and Bode Sowande. Of late, Ola Rotimi has joined this category with his play, *If*. Kole Omotoso is quite vocal about the position he has taken:

> The percentage of people who have made it in this country [Nigeria] ... position-wise, money-wise, the easy things of life, is such that it is too small, and for people to easily forget is so disturbing. You drive through villages and you see this destitution, you see these people whom nobody has ever given any representation, nobody wants to talk about. Most writers have

been concerned with the elite, and the elite for me is very empty ...
My own commitment is to awaken the conscience of those who
have made it; that's why there is this preoccupation with characters
who are dejected and rejected and neglected.[1]

And while he does not see himself as becoming an activist to
put things right, he is committed to a specific social
ideology—that the rich should become poorer and the poorer
richer in a process of "levelling up." He holds strongly that
unless the Nigerian society accepts this approach of a
simultaneous increase and decrease in wealth, its doom is
inevitable.[2] This is Omotoso's method of bringing social
equality or, to use Marxist phraseology of calling for a
"classless society."

It is not only Omotoso who calls for a classless society;
indeed, the whole "Ibadan-Ife Group"[3] is concerned with it.
When the group met in the 1977/78 academic year to review
its activities, its members condemned Nigeria's foremost
playwright, Wole Soyinka, for his lack of commitment to
Marxist cause in his work. Wole Soyinka who was not
present at the conference attended a later session with his
rebuttal, "Who is Afraid of Elesin Oba?"—a paper that
castigates the Marxists for talking and not acting.

The fact about Soyinka's plays is that while they have
some Marxist ideas, they do not peddle Marxist ideology and
Soyinka has never really openly tagged himself a Marxist
either in speech or in writing. He has, in reality, never
produced a work that devoted itself entirely to class struggle
in the Marxist sense of it. On the contrary, he has eschewed
very facile ideological programs, and has gone to the extent
of almost casting scorn at the pedlars of ideology who
lament "the lack of a 'solid class perspective'" in his work.[4]
He has said, when interviewed about his plays, that:

A lot of people find it very easy to say what their values are, to
encapsulate everything, by saying: "The values I stand for are the
Marxist values of society." Ask them to go deeper, how exactly
are you going to apply this to the situation of famine, of
indifference of your government at this particular time and they'd
probably reply: "Oh it is not yet the historical moment to confront

the reactionary, capitalist elements in society who ultimately are responsible for creating this situation of famine in our country" ... They will never commit themselves to a direct activist programme both for the amelioration of this particular disaster or for a confrontation with the indifferent regime which must accept responsibility for it ... I do not want to fall into the trap of what I call professional mouthers, the parrots of ideology.[5]

While Soyinka believes in the values of an egalitarian society—egalitarian in justice, economic welfare and the right of each individual to achieve maximum fulfillment— and in the "legal robbery of the exploiters and the acquisitive monopolists in society" and in the retention of the means of production and the accruing material benefits by the people, he dissociates himself from "those pseudo-Stalinists- Leninists and Maoists who are totally unproductive and merely protect themselves behind a whole barrage of terminologies which bear no relation to the immediate needs of society."[6] Elsewhere he points out that a creative work is "not a thesis on the ultimate condition of man" and that to ask for a "'solid class perspective' in such a work curtails creative and critical options."[7]

Because Marxist ideology forms the basis of the plays examined in this chapter, a look at the basic tenets of Marxism becomes imperative to an in-depth understanding of the plays. More importantly, Karl Marx and Friedrich Engels had interest in drama, especially in revolutionary tragedy, and had on one occasion written out their concept of drama in reaction to Lassalle's play, *Franz von Sickingen*.[8]

What is considered Marx's most important contribution to socio-political theory was his general mode of analysis, the "dialectical" model, which regards every social system as having within it immanent forces that give rise to contradictions ["disequilibria") that can only be resolved by a new social system. This mode of analysis has become one of the theoretical structures influencing the scenarios of the plays of Nigeria's Marxist dramatists.

Marx believed that the era of mere philosophical understanding and theoretical interpretation of the world was no longer of importance to man; the contemporary man must be concerned with the transformation of both the world itself and men's consciousness of it. In the Preface to the *Critique of Political Economy*, he points out that in carrying on social production, men enter into definite relations that are indispensable and independent of their will. Such relations correspond to a definite stage of development of their material forces of production. The sum total of these relations of production constitutes the economic structure of society, the real foundation of a legal and political superstructure, and to which correspond definite forms of social consciousness. Because the economic structure is of such vital importance, the mode of production in material life determines the general character of the social, political and intellectual processes of life. The outcome of this determinant factor then is that no longer does the consciousness of men determine their existence, it is, on the contrary, their social existence which determines their consciousness.

Marx also regarded "struggle" as the law of life and of existence. In *The Communist Manifesto* (1848), he enunciates, with Engels, the proposition that all history has hitherto been one of class struggles. He points out that there are two basic classes around which other less important classes are grouped. These two major classes—the bourgeoisie and the proletariat—oppose each other in the capitalist system. The bourgeoisie refers to the class of capitalists, the owners of the means of production and thereby the employers of wage-labor. Proletariat refers to the class of wage-laborers who, having no means of production of their own, are reduced to selling their labor power in order to survive. Simply put, they are the workers. The *Manifesto* believes that only the victory of the proletariat in a final and total struggle with the bourgeoisie can put an end to class society forever. It calls on all working men of all countries to unite, and emphasizes that the proletarians have nothing to lose in the struggle but their chains of oppression and servitude, and that they have a whole new world to win.

Marx taught that with the development of capitalism, the class struggle takes on an acute form. The bourgeoisie produces its own grave-diggers, for the fall of the bourgeoisie and the victory of the proletariat are equally inevitable. When man has become aware of his loss, of his alienation, it will be possible for him to proceed to a radical transformation of his situation by a revolution. This revolution will be a prelude to the establishment of the reign of liberty. In the place of the old bourgeois society with its classes and class antagonisms, there will be an association in which the free development of each is the condition for the free development of all.

Marx holds two view on revolution. One is that of a final conflagration—a violent suppression of the old conditions of production which occurs when the opposition between bourgeoisie and proletariat has been carried to its extreme point. The other conception is that of a permanent revolution involving a provisional coalition between the proletariat and the petty bourgeoisie rebelling against a capitalism that is only superficially united. Once a majority has been won to the coalition, an unofficial proletarian authority constitutes itself alongside the revolutionary bourgeois authority. Its mission is the political and revolutionary education of the proletariat, gradually assuring the transfer of legal power from the revolutionary bourgeoisie to the revolutionary proletariat.

The Marxist credo becomes effective as it expresses with eloquent ferocity the grievances of the poor while prophesying retribution and a happy ending. For the state, once captured by the class-conscious vanguard of the proletariat, would take over the means of production from the capitalists, and a brief "dictatorship of the proletariat" would establish a truly communist society. The state would then wither away and man at last would become fully human in a classless society.[9]

Because revolution is central to Marxist plays, something must be said about it both in general terms and in the Nigerian situation. Nigeria's Marxist ideologues, in their campaign for a classless, egalitarian society, use their plays to preach about a revolution. But revolt by the masses is not achieved by preaching. In contrast to revolt by individuals, revolt by the masses as in a political revolution, indicates that a vast social organization has ceased to function. Ordinarily, this revolt is thought to begin when there is an outbreak of violence, but violence is merely symptomatic of an underlying change which has already taken place. The real revolution occurs far beneath the surface when the underlying attitude of the citizenry can no longer tolerate existing patterns of social control. Usually, one segment of the population has suffered economic and political repression at the hands of another. When such conditions prevail—one could easily recall alleged examples from the pre-1967 Nigerian Civil War occurrences—almost any incident may lead to an actual outbreak of violence.

Generally any revolution tends to go through several stages. It does not just occur because someone preaches it. At first, there is only unrest on the part of individuals. Crime and vice increase, class antagonisms develop, governments become inefficient, and, overall, there is a drift towards change. Gradually, collective unrest replaces individual unrest. Because discontent is contagious, it spreads through the repressed segment of the population. The intellectuals gradually lose faith in current leadership and become infected with the discontent of the repressed classes. Again, the Nigerian Civil War serves as an example, when, it is alleged, the dons of the University of Ibadan were so touched by national occurrences that they drew up the case for the secession of the Eastern Region of Nigeria.[10] As leaders of public opinion, they lend their influence and stature to the revolutionary movement. They give it an ideology which takes on a religious aura and provides the revolution with the spiritual element it needs. They help develop organization and formulate issues to accompany the new ideology.

When a great revolution finally breaks into the open, it encounters virtually no opposition from the masses. The people are united and the old order appears to be all wrong. But reaction against repression will lead to the successful overthrow of the old order only if the ruling order is weak or degenerate. If the old order is weighted by internal weakness, then it gives way to a concerted revolutionary attack, and the new order is ushered in.

When a revolution succeeds in its assault on the old order, proponents of the latter may appear to acquiesce and to remain quiet. But they form the core of a possible counter-revolution. In the Nigerian experience, General Murtala Mohammed overthrew the government of General Yakubu Gowon in a popular revolution after the latter seemed to have outlived its usefulness in July, 1975. Then on February 13, 1976, a counter-revolution was triggered off by members of the old order of General Gowon, and though they succeeded in assassinating General Mohammed, the counter-coup d'etat was very unpopular; it met mass demonstration and did not succeed. And Paul Landis tells us that even after the actual struggle is over, whether successful or not, the revolution is not finished.   The problem of establishing and maintaining social control is not that simple.[11]

Nigerian dramas of Marxist ideology seem to be weakened by their desire to preach a revolution. A true revolution is not preached; it is executed. Perhaps, it is this essence that Wole Soyinka realizes when he lashes out at playwrights involved in them as "parrots of ideology" who flee away from engaging in realistic action and confrontation with those responsible for the inequality and suffering they preach against. Soyinka might be right in his condemnation of them for one of the Marxist playwrights considered in this chapter, asked if he ever foresees himself as becoming an activist, answered in the negative. Having delineated some of the socio-political problems, he feels it would be too much for him to solve them in practical terms.[12]

The mission of these literary apostles of Karl Marx in Nigeria is one of singular difficulty. They formulate their indictment against the bourgeoisie supposedly in the interest of the exploited working class. Those in the bourgeoisie are lampooned, and the playwrights whisper in their ears sinister prophecies of an inevitable catastrophe. Like angry young

men, their dramatic criticism of the bourgeoisie is often
bitter, witty, and incisive.   But their dilemma is that the
society and the masses they are fighting for do not seem to
take them seriously. The masses cannot comprehend how
university lecturers who themselves are regarded as
belonging to the bourgeoisie would now come to lead them
to fight against their class. The people see in their writings
emblems of a historical precedent, as in England, when the
bourgeoisie took power from the aristocrats.   The
aristocracy, in order to rally the people to it, had waved the
proletarian alms-bag in front for a banner. But the people,
as often as it joined, saw on its hindquarters, the old feudal
coat of arms, and therefore deserted the aristocrats with loud
and irreverent laughter. This seems to be the sort of reaction
these Marxist dramatists evoke in the audience.   Perhaps,
they may find their true audience in the future if the events
they depict in the fictive world of their plays take on so much
resemblance with the events in the real world of Nigeria that
both the fictive and the real cannot be separated. Moreover,
the Marxist ideology in the plays must survive time and
prove that there is something in the plays more than
fashionable intellectualism.

Femi Osofisan has written many plays but only two of
them can really be said to be related to Marxist ideology, and
even one of these, except for some minimal references, is
more in tune with ordinary social drama than Marxism.   In
Once Upon Four Robbers, his concern is with the "callous
contradictions" of an "unjust [Nigerian] society" that give
rise to armed robbery.[13] The contradictions he refers to
stem from "rapid modernization" in which side by side cars,
boutiques,   supermarkets   and   amusement   zones   are
congested hospitals, crowded schools and "sprawling slums
and ghettos." The positioning of extreme wealth by extreme
poverty leads to the "manufacture" of "potential assassins" in
the Nigerian society. Osofisan argues that if armed robbery
is a disgrace and a death-affirming reality in Nigeria, so do
hunger and unemployment. His ultimate intention in writing
the play however is to "shock" the public into a "new
awareness so that its attitude of "passive acceptance or sterile

indignation" may be channelled toward a "more dynamic, more enraged determination" to confront itself.

Though the play's concern is with armed robbery, Marxist undertones are detectable in it. When those in government cheat the public and make themselves synonymous with the government (pp. 39-40), when the rush is to amass wealth and to use this to change the true course of justice (pp. 33, 12, 13) and when "too many people ride their cars along the sore-ridden backs of the poor" (p. 17), there is bound to be a revolution that will alter irrevocably the course of events:

> MAJOR ... Serg, today that law is on the side of those who have, and in abundance, who are fed and bulging, who can afford several concubines. But tomorrow, that law will change. The poor will seize it and twist its neck. The starving will smash the gates of the supermarkets, the homeless will no longer yield in fear to your bulldozers. And your children, yes, your dainty, little children will be here where I stand now, on the firing block ... (p. 53)

The important role that ideas play in a Marxist revolution is set forth in the play when Sergeant disclaims his brother, Hasan, and refuses to save him from impending death because they have no ideological bond:

> Blood is an accident. It's only our ideas that bind us together, or rip us apart. Hasan and I are on opposite sides of the street. All I can do is hope that he has a decent trial ... (p. 58).

Though *Once Upon Four Robbers* is written after *The Chattering and the Song*, in ideological content it seems to precede the latter play. *The Chattering and the Song* is a more mature play in which what are only Marxist echoes in *Once Upon Four Robbers* are given detailed expression. The play is set in a bourgeois environment in which the central character, Sontri, protests against the bourgeoisie, his own class. He belongs to a revolutionary group—the Farmers' Movement—that is determined to overthrow the government. There is a revolution and a counterrevolution in which some members of the Farmers' Movement are arrested, but the leader of the Movement escapes the purge and converts other powerful people to carry on the revolutionary struggle.

The treatment of the play in its parts is imperative to a coherent understanding of its Marxist intentions.   It is divided into four parts—Prologue, Part One, Part Two, and Epilogue.

The Prologue establishes some capitalist, bourgeois and consumerist tendencies in preparation for an attack. A house with a garden at the back is shown, and wealth is displayed through evidences of a wild party and drunkenness. The rape of the poor and the weak, the inordinate acquisition both of things and of persons, the "strangled scream of the people," deception of the people by those who claim to be serving them, seduction of the poor with wealth, and covetousness—all these evils which Marxists attribute to a bourgeois and capitalist society are established in the Prologue of *The Chattering and the Song*. The people who exploit the poor think of "this moment is us. Us only" (p. 5),[14] and are therefore unaware of the evil things, of the harm, they perpetrate against the people. They do not see the anger welling up in the masses. So revolution, a core element in Marxist ideology, would take the bourgeois oppressor unawares.

In Part One, there are more revelations of, and vicious attacks on, the system: females follow the bourgeois, there is perversion of justice and ideas are misplaced. There are indications of some instability revealed in the "chattering" and "song" of weaverbirds as they escape to a "host government for political asylum" (pp. 16-19). The "chattering" and "song" from which the play derives its title, are a metaphor for "commotion" or "a violent disturbance ... Like a riot" (p. 17). The weaverbirds represent the masses, and when Funlola, a representative of the bourgeoisie, pulls down the birds' nests because she thought "they were causing too much commotion" (p. 17), the bourgeois class is expelling the proletariat because it does not want to see and listen to the latter. The masses have become an offensive class that must be segregated from the powerful affluent class. The coming of "the piercing knife of Truth ... the blade of Life" (p. 15) and the action of the weaverbirds that cannot be stopped from singing (p. 47) are prognostic of a bloody revolution in which the thesis (bourgeoisie) will be confronted by its antithesis (proletariat) to usher in a new day, a synthesis (classless society). Part One also exposes all the malpractices of the ruling bourgeois government and sets the final, concrete situation for the revolution.

Part Two starts off the revolution in a play-within-a-play. The king, faced by an agitator, one of the leaders of the masses, finds that he cannot kill him the conventional way by hanging, poisoning or firing squad; he wants his scientists to invent a new method of getting rid of undesirable elements. But the agitator is quite eloquent and he educates the masses, including the king's guards:

> Soldiers, listen to me! I am going to release you, but only after you release your minds. No one can do that for you but yourselves. Think! Think! with me! For it is that alone that will free you of your shackles ... Look around you. Look into your past, look into your future. What do you see? Always the same unending tale of oppression. Of poverty, hunger, squalor, and disease! Why? Ah, you and your people, you are the soil on which the Alafin's tree is nourished, tended until it is overladen with fruit! And yet, when you stretch out your hands, there are no fruits for you! Why? Only *your* limbs are gaunt with work and want, only *your* faces are wrinkled and hollow with sweating and not getting! Alafin and his men are fed and flourishing, but they continue to steal your lands. They are rich, their salaries swell from the burden of *your* taxes! Their stores are bursting, *your* children beg on the streets. I am begging you, please, fly out of your narrow nests. Come follow me, raise a song to freedom! NOW! (pp. 41-42)

This education of the masses is important in Marxist ideology, for to free the shackles on the body, one must first unchain those of the mind. With shouts of "Freedom!", the soldiers converge on the king, the apex of bourgeois conception: a true Marxist revolution disregards monarchical claims to divine rights which are used to perpetrate oppression of the masses.

The play-within-the-play is used to begin the revolution before anyone knows it—but on the wrong footing. It is not the expected revolution by the masses but a betrayal and an arrest of the right revolution even before it begins in earnest. One of the leaders of the Farmers' Movement, Sontri, who will seize power and proclaim a new republic is under the arrest of the secret police, betrayed by a friend whose fiancee he had snatched away to marry (p. 46).

In Marxist belief, it is good that Sontri is arrested because he would be a sober man to the revolutionary spirit when released. Says Leje, a cunning leader in the revolutionary movement:

> We need anger to start a revolution, even a great anger, but once it has started, it will get rid of us, unless we meet it with cunning and compassion. That's why Sontri needed the arrest, Mokan [the betrayer] was helping us without knowing it. (p. 51)

Sontri's arrest is also good to the revolution on another level. Selfish motives, as Sontri's matrimonial concerns, do not come into a revolution. The revolution must be geared to seek the higher goal of mass liberation through class struggle. Class struggle against presidential or monarchical exploitation of the masses must take precedence over an individual's marital affairs or selfish vengeance.

Though Sontri is arrested, the revolution is far from being crushed. With the presence of crafty leaders like Leje, Sontri's optimism that the revolution is alive is more than the mere self-consolation of a man who laughs when he should cry:

> There's nothing you can do to stop the birds from singing. Mokan, the revolution is already on wing, you cannot halt it! (p. 47)

The Epilogue shows the emergence of Leje and Funlola as leaders in the Farmers' Movement and their willingness to further the course of the revolution once Funlola's initial suspicions of Leje are allayed. More than this, the Epilogue is important for its statement of what the ideal revolution

should entail—personal sacrifice and comradeship with the
down-trodden. These would usher in victory. The
Movement needs all capable people. The whole world is a
farm and all hands must toil both to cultivate it and eat of its
fruits (p. 53).

At the end of the play, though the playwright states that
the play does not end, everyone in the theatre, the actors and
the audience, dance in a movement of harvesting to the
Farmers' Anthem. It seems to me a Brechtian formula of
carrying the action from stage to life and Osofisan's way of
making everyone a farmer. Farming, in the play, thus
becomes a leveller of humanity and a panacea for all the
problems posed in *The Chattering and the Song*:

> When everyone's a farmer
> We'll grow enough food
> . . . .
> No insurrection
> . . . .
> Less exploitation
> . . . .
> No more injustice
> . . . .
> No more oppression
> . . . .
> No alienation
> . . . .
> But brothers and sisters
> Sharing everything. (pp. 56-57)

Osofisan's Farmers' Anthem seems to suggest the idea
of a commune in its meaning of a small, rural community
with common interests and shared or common property.
Though the song may fit the ideological intention of the play,
it does not conform to the actions in the play. It is misplaced
in that nowhere in the play is it used either to further the
revolution or to unify the farmers behaviors or to act as a
code by which the farmers could identify themselves.[15]

On another level, the anthem is also faulty if its contents
are addressed to the Nigerian audience, and if that audience
is expected to carry the actions into real life—as is suggested

by the active participation of the audience in this "endless" play. The fault is that of the playwright's poor perception of a contemporary society, whatever its ideology. The possibility of everyone in Nigeria or elsewhere becoming a farmer is nonexistent. If everyone is a farmer, there would even be no farming since there would be no professional bodies to make the steel and shape the implements that farmers would need for farming. He sees farming as a remedy for wars, oppression, and exploitation. This is where he fails to look at history to see that even when most countries, including Nigeria, farmed in those olden days, there were wars, oppression and exploitation. If Osofisan's intention is really to make everyone a farmer, he is guilty of not studying the society he is writing for seriously; if he is simply creating an illusory art work, he is guilty of infidelity to Marxist preoccupation in which art is geared towards concrete life actions. Thus the Farmers' Anthem creates a problem for an otherwise good play.

In terms of theatrical architectonics, Kole Omotoso's *Shadows in the Horizon* is not as accomplished as Osofisan's *The Chattering and the Song*, yet it seems superior to the latter in its Marxist intention. Especially intriguing is its fidelity to the treatment of tragedy as it is conceived in Marxist doctrine.

In Marxist ideology, all great revolutions are at the same time expressions of sharp class contradictions and antagonisms and of radical attempts to resolve them. When they succeed, they constitute true historical leaps because an immense area of humanity which up till the revolutions lay fallow, is suddenly opened to the creative activity of human beings. Marxists have always been thrilled by the changes that revolutions bring to people and to history. Marx himself had referred to revolutions as the locomotives of history while Lenin saw them as true popular festivals. Their concept of revolutions does not mean that revolutions rest on beds of roses. Often times, revolutions are bloody: there is violence and pain, suffering and death, with an intensity that depends on the degree of resistance put up by the dominant classes to the eruption of the new. But what is decisive is the creative action that starts in the first moments of victory. A victorious revolution, by unleashing the creative energies of the people, escapes the prison of tragedy. This and many other ideas are expressed in *Shadows in the Horizon.*

In a Note to the play, Omotoso calls for the "destruction of all bogeys" that obstruct true vision, for the "demolition of all shadows in [the] horizon" so that the quality of the lives of those who live in Nigeria may be redefined (p. iii).[16] And he dedicates the play subtitled "a play about the combustibility of private property" to the "day when those who have not shall not be satisfied with their nothing" (p. vi). All these give indications of a call for a radical change— and by the content of the play, a violent revolution till power is given to the people. The play does not negotiate for peace. It seems to affirm that the road to peace between the dominating bourgeois class and the dominated laborers is through violence because any other means of negotiation will protect the interest of the former and reduce the latter to utter servitude.

In Femi Osofisan's *The Chattering and the Song*, the true revolution is yet to start; in *Shadows in the Horizon*, by Kole Omotoso, the revolution has already begun and the Hon. Clement Bamigbade, merchant, trader, and politician, the chief representative of the bourgeoisie, is in trouble with his property. Dressed in white lace and bejewelled, he has salvaged a few cars, houses and trunks from the "ignorant masses" (p. 1). To Bamigbade, wealth is a gift of God and if there are paupers, it is because they have not been blessed with property—by God. He wonders why any creature of God would not have respect for property and treat other people's property as if it were his. His idea of respect for property is to the extent of adoration so much so that in the moment of crisis, he protects his property and forgets everything about his family (p. 2). One is reminded of Ben Jonson's *Volpone*, in which gold takes on a living spirit to be worshipped and greeted at sunrise.

Other members of the bourgeois class are also presented and we see that like Bamigbade none of them has any redeeming quality. Captain Atewolara is a howling fiend who would shoot someone's brains out because of his property. Both Bamigbade and Atewolara have deteriorated to bestiality, and Professor Kofo Orimoogunje, Head of Department, Hi-Rated Studies, University of Ibadan (p. 7), soon relinquishes commitment to his legitimate profession, turns businessman and abandons civilization to become a fierce beast, much fiercer than the other men:

As soon as those people [Bamigbade and Atewolara] come, I'm going to shoot them and all this will belong to me, everything here. The houses, the taxis, everything will be mine. Very simple. Just pull the trigger, like this. But the report of the gun? What about the noise of the gun? That would bring witnesses. And anyway, while I'm busy shooting Atewolara, that cunning businessman would go behind me and do something foul. Or if it is the merchant I decide to shoot first, the retired security man is going to recall all his wartime experience and save himself, and then kill me. No. I must think of something else. Something quiet. Something deadly. Poison! (p. 17)

The situation Omotoso presents here is one of the survival of the fittest savage as members of the bourgeoisie fight not only against the masses, but against themselves. Wealth is portrayed as eroding society, taking it back to its days of disorder when no society in its definition as civilized community existed.

In the seventeenth century, the philosopher Thomas Hobbes (1588-1679) had pictured man as he must have existed in the state of nature when there were no controls and hence no order and security. In this original condition man to man was a wolf. The problem was how to achieve social order from this original chaos. By means of introspection, it is revealed that original man was endowed by nature with certain passions and with reason. Natural selfishness led each man to seek his own welfare and thus brought him into conflict with others. It was war of every man against every man. However, reason dictated to him how he might better secure his individual ends and certain convenient articles of peace were arrived at upon which agreement was drawn.

Omotoso is showing that the inordinate ambition of the
bourgeois class to accumulate property at the expense of
everyone else and with any means is an abandonment of the
agreement rational man had entered with himself and others
to form a civilized community. By abandoning civilization
based on rationality, the three men—Bamigbade, Atewolara
and Orimoogunje—if they be called men, have forsaken
society, and are therefore seen, at the beginning of the play,
trying to escape from it. They have deteriorated to the
chaotic days depicted by Hobbes when man was a wolf to
man. It is appropriate then that at the "layby on a motor
way" where they gather in their first step towards leaving
normal society, each man tries to kill the other.

To emphasize that the society is ripe for a change, the
play depicts the physical separation of residential areas
between the wealthy and the poor. While the latter occupy
an area which is dirty, unclean and unhealthy for bringing up
children and whose occupants are referred to as "animals" by
the wealthy, the former occupy luxurious areas like Ikoyi
under the unfailing protection of "policemen, soldiers, navy
and airforce personnel" (pp. 4-5).

The revolution is slow in its movement to alter the
existing social structure not really because the bourgeois
class is too powerful to be challenged effectively, but that the
two rebellious labor unions are at first also opposed to each
other. But later they unite. Unity is important in Marxist
teaching; Marx and Engels had called on all working men to
unite so as to be able to change things and achieve their
desire. The unity of the workers in the play makes them
reconcile to a concerted action. The propertied men,
overwhelmed by the sudden turn of events and aware of a
portentous doom, begin to flounce about, thinking of the
next line of action. They come to an agreement, by a vote of
two to one, Bamigbade dissenting, to draft a petition to the
Workers' Union. Professor Orimoogunje is the scribe, and
the petition adopted by the others with a nod reads thus:

Petition addressed to the Union of Comrade Servants from their
Comrade Masters. To the members of the Union of Comrade
Servants, sincere greetings from your Comrade Masters. We all

comrades, servants and masters, must not forget that even the Almighty Himself did not create the fingers of the hands equal. It is true that all the fingers of the hand are not equal, but they are all called fingers. There are small fingers; there are long fingers, and there are also big fingers. Each finger has his duty and his responsibilities. It is therefore with this eloquent parable in mind that we your comrade masters declare that it is our responsibility to provide for you, to protect your families and to do everything in our powers for the good of those you love. By the same token our comrade servants must do everything for our convenience in order that we may better execute our responsibilities to you. We therefore call on you comrade servants, dear and beloved comrade servants, to return to the path of rectitude and assume your responsibilities to us. Only then shall we be in a position to sit together in a comradely atmosphere, servants and masters all, to discuss what you call your grievances ... (p. 15)

I have quoted this petition at length to point out that it entirely violates what most Marxist revolutions have often claimed as central to them—égalité. The petition is firmly erected on what the workers are rejecting. It assumes that the master/servant relationship still exists even at this turbulent time when what the workers want is a destruction of that structure to build one of equality. Instead of the bourgeoisie to initiate a peaceful dialogue before telling the angry and rebellious workers to assume their usual servant role, it puts the latter before the former. The play shows here then that the bourgeoisie cannot grasp the situation and take the pulse of the revolution. Because of this lack of understanding of the true situation, it is unable to stem the disaster that is to come. The revolution becomes irrevocable.

Before the revolution reaches its climax, Professor Orimoogunje is killed by members of his bourgeois class and his property is shared between Bamigbade and Atewolara. But Bamigbade is soon caught up with by the masses who demand his probe. There is a moment of tyranny by the masses, comparable to Marx' "dictatorship of the proletariat," in which Bamigbade's activities are publicly probed. He is found guilty and condemned to loss of property and life. Atewolara, cleverly escaping the wrath of the masses, becomes the executioner of his fellow propertied man, and for a certain perfection of his art of deceit, he becomes not only the grand inheritor of Bamigbade's wealth but the new head of government. No sooner is he on the throne than he issues a decree which, by banning the Workers' Union and making public office synonymous with his name, resorts to the old order:

> LISTEN TO THE FOLLOWING ANNOUNCEMENT. PUBLIC LIFE. ONLY BRIGADIER ATEWOLARA CAN LEAD A PUBLIC LIFE. ALL OTHERS MUST LEAD PRIVATE LIVES. PRIVATE PROPERTY: ALL PRIVATE PROPERTY IS MADE PUBLIC PROPERTY SO THAT IT MAY ACCORD WITH MY PUBLIC LIFE. THE UNION NO LONGER EXISTS. (p. 34)

The revolution thus suffers an eclipse as the old is entrenched in Atewolara. Representatives of the bourgeois class come to congratulate him and identify with his regime. But Atewolara's ascendance is only a partial eclipse of the way of life the masses have fought for; the revolution breaks again, and this time it is more bloody and much fiercer— partly due to the resistance put on by Atewolara, and partly to the grim determination of the workers to end it once and for all. The ruler's property and his throne are set ablaze, and the play ends in conflagration. In the final analysis, power is back to the masses.

Though there has been a lot of pain and violence, suffering, death and destruction, and though the leaders of the Workers' Union—Bibilari and Alogbo—do not live to see the dawn of the new era they had helped to usher in, *Shadows in the Horizon*, by Marxist standard, is not a tragedy. The workers are victorious and what is decisive is the creative action that starts in the first moments of victory. This is where the concluding argument, even as the fire rages, between Atewolara and the Workers becomes important:

ATEWOLARA: No, you cannot build from ashes.
               No, you cannot build from ashes.
               No, you cannot build from ashes.

WORKERS: But we have to build
                    But we must build
                    Yes we have to build. (p. 44)

What the people are burning down is the bourgeois edifice;
in its place, they are prepared to create a new world whose
foundation is the masses.   By destroying the bourgeois
world and setting itself up successfully, the revolution is
victorious.   By its preparedness to build, the revolution
unleashes the pent-up creative powers of the people and thus
escapes the prison of tragedy. That destructive fury that has
successfully   dethroned   the   old   order   becomes   an
aggressively creative fury to set up a new world of equality,
a classless society.

        The presence of Marxist ideology in Nigerian drama is a
fact that must be acknowledged. That it competes fairly well
with   the   main   stream   of   socio-political   dramas   is
contentious.   But whether the impetus that Marxist plays
gather at the moment is a mere euphoria that accompanies an
intellectual fashion, and as a fashion might soon lose its fire,
or whether there is a deeper commitment and sincerity than is
at first obvious, cannot be ascertained now: only the test of
time has the answer.

THE GATHERING
OF THE TRIBES

•9•

Among the aims of FESTAC '77 was the promotion of a "better international and inter-racial understanding" and the facilitation of a "periodic 'return to origin' in Africa by black artists, writers and performers uprooted to other continents."
International Festival Committee

The issue of national unity has been a thorny one in Nigeria. It gained prominence during the military coups of 1966, and especially in the tribal antagonisms that flared up in Northern Nigeria in which thousands of Easterners, mostly Ibo, were killed.[1] It led to a secessionist movement and culminated in a bloody civil war for reunification. Many plays have made references to this problem of unity. In *The Cassava Ghost*, Kamanu says, "Our main trouble is unity ... if there can be unity in this country ... believe me, our condition will be changed ... There'll be nothing under the sun we can't do" (p. 8), while Tina sees some unity in the fact that women in "The North, South, East and West speak with one voice ..." ready to "fight together, win together or die together" (p. 9). She condemns those who disunite the country by their emphasis on, "He's of this or that tribe ... as if we've not been one people ..." (p. 31)[2] *The Road to Ibadan* and *Echoes from the Lagoon* have some reflections on the civil war that was fought to unite the country while *Old Wines are Tasty* shows how politicians are more interested in ethnic fights than in truly national affairs.[3] All these plays have

touched on the issue of unity among other things; it is in
Wale Ogunyemi's *Langbodo* one sees the problem examined
in greater dimensions.

   Langbodo is by no means a great play. Its importance
is its ambition—to use all the predominant diverse cultures
of a multi-ethnic Nigeria in a unifying manner in the play.
Says the playwright in the Preface to the play:

> I wrote this play drawing much from the diverse cultures of
> Nigeria. It starts with Oyo State [Yoruba culture] as a spring board
> catapulting the sojourners to Anambra State [Ibo culture] and from
> there to the North [Hausa-Fulani cultures], coming down to the
> Rivers [Ijaw culture], leading them to Bendel [Edo culture] via
> Cross Rivers [Efik-Ibibio culture] only to be superimposed upon
> by Oyo, the initial starting point.

He advises producers to "feel free to relate the play to the
contemporary event and adapt the songs and sequences to
reflect and embrace the cultures of the Country in mounting
the production."

   The play uses the imagery of hunters on a journey to
Mount Langbodo, a fabled land that can only be reached by
going through the Forest of a Thousand Daemons (p. 6).
Such an odyssey is necessary towards eliminating things that
can disperse and disunite a nation. For, any leader of a
country that can have in his possession a particular object
from Mount Langbodo is spared in his nation "the horrors of
war, disease and famine such as we have known for so long
and it would win an abundance of peace and well-being; its
fame resounding to every corner upon earth" (p. 6).
Although one man may be bold enough to undertake the
journey, Akara Oogun points out that the duty of saving a
nation and of uniting it is a task for everyone, and not just
for one man:

> I want you to send a crier round the entire land to summon all such
> seasoned hunters as I and send us together on this quest that my
> head goes not forth alone to combat death.   Nor will this be
> enough.   Send messengers to all the neighboring villages and
> homesteads that their bold hunters may join us on this mission to
> Mount Langbodo. (p. 7)

The description and attributes of the various hunters are important to the theme of unity that the play dwells on. The hunters are seven in number, and seven in some Nigerian ethnic groups is a magical number and a metaphor for plurality and,or incompatibility. Akara Oogun is a "Compound of Spells" who is beyond the harm of witches and sorcerers (p. 5). Kako "of the Leopard Club" is a descendant of ghommids. His astonished parents— "mother, a gnome," "father, a dewild"—abandoned him in the hollow of a tree when they found that their child was "almost human" (pp. 8-9). The third hunter, Imodoye, was snatched away from the human race by a spirit when he was only ten. For seven years he had lived among spirits where he became "well versed in charms, wise and very knowledgeable" (p. 10). Olohun Iyo, "the Voice of Flavour," is like the mythical Orpheus. When he drums smoke rises in the air; when he sings, trees begin to dance. He knows the music of incantation (pp. 10-11). Elegbede, the fifth hunter, was born with three eyes—one of the eyes being fixed at the occiput. His mother cast him into the bush for being a human aberration. There in the forest he lived among baboons and wild animals. Elegbede understands the language of birds and animals (p. 12). Efo Iye is "partly human, partly cockatoo." He is a very good archer (p. 12). The seventh and last hunter is Aramonda, "the miraculous man." When it is cold he is hot and when hot he is cold. "Everything about him is the wrong way round" (pp. 13-14).
   The idea behind these fairy-tale characters is to point out the many diverse groups that make up the country. More than this, it shows that these otherwise incompatible people are united in pursuing the King's order, and King is the personification of the country. However different people are, the play seems to say, they must be together in a common effort to uplift the country, the one thing they can count on as belonging to each and everyone of them. The hunters will dare anything once it is at the King's behest:

If I see you [the King] as a sponsor
I could dare the ancestral spirit

If you are my sponsor
I could confront Orisa ...
The fear of your person is what will kill your enemies
It is the King I will ever dread ... (pp. 10-11)

And in the dialogue between Imodoye and the King's Retinue the play is imbued with a patriotic fervor that is supposed to be a bond between a citizen and his country:

IMODOYE   ... No matter how pleasant is the foreign land ...
RETINUE   He who boasts a home always returns home.
IMODOYE   No matter how delightful these strange lands may be to us, we will not fail to remember our home. If our town is so small that it looks like a bird's nest
RETINUE   Yet, the town is still our town
IMODOYE   It is the people who must turn the small town into an important one.
RETINUE   Yes.
IMODOYE   But whoever says that his birth-place is no longer his, that person is a half-witted fool. (pp. 14-15)

The diverse hunters, united by a common patriotic duty, must go to Mount Langbodo, and no matter how pleasant they find this foreign land, their firm purpose will make them return to their land of birth.

We are also given some insight into the fact that not only is one's country preferable to a foreign land but that national duty must take precedence over family, and by extension, clannish and tribal affairs.   When Paminku, Kako's wife, tries to dissuade him from undertaking his assigned national duty till they can consummate their marriage, Kako replies firmly:

Please explain to her that my country's duty is more important to me and I won't combine a woman's problems with my duty. (p. 20)

Langbodo also points out that the issue of unity and patriotism is not only relegated to human sphere; even spiritual forces act for and against achieving national unity. First Medium is against patriotic endeavors:

Fools! Fools all! for accepting such a risky assignment. I can
understand a duck falling down beside his dead mate and dying in
sympathy; that is loyalty to the point of death. I also can
understand a viper laying down her life for her children, for
assuredly she knows her children will not renounce her in the end
and take after lizards—that also is honesty and trust. But if it
comes to suffering for a country full of rogues and dishonest
people, count me out!... Let those idiots bound for Mount
Langbodo appease Ogun,[5] let them pacify Sango,[6] even if they
propitiate all the four hundred and one deities in the pantheon, I
swear, they will never return for I shall spell their doom, that their
quest may two-fold be sorrow and disaster for all ... (pp. 17-18)

Throughout the play, the exploits of First Medium are
inimical to national progress and unity.

In contrast to First Medium, Second Medium is the
spirit of man's unity and successful venture. She sees First
Medium as a "trouble maker and an enemy of [his] country."
Her concern is the welfare of mankind and she feels the
plight of the hunters and their success should be, not only
her concern, but that of everybody (pp. 18-19). Throughout
the play, these two characters act as contradictory forces as
they propel the hunters towards disintegration and
integration; in them they further exemplify the issue of unity
and disunity in a country that the play treats.

In trying to perform duties that are essential to make a
country unite solidly, problems must necessarily present
themselves. The problems take on such importance that they
tend to disunite and decimate even those who have set out
with one mind to achieve something. Attempts are made at
resolving them but each resolution brings in another problem
so that the hunters discover that their journey to Mount
Langbodo is a real odyssey which only a few, and ultimately
one, of them may survive.

Problem 1: Paminku has been married to Kako only a
few months. She wants her husband to put her in a family
way before undertaking the "dangerous adventure" to Mount
Langbodo. When Kako refuses to postpone the journey she
"winds herself round Kako," refusing him permission to

leave. Although inadvertent, her tangling with Kako may "render his charm impotent" since she is in her menstrual period (p. 2).

Resolution: Kako savagely beats his wife. But the beating brings disaffection and anger between Kako and the members of the Mount Langbodo team. Kako threatens to dissociate himself from the journey and he is barely prevailed upon by Aramonda's intervention (p. 22).

Problem 2: The hunters now leave for Mount Langbodo. They find themselves encircled by impenetrable trees. They make futile attempts to cut down the trees as beasts, ghommids, crickets and birds laugh at their ordeal. Elegbede kills one of the two mocking birds. He is accused of hostility to an innocent bird and a quarrel breaks open among the hunters again (pp. 23-24).

Resolution: The resolution of the problem of the encircling trees is tied to the first problem about Kako and his wife. Paminku, Kako's wife, is now dead (p. 25). Her merciless death in the hands of her husband brings natural sympathy—the closing in of trees on the hunters. To free the hunters, a bird must be killed as a sacrifice to appease the wrath of Paminku (p. 24). So when one of the mocking birds is killed, the trees open and the "hunters meander their way through them" (p. 25).

Problem 3: A bird has been killed for sacrifice but it is the wrong bird. The hunters find themselves in "the city of the King of Birds," a town forbidden to anyone who wantonly kills a bird (p. 25). The hunters are arrested by the birds. To regain freedom, they must fight the terrible Sand Elves, enemies of the birds (p. 28).

Resolution: Hunters fight and win the Sand Elves with the help of Mother Earth, personified as Second Medium (pp. 28-30).

Problem 4: The birds are overwhelmed with joy at the conquest of their inveterate foe, the Sand Elves, by the hunters. They arrange a celebration of victory. During the celebrations, the hunters become rude to the Ostrich, King of Birds (pp. 30-31). They insult it, pushing it from its throne, from man to man, till Elegbede commits the ultimate offense by "racking" the Ostrich on the head (p. 32).

Resolution: Angered by the treatment the hunters have given to the birds, Efo Iye (half-man, half-bird), decides to abandon the hunters and go with his other half, the birds. So the hunters lose one of their men. More than this, the birds go to war on the hunters. The hunters barely survive by taking flight.

Problem 5: Their war with and flight from the birds make the hunters very hungry. They decide to hunt for some animal for food. But whenever they take aim, a ghommid wails and scares the animal away. Angered at this the hunters abuse and attack Egbere, the ghommid (p. 34). They thus lose the help and sympathy of one whose concern is the welfare of man (p. 35).

Resolution: Imodoye appeases Egbere's wrath (p. 35). In return, the ghommid gives some protective charms to the hunters. Imodoye is so taken up by the wisdom of this strange being that he deserts his own people and goes with the ghommid (p. 36). The hunters are thus decimated again because of the lack of a firm, united front.

Problem 6: The hunters are still hungry. They hear some weird music from a tree and think that it is an animal trapped in it. Kako hits the tree and the boulder opens. The hunters find themselves confronted, not by an animal, but by Agbako, the creature "God created ... to cause mishap in the world" (p. 38).

Resolution: The hunters try to run away but they are unable because they are under the magical influence of Agbako. They engage him in a fight; they are severely beaten and rendered unconscious. Spirits of the woods who had watched the fight revive the hunters (p. 40).

Problem 7: The hunters' search for meat to eat along with their yam makes them kill a pet that belongs to Were Orun, "the lunatic of heaven" (p. 42). This brings a fight between Were Orun and the hunters.

Resolution: Were Orun is killed by the hunters (p. 44).

Problem 8: As the hunters flee from where they kill Were Orun so that "more terrible things" may not happen to

them, they meet First Medium who misleads them and tries
to drown them in a river.

Resolution: Second Medium rescues the hunters from
the disastrous machinations of First Medium and leads them
to a town where they "will be a part of the celebration." But
she warns them not to be "vainglorious in the town so that
[they] may not all die because of women" (p. 53).

Problem 9: The hunters cannot avoid the temptation of
seductive women and they cling to them, including the
Chief's favorite wife, much to the anger of their husbands.
Akara Oogun is accused of stealing away the Chief's wife
and sentenced to death by the people but he kills his main
accusers and runs away (p. 60).

Resolution: The townspeople raise a war cry against the
hunters. Hunters run away, except Aramonda and Kako
who are killed, the former "on top of a woman. Aramonda
died making love to his neighbor's wife" (pp. 60-61).

While *Langbodo* thus presents problems that must be
met in forging the unity of a nation, it also points out that
however divisive these problems may be, they are not
insurmountable. They can be overcome, although the lack
of a perfect resolution of each problem seems to indicate that
men must keep on trying until a true answer is met.
Moreover, by displaying the culture of the major tribes that
make up Nigeria, from the Yoruba praise-singer and
"Kabiyesi"[7] exclamations, the "Sharo" of the Fulani and the
"Bori" of the Hausa [8] to the special training given to
"seductive" Efik and Ibibio women and the paraphernalia of
a dignified Edo King, the play tries to show how the respect
the various tribes have for culture is a unifying element.
Indeed, the playwright testifies that "all black people of the
world have a common culture."[9]

Second Medium also strikes the strong note of the
importance of unity towards achieving things and crossing
safely Nigeria's ocean of problems when she says, as she
gives each of the hunters a paddle with which to steer the
canoe of which she is the helmsman, "It's going to be team
work, and united, we shall cross without accident" (p. 51).
And when First Medium raises a storm through incantation

to thwart the progress of the hunters in achieving their
objective, Second Medium encouragingly tells them that
"Storm will come and storm will go but we will not go with
the storm" (p. 52). Appreciative of what Second Medium
has done for them, the hunters tell her how they look
forward to meeting her in the future. She dashes all such
hope in her reply. This is important to the over all message
of the play. Second Medium has always acted to them as a
deus-ex-machina. She now points out indirectly that there
shall not always be a Second Medium to rescue men from
the national problems that tend to divide them; such
problems are man-made and must be resolved by man.

Of the seven hunters who set out for Mount Langbodo,
only three arrive there (p. 64). They find that the unity and
welfare they seek for their country can be achieved through
the effort and experience of every citizen and not through
acquisition of a magical object:

> OBA   Nothing to give, nothing to take, nothing to discuss, good
> hunters. What you come here for has already been given to
> you in bits on the way and your people need nothing more
> upon which to build a united country.
> AKARA OOGUN But that object in your possession ...
> OBA   It is not when you lift your garment up and show your
> stomach to the world that the world will know you are well
> fed. Those beautiful words of advice, those touching and
> penetrating words of admonition are enough. Let your people
> love one another that they may value self-respect. If they hold
> dear the dignity of their persons, they will not thieve, they
> will not gossip, they will not be false, they will not be
> disobedient, they will not go to war and afterwards nurse the
> grudge of war against the vanquished. As you pass through
> your journey in the world, meeting with good luck and
> encountering the bitter, accept everything cheerfully. Behave
> like men and remember that God on High helps only those
> who help themselves. Let your people help and love one
> another. (pp. 65-66)

But the ruler of Mount Langbodo still gives the hunters an
elephant tusk—"a symbol of peace and plenty"—not as what

will enable them to build a united country but as an emblem of their arrival at Mount Langbodo.

In the final analysis there is no arrival at Mount Langbodo. As the inimical First Medium reveals to Akara Oogun, the only hunter who finally survives the odyssey, "Mount Langbodo is in your home, your street, your town, your village, your country." As long as the people are corrupt, self-centered and do hate themselves, the seeds of the total annihilation of the nation are firmly sown in their fertile soil (pp. 67-68). It is in their nation that these ills exist, and not in the hostility they encounter in their journey through the Forest of a Thousand Daemons to Mount Langbodo.

When First Medium snatches "the symbol of unity" from Akara Oogun, the latter cries to his compatriots, the very people who had sent him on the dangerous adventure to Mount Langbodo, to help him and to prevent First Medium from taking the elephant tusk away. He appeals to them not to allow those brave hunters who lost their lives in the quest for the object of unity to die in vain. The people and the King refuse to appreciate Akara Oogun's achievement; they jeer and laugh derisively at him and deny him any help (pp. 68-69). This is the concluding pessimism of *Langbodo*. It seems to say that things have gone so bad that no one cares for national unity, not even the King himself, the supposed head of the country and on whom everyone meets. We are dismayed and shown the hopelessness of fighting for national unity as the "King moves to Young Akara Oogun and turns him over with his leg. He hisses, and leaves" him there (p. 69). But the playwright tries to redeem this pessimism by calling for a solid Kola and not the segmented. The former unites, the latter disintegrates. It is the image of the solid Kola that the playwright wishes the tribes of Nigeria to think about.

Though *Langbodo* is not the best of Ogunyemi's plays, it is an important dramatic work in the history of Nigeria. in January-February 1977, a world event—Second World Black and African Festival of Arts and Culture (FESTAC '77)—took place in Nigeria. Among the aims of the festival was the promotion of a "better international and inter-racial understanding" and the facilitation of a "periodic 'return to origin' in Africa by black artists, writer and performers uprooted to other continents."[10] It was during this festival of arts and culture that *Langbodo* was presented as Nigeria's entry in drama.[11]   Thus presented at a world festival, *Langbodo* becomes a gathering of the tribes on two levels. On one level, it is the gathering of the many ethnic groups and tribes that make up Nigeria. On the other level, it is the meeting of the different nations of the world in a festal calling. It especially refers to the blacks in diaspora, and the many problems—past and present—that have made the reunion of all blacks in their root as difficult and impossible as Mount Langbodo. The pessimistic ending that scorns the idea of unity that is central to the play seems to laugh at the idea that the gathering of the tribes of the world could produce something worthwhile.   But there is no denying what Langbodo wants: a "solid kola [unity] and not the segmented [disunity], for the first—solid kola—is what secures a man to this world while the segmented scatters him to the winds" (p. 69).   Thus is the play torn between optimism and pessimism, although the latter seems to outweigh the former.

CONCLUSION:
THE DRAMA OF THERAPY

•10•

Political leaders seem so aware of the presence of drama that even as some have attacked it for trying to dethrone them, as Chief S.L. Akintola did, others already dethroned have sought some consolation in the wisdom of drama.

Socio-political theatre has had a vibrant existence in Nigeria. It has played many useful, and one may add, controversial roles. It has always found ways of responding to the changes and challenges of a newly independent nation.

At the celebration of Nigeria's independence in 1960, theatre assumed an advisory role as it seemed to suggest in Soyinka's *A Dance of the Forests* that independence should be approached with caution, and not with euphoria. Says Oyin Ogunba, of the play:

> ... It poses the question whether the new community is a mere, fortuitous assemblage of people brought together by a common, temporary excitement, with the prospect of an easy dispersal once the excitement cools down, or whether it is something that will develop into a union with a more or less sacred political bond.[1]

The play thus advises the country to enter into sober reflection at independence. There seems to be a realization by dramatists that independence is not a bed of roses; rather independence brings its own burden as man realizes with Jean-Paul Sartre that "man is doomed to be free."

Theatre has also played the role of a critic in the Nigerian socio-political system. In this function, it has occasionally met with hostile reception. In 1964, Hubert Ogunde's *Yoruba Ronu* indicted the government of Chief S. L. Akintola, Premier of Western Nigeria, and attacked his method of political ascendancy. The Premier retorted with a ban, declaring Ogunde's theatre an "unlawful society"[2]. It has been a critic of all forms of political malpractices, oppression and war. And this is where a play as *Madmen and Specialists* and the sketches in *Before the Blackout* are as important as *Yoruba Ronu* in their direct critical involvement in the pragmatic politics of their time.

Closely allied is the function of theatre as a recorder of socio-political events. For though events are not entered in their exact historical perspectives—theatre is not history—the critical and artistic touches given the events by drama allow the occurrences to be revisited and examined in their true perspectives by future generations. One can forever recall the agony of the Nigerian Civil war that *Madmen and Specialists* and *The Road to Ibadan* dramatize and can trace the roots of future political impropriety to *Before the Blackout*.

In his "Resolution" of 1920, Lenin had proposed that politics and art be imbued with the spirit of class struggle. Implicit in the proposal was also the statement that "if the revolution can give art a soul, art can give the revolution a mouth."[3] Lenin was not the first to follow this line of thought. Before him, Karl Marx and Friedrich Engels, in separate letters with similar contents to Ferdinand Lassalle, had pointed out in 1859, that one of the weaknesses of *Franz von Sickingen*, a play by Lassalle, was that it did not give close attention to the real struggle—that of the peasant versus the nobility—and had dwelt on a less important selfish struggle between a noble and a prince. They contend that the play would have been imbued with a stronger class conflict and "tragic collision" between the nobility and the emperor/ empire or between the peasants and the priests[4]. And over the ages, many plays have been given the ideological flavor depicted by Marx and Engels. We find this as a new trend in

Nigerian drama as playwrights such as Femi Osofisan, Bode Sowande, Kole Omotoso and Ola Rotimi employ Marxist didacticism in plays. Theirs is the first stirring of a revolutionary way of thinking--that Marxist ideology could solve Nigeria's political and socio-economic problems. In their hands, drama plays an ideological role.

Socio-political theatre in Nigeria has also served as a weapon with which to fight social ills and political malpractices. By exposing and castigating those who behave in an aberrant manner, it helps prevent future occurrences of such acts. It shows how men may live. This is the importance of such plays as *Yoruba Ronu*, *Farewell to Babylon*, *The Road to Ibadan* and *Opera Wonyosi*. In this function as a weapon to correct chronic problems, theatre also serves as a moral equivalent to war.

The future of socio-political theatre seems great because of its capability. It is capable of insisting on an image of change and of perfection as its target. This is a radical perspective but it seems to me that the future of Nigeria's socio-political theatre lies in it. As long as there is room for improvement—and Nigeria is far from being a perfect nation—this type of theatre is bound to prosper. Ultimately, it may prove more useful for the survival of the country than cultural drama.

In a country that has experienced many coups as it seeks a better society and a workable socio-political platform, socio-political theatre is of vital importance. Political leaders seem so aware of the presence of drama that even as some have attacked it for trying to dethrone them, as Chief S. L. Akintola did, others already dethroned have sought some consolation in the wisdom of drama. The prime example is General Yakubu Gowon, Head of State and Commander-in-Chief of the Nigerian Armed Forces, 1966-1975, who, when he heard in Kampala, Uganda, where he was attending a summit meeting of the Organization of African Unity, that

his government had been overthrown, resigned himself to
fate in the words of the dramatist par excellence:

All the world's a stage
And all the men and women merely players.
They have their exits and their entrances.[5]

The words were a tribute to drama and a soothing therapy
for a soldier-politician in a moment of distress and of truth: a
moment of distress, because he had lost his throne; and of
truth, because he had become the Head of Government by
ousting Gen. Aguiyi-Ironsi in a coup and now the wheel
comes full circle as another soldier tells him that his role is
ended and he must make his final exit.

But beyond the role of criticism and of providing
individual consolation in moments of distress, socio-political
drama is a drama of therapy because it is an integrative force
in a multi-ethnic Nigeria. In the issues it touches, in its
multi-ethnic playwrights and audience, such drama exhibits
the qualities necessary to nation building.

The issues raised by the socio-political plays examined
in this study are, in essence, directed towards integration and
nation-building. They can be isolated into three categories:
unity, social harmony and democracy.

There is a recognition in the plays of the importance of
unity in the achievement not only of self-governing status
but of the overall development of Nigeria. *The Cassava
Ghost*, for example, realizes the multi-ethnic birth of Nigeria
but strongly points out that Nigeria as a nation must not
allow its historic ethnic diversity to detract it from its
attainment of independence as one nation from the colonial
power and of maintaining that unity. It shows that
remaining as an indivisible entity is Nigeria's prerequisite to
survival and to achievement of many goals. Once there is
unity, it says, "there'll be nothing under the sun we can't
do."[6] And, later in the play, everyone is happy that "the
North, South, East and West [a metaphor for the different
ethnic locations in Nigeria] speak with one voice now." And

with the unity achieved, the citizens are willing to "fight together, win together or die together."[7]

Langbodo's central issue is the importance and necessity of national unity towards survival. While the play shows the problems that must be encountered in the search for national unity, there is a pointer to the fact that these problems are not insurmountable. The play encourages the ethnic groups to come together and do everything required to achieve national unity. The unity of the country is not for one man or one ethnic group, it is a duty for everyone. Like The *Cassava Ghost, Langbodo* emphasizes that fame, peace, and well-being and the avoidance of horrors of war, disease and famine can only be achieved through unity. Towards this, no personal and ethnic sacrifices can be too great.[8] Indeed, the play encourages the nation to seek a "solid kola [unity]" which "secures a man to this world."[9]

Another integrative quality exhibited by Nigeria's socio-political plays is their concern with the issue of social harmony. Most of the plays dealt with in this study fall into this category. There is a realization that social harmony brings people together. The Marxist and Socialist plays like *Shadows in the Horizon, If,* and *The Chattering and the Song* seek this harmony by advocating that the gap between the rich and the poor be bridged; indeed, the plays seek egalitarianism in everything.[10] Other plays, most notably *The Night Before* and *The Strong Breed,* advise that political propriety and Christ-like qualities in leadership are important in nation-building. Others, like *Madmen and Specialists* and *The Road to Ibadan,* argue that what the nation wants is that supreme love that can render fratricidal belligerence impossible. Social harmony can be achieved only through brotherly forgiveness and rational approach to issues, no matter how trying they may be.

A third category of plays dwells on the importance of a true understanding of democracy to nation-building. Just as *Before the Blackout* advises that politics should not be based on ethnic affiliations and castigates "regionalized" politics as harmful to true national integration and democratic processes, *Old Wines are Tasty* rebukes the mentality that sees "Opposition Party" as a "new way of ruling people" which turns "friends into enemies" and makes brothers kill each other.[11] Other plays, especially *Kongi's Harvest*, *Farewell to Babylon* and *Opera Wonyosi*, point out that dictatorship may not be a desired alternative to democracy. In revolting images they depict the manner in which dictatorship stifles popular activities and self-expression. In a multi-ethnic nation like Nigeria, the free expression which democracy assures is a way of bringing out burning issues. Issues when expressed give rise to possible solution; when stifled they boil within and explode, often times in violence. And violence often leads to anarchy and national disintegration. The advocacy for a free, democratic society by these plays, then, is geared towards a formidable nation-building.

The playwrights themselves seem to be an integrative force in Nigerian society. They belong to different ethnic groups yet have one voice in their advocacy of unity, social harmony, and a true democratic process as necessary to nation-building. Their unanimous approach to these issues and the fact that what they write about is concerned with the nation and not with any particular ethnic group seem to exemplify what they say in their plays—that the nation belongs to all and not to one ethnic group and that the task of building a healthy, strong and virile nation is for every Nigerian. From Sonny Oti and Samson Amali in the North through Wole Soyinka and Femi Osofisan in the West and John Pepper Clark and Zulu Sofola in the Midwest to Elechi Amadi and Ezenta Eze in the East, all speak with one voice as they say that Cain should not kill Abel and that both brothers have a duty to build if they are to live in Paradise.

Another level in which the playwrights show themselves as an integrative force is in their dramatic architectonics. In some of the plays the characters are multi-ethnic. In *Langbodo* and *If*, for example, there is an interaction of characters from the major ethnic groups in Nigeria. There are Essien (Efik group), Oba (Edo and Yoruba groups), Akara Oogun (Yoruba), Garuba (Hausa-Fulani), Chinwe (Ibo), and national and international characters like Papa, Mama, and Betty. Moreover, the plays are thematically nationalist and not ethnic. Themes of war, leadership, political practices, dictatorship, unity and bridging the gap between the poor and the rich are national ones. Even when a play like Sofola's *Old Wines are Tasty* uses an ethnic background, it is merely as a trampoline from which to leap to national issues. The play may be focused on Olona in the midwestern area of Nigeria, but the influencing factors and center of the play are from Lagos, Nigeria's capital. And some of the playwrights have successfully based some of their plays on ethnic groups other than theirs, although most of such plays are more cultural than socio-political. Prime examples are Soyinka's *The Swamp Dwellers* which is based on the Niger Delta culture, and Sofola's *The Wizard of Law* with a Yoruba background.

The audience to whom these plays are directed is elitist, elitist in the sense that it is one that has acquired the use of English. But even within this limit the audience is an integrated, national one. The plays belong to any English-speaking audience in Nigeria; hence, they have been produced in all parts of the country and they are immensely popular. The main reason for their popularity is that the issues they give expression to are not ethnic and localized; they are issues that affect the life of every Nigerian as he tries to understand the country's socio-political events and to determine what ways national problems could be solved. What gives life to these plays is the kinship the audience feels with the contents of the plays. During their productions, the playwright and his ethnic group are forgotten, and rightly so; only the issues come to the fore.

Socio-political drama also appeals to a national, English-speaking audience on another level—its freedom from affiliation to an ethnic culture. Because Nigeria is multi-ethnic, a culture-oriented playwright, even when he writes in English and can be understood verbally by any Nigerian literate in English, is handicapped by the fact that people outside his ethnic group may not easily understand the cultural force in the play. Occasionally, then, he has to be an "interpreter" of his own work through theoretical and critical writings. And when the plays are produced, they are interesting and fascinating only as cultural displays. On the other hand, socio-political plays have the advantage of appealing to a wider audience literate in English because they need no interpreter; the audience does its own interpretation because it understands the issues focused on. The audience discusses the plays orally and in national papers. There is no immediate affinity to a specific ethnic group. They are "national" dramas.

It needs be made clear that there is no incompatibility between socio-political drama and Nigerian culture. Occasionally, socio-political drama draws from the culture. In such instances, the culture is simply at the disposal of the central socio-political issue and the cultural interpretation is not required towards understanding the play. In *Langbodo*, for example, a multi-ethnic culture even enhances the message of the play. The central focus of *Langbodo* is unity; and the use of ethnic cultures from the Northern, Eastern, Central and Western areas of Nigeria simply appreciates the problems that could be encountered and amplifies at the same time the necessity and possibility of unity. It portrays the resolutions of the problems raised and unequivocally states that only a united people can survive. Indeed, to the playwright, *Langbodo* affirms the idea of unity in diversity, as he states that "all black peoples of the world have a common culture."[12]

Finally, it must be said that though socio-political drama sees criticism as one of its functions, its incisive criticism and portrayal of alarming scenarios in the socio-political set up are not intended to destroy the delicate fabric of the Nigerian society. Rather the plays are the writings of genuinely patriotic dramatists, sad that such angst-ridden situations should arise and hoping that by using drama to portray the problems and issues such situations could be altered. The plays are directed to "heal" and not to "inflict" national wounds. When *The Cassava Ghost* points out aspects of disunity and when *Langbodo* shows the odyssey one goes through in forging unity, it is out of genuine desire to see the existence of true unity and the solution to those problems that tend to foster disunity. When *Before the Blackout, Old Wines are Tasty, The Trials of Brother Jero, Jero's Metamorphosis, Our Husband has gone Mad Again* and *If* are critical of political leadership, they are as concerned as *The Old Masters* that cries out that "what we want is a leader."[13] Even as these plays are critical of leadership they point a finger to the possibility of the emergence of the right leadership to heal national wounds. Eman in *The Strong Breed* gives such optimism as he heals those who send him to death by arousing a change of attitude in them. When *Farewell to Babylon, Kongi's Harvest* and *Opera Wonyosi* depict the lower depths of dictatorship, it is to point out why Nigeria (and Africa) should avoid such a form of government because it cannot remedy national malaise; rather, dictatorship brings anguish and death to those who have the right to full life. *If, Shadows in the Horizon* and *The Chattering and the Song* may advocate Marxist ideology, but they are not interested in revolution per se; their main concern is to bridge the gulf between the rich and the poor and to make life abundant for all. When *Echoes from the Lagoon, The Road to Ibadan* and *Madmen and Specialists* reflect on war, it is to show that fratricidal warfare is not a healing balm to national sores, that man should reject war. For it is only in the abnormal theatre of war that human animals equate destruction to production, when people get medals, awards and honor for killing, mutilating, arson, violence, damage—negative acts that in normal civilization are ignoble and attract public penalty and outcry. All these plays are in a sense critical but their criticism is aimed at achieving a healthy national integration and at healing a national malaise. In this, socio-political drama in Nigeria is a drama of therapy.

APPENDIX A

BRIEF BIOGRAPHICS OF PLAYWRIGHTS

ELECHI AMADI

Elechi (Emmanuel) Amadi was born in 1934, in Aluu, Rivers State, Nigeria. He attended Government College, Umuahia and the University College, Ibadan. After a brief civil work, he joined the Nigerian Army. Indeed, he had two short careers in the army that were interspersed with teaching. For some time he also headed the Rivers State Ministry of Education.

Amadi has written many novels and a couple of plays. His most important works are *The Concubine* (1972), *Sunset in Biafra* (1973), *Isiburu* (1973), *The Great Ponds* (1975), *Peppersoup* and *The Road to Ibadan* (1977), *The Slave* (1978), *Ethics in Nigerian Culture* (1982), and *Estrangement* (1986).

JOHN PEPPER CLARK (BEKEDEREMO)

Born in 1935, in the Ijaw area of the Niger Delta, J. P. Clark was a Professor of English in the University of Lagos, Nigeria. He is a playwright, poet and critic. His published works include *Song of a Goat* (1967), *Poems* (1962), *Three*

Plays (1964), *Ozidi* (1966), *A Reed in the Tide* (1968), *America, Their America* (1969), *Casualties* (1970), *The Example of Shakespeare* (1970) *The Ozidi Saga* (1977), and *Mandela and Other Poems* (1988). On retirement from his academic Position at the university he formed the PEC Repertory Theatre in Lagos in 1986. Author of *The Bikaroa Plays: The Boat, The Return Home, Full Circle* (1985), J.P. Clark is also the author and producer of two documentary films: *The Ozidi of Atazi* and *The Ghost Town*. He is a founding member of the Society of Nigerian Authors.

EZENTA EZE
The second son of a paramount chief of Mgbowo in Eastern Nigeria, Ezenta began his education at C.K.S., Aba. He also attended St. Charles, Onitsha, and Aggrey Memorial College, Arochukwu. After college he left Nigeria for Liberia where he took a teaching job for some time. From Liberia he went for further training in the United States. He obtained a Master's degree in creative writing at San Francisco State University. He also lectured in Drama and headed the Department of Journalism at the University of Nigeria, Nsukka.

Ezenta Eze had written critical and journalistic essays. However, his chief reputation lies on his first published dramatic work, *The Cassava Ghost* (1974). His untimely death cut short a promising career as a writer and lecturer.

RASHEED GBADAMOSI
Born in Lagos, Nigeria, Rasheed Gbadamosi attended the Methodist Boys' High School in Lagos and got his first degree at the University of Manchester, England. He also studied at the University of New Hampshire in the United States and obtained a Master's degree in Economics. During the military regime of General Yakubu Gowon, Gbadamosi was made the Commissioner for Economic Development and Establishments in Lagos State. He writes plays and short stories. Among his published plays are *Trees Grow in the*

Desert, Behold My Redeemer and *Echoes from the Lagoon* (1973).

HUBERT OGUNDE

Born in Ososa, Ogun State of Nigeria, in 1916, Hubert Ogunde had an early association with the traditional Alarinjo Theatre. After his education in Ososa, Lagos and Ijebu-Ode, he became a teacher and organist from 1933-1940. In 1941 he joined the Nigeria Police Force and worked in Lagos; he resigned from the Police Force in 1945 to devote time to professional pursuits in the theatre.

Ogunde's theatre was a travelling theatre that had toured many West African countries, Canada, U.S. and Britain. His commitment to topical issues had made him experience the wrath of the different Nigerian governments, especially the British and Akintola administrations. The latter banned Ogunde theatre in Western Nigeria in 1964. He founded the Union of Nigerian Dramatists and Playwrights in 1971 and became its first president. He was head of a committee charged with creating a cultural troupe for Nigeria. The troupe is expected to go on international tours.

Among Ogunde's many plays are *The Garden of Eden and the Throne of God* (1944), *Worse Than Crime* (1945), *Tiger's Empire* (1946), *Strike and Hunger* (1946), *King Solomon* (1948), *Swing the Jazz* (1948), *Bread and Bullet* (1950), *My Darling Fatima* (1951), *Song of Unity* (1960), *Yoruba Ronu* (1964), *Truth is Bitter* (1964), *Aiye* (1972), *Nigeria* (1976) and *Igba t'o de* (1977). Hubert Ogunde died in 1990. He is fondly referred to as the "Father of Nigerian Theatre."

WALE OGUNYEMI

Wale Ogunyemi is a native of Igbajo, Oyo State, Nigeria. Born in 1939, he grew up to love shrines and groves through the influence of his grandmother. He thus witnessed many rituals, ceremonies and masquerades which were later to influence his plays.

Ogunyemi works in the Research Division of the Institute of African Studies at the University of Ibadan,

Nigeria. An actor and a playwright for the stage, television, and radio, Ogunyemi has published such plays as *The Scheme* (1967), *Be Mighty Be Mine* (1968), *Aare Akogun* (1969), *Eshu Elegbara* (1970), *The Ijaye War* (1970), *Poor Little Bird* (1972), *Obaluaye* (1973), *Langbodo* (1979), and *Eniyan* (1987). His play, *Langbodo*, was Nigeria's entry in the drama division of World Black and Africa Festival of Arts and Culture (FESTAC) in 1977.

KOLE OMOTOSO

Born in Akure, Ondo State, in 1943, Kole Omotoso attended Oyemekun Grammar School and King's College, Lagos. He took a degree in Arabic and French at the University of Ibadan before going to the University of Edinburgh for a doctoral degree in Modern Arabic Literature.

A novelist, playwright and critic, Omotoso now lectures in dramatic literature at the University of Ife, Nigeria. Among his published works are *The Edifice* (1971), *The Combat* (1972), *Shadows in the Horizon* (1977) and *Memories of our Recent Boom* (1982).

FEMI OSOFISAN

One of Nigeria's younger playwrights, Femi Osofisan received his education in Ibadan, Nigeria, and France. He is currently the Professor and Head of the Department of Theatre Arts, University of Ibadan, after holding a similar position in Benin University. Though he has written a novel, *Kolera Kolej*, and edits a poetry book, *Opon Ifa*, Osofisan's fame lies in the theatre where he writes, directs and acts. He is the founder of a semi-professional theatre troupe, the "Kakaun Sela Kompani." His published plays include *The Chattering and the Song* (1976), *Who's Afraid of Solarin?* (1978), *Morountodun and Other Plays* (1982), and *Once Upon Four Robbers* (1980). His *Eshu and the Vagabond Minstrels* set a record of the longest running production in 1986. He is currently working on a Nigerian Government commissioned play on return to civil rule. A recognized international scholar and writer, Osofisan is at the moment (April 1991) a visiting Professor at Iowa

University. He is an energetic playwright, poet, actor and director.

OLA ROTIMI

Born in 1938, in Sapele, Bendel State, Nigeria, Emmanuel Gladstone Olawole Rotimi is said to have started acting on the stage at the early age of four. After attending Methodist Boys' High School in Lagos, he went to Boston University for a first degree in drama. He also studied at Yale University for a Master of Fine Arts degree. For many years he worked at the Institute of African Studies at the University of Ife, Nigeria. He is now the Dean of Faculty of Arts at the University of Port Harcourt, Nigeria.

Though an actor and a director, Ola Rotimi is a published dramatist. His plays include *The Gods Are Not to Blame* (1971), *Kurunmi* (1971), *Ovonramwen Nogbaisi* (1974), *If...* (1983), *Our Husband Has Gone Mad Again* (1977), and *Hopes of the Living-Dead* and *Holding Talks: An Absurdist Drama* (1977). His plays have won him many national and international awards.

ZULU SOFOLA

Zulu Sofola teaches at the Department of Theatre Arts, University of Ilorin, Nigeria. Born in Issele-Uku, Bendel State of Nigeria in 1935, she is a graduate of the Catholic University of America, Washington and Virginia Union University, Richmond. She is Nigeria's foremost female dramatist. She has published and directed such plays as *Wedlock of the Gods* (1972), *King Emene* (1974), *The Wizard of Law* (1975), *The Sweet Trap* (1977) and *Old Wines are Tasty* (1981).

BODE SOWANDE

Bode Sowande, a teacher at the University of Ibadan, Nigeria, is a playwright, actor and director. He writes not only for the stage but for the radio and television. A graduate of the University of Ife, Nigeria, and of Sheffield University, England, Sowande is the founder of a group of performing artistes, the Odu Themes. Among his published plays are *Farewell to Babylon, The Night Before* and *A Sanctus for Women*—all published in a single volume in 1979—and *Flamingo and Other Plays* (1986). He is currently running an entertainment house in Ibadan.

WOLE SOYINKA

Born in Abeokuta, Nigeria, 1934, Wole Soyinka attended the University of Ibadan, Nigeria, (then University College, Ibadan), 1952-1954, and the University of Leeds, England, 1954-1957. After his graduation he worked with the Royal Court Theatre, London, as play reader until 1959 when he returned to Nigeria. In 1960, he formed a theatre company in Lagos, The 1960 Masks. He was a Rockefeller Research Fellow at the University of Ibadan, 1961-1962, and a lecturer at the University of Ife, Nigeria, for the next two years. He formed the Orisun Theatre group. During the political turmoil of 1964-65, Wole Soyinka was arrested and acquitted for a 'pirate' radio broadcast that condemned electioneering malpractices in the Western Region of Nigeria. He became a Senior Lecturer and Acting Head of the Department of English at the University of Lagos from 1965 until 1967 when the Federal Military Government of Nigeria arrested and detained him in prison for his activity in the Civil War. Released in 1969, he was appointed Acting-Head of the Department of Theatre Arts, University of Ibadan. In 1971 he went on self-exile to Britain and Ghana until the government that detained him in prison was overthrown. He was Professor and Head of Literature at the University of Ife, Nigeria, before he retired in 1985. The following year he won the prestigious Nobel Prize in Literature, the first African to have done so, and received the CFRN (Commander of the Federal Republic of Nigeria) award from the Nigerian Government (1986).

A prolific playwright, poet and novelist, he is the author of such plays as *A Dance of the Forests* (1963), *The Lion and the Jewel* (1963), *The Trials of Brother Jero* (1964), *Kongi's Harvest* (1967), *The Swamp Dwellers* (1964), *The Strong Breed* (1964), *The Road* (1965), *Madmen and Specialists* (1971), *Before the Blackout* (1971), *Jero's*

Metamorphosis (1973), *The Bacchae of Euripides* (1973), *Death and the King's Horsemen* (1975), *Opera Wonyosi* (1981). Among his Collected poems are *Idanre and Other Poems* (1967) and *Poems from Prison*(1969). In other areas of literature, he has written *The Interpreters* (1965), translated *The Forest of a Thousand Daemons* (1968) from its Yoruba original and immortalized his experience in gaol in *The Man Died* (1972). His other works include an autobiography, *Aké: The Years of Childhood* (1981), *A Play of Giants* (1984), *Requiem for a Futurologist* (1985), *Art, Dialogue and Outrage* (1988), and *Isara* (1988). He is a member of the International Theatre Institute and a Visiting Professor at Cornell University, Ithaca, New York. He gave a lecture at the University of Kansas, Nov. 1990.

GORDON TIALOBI
Gordon Tialobi was born in Warri, Bendel State, Nigeria, in 1940. After his education, he went to London in 1963 where he still lives. Apart from acting in many BBC African Theatre productions, Tialobi is also a designer and a sculptor. He also translates Yoruba Poetry to English. *Full-Cycle* (1973) is the first of his works to be published.

APPENDIX B

PLOT SYNOPSES OF MAJOR PLAYS

The Road to Ibadan by Elechi Amadi

Main characters: Wigo, a student nurse; Dokubo, an undergraduate; Captain Koko, Army Commander and Sylvanus, Capt. Koko's Batsman.

ACT ONE
Scene i
The war is raging and the town where Wigo and Dokubo live is being evacuated. Both are students in Ibadan. They are also lovers who hope to be married some day. Dokubo tries to persuade Wigo to go with him to Ibadan so that they can resume studies; the war is being fought in the East while normal activities go on in the West where Ibadan is located. Wigo is unwilling to go; she does not want to leave her mother alone, especially as her father had died.

Scene ii
The evacuees are still running from the war zone. Mrs. Weli, Wigo's mother, is killed in the confusion that accompanies a cross-firing in the night.

ACT TWO
Scene i
The refugees are hungry. Food is scarce to get to buy. A thief, Julius, plays on their desire to buy cheap food to dupe them of their money. When they realize their folly they raise a commotion. The disturbance startles a rat which the refugees pursue for food. Meanwhile, another thief seizes the opportunity so steal money and clothes belonging to Wigo and Dokubo. There is an uproar as other refugees realize their belongings are missing. A loud volley of rifle fire follows the uproar in which some of the refugees are killed. Among the dead is John, Wigo's brother. Wigo and Dokubo are taken away by the soldiers.

Scene ii
Wigo and Dokubo are taken to a military unit where they find that the Commander, Captain Koko, is acquainted to Wigo. Capt. Koko, however, tries to distance himself from Wigo and to act formally. Dokubo is given military uniform to do jobs around the house while Wigo is to take charge of nursing wounded soldiers.

Scene iii
Captain Koko thanks Wigo for doing a good job for the sick soldiers; he also tries to drop his formal approach to her. Wigo returns the thanks but reminds Capt. Koko to hold to his ideal of "no references to personal relationships." Their relationship, she emphasizes, is to be that of an officer commanding a fighting unit to a refugee taking shelter under him.

Scene iv
Dokubo tells Wigo they should escape and go to Ibadan. Wigo again refuses. She feels she has a sense of

achievement any time she nurses a soldier and he recovers. Dokubo is not pleased by the argument and accuses Wigo of making love to the captain.

ACT THREE
Scene i
Capt. Koko's unit is surrounded by enemy soldiers and he himself leads the counter attack. He is wounded and carried off the battle field to be looked after by Wigo.

Scene ii
Dokubo is arrested for betrayal. He is said to have inadvertently shown the enemy the route to Capt. Koko's unit by trying to escape to Ibadan. His fate is in the hands of Capt. Koko.

Scene iii
Capt. Koko invites Wigo to dinner and tells her he still loves her as he did years ago. He had joined the army out of frustration when Wigo had rejected his proposition for marriage.

Scene iv [1]
The enemy bombards Capt. Koko's unit at night. Capt. Koko summons his officers for a meeting on the situation, and they plan some strategy. Capt. Koko's love for Wigo involuntarily surfaces in his discussion with the officers and he is embarrassed.

Scene v
Capt. Koko decides to send Wigo and Dokubo away to their school in Ibadan in a military plane so that he may avoid a "slackness" in his duty as a result of his unrequited love for Wigo. Wigo asks to stay a few days longer but Capt. Koko refuses. As they embrace passionately to say goodbye their union is forged as "Mrs. Koko" and "my Captain."

Ozidi by J. P. Clark

Main characters: Azezabife the Skeleton man, Oguaran the Giant, Ofe the Short, Agbogidi the Nude, Ozidi (father), Temugedege, Ozidi's idiot brother; Orea, Wife of Ozidi; Ozidi (Son); Oreame, Ozidi's grandmother; Tebesonoma of the Seven Crowns; Odogu the Ugly; Azema, Odogu's mother; Engarando the Smallpox King.

ACT 1
Scene One

Seven Virgins present offerings to the invisible "People of the Sea" so that all may be well with the community. Council of State of Orua meets to select a new king; the throne is vacant after those elected had died within a short reign. Ozidi's family is told to accept the throne. Ozidi refuses but his idiot senior brother, Temugedege, accepts.

Scene Two

Temugedege is king but his subjects do not come to pay the traditional respects to him. Even the councillors who proclaimed him king refuse to come to see him. He does not receive the usual gifts and tributes and asks his brother, Ozidi, to make sure they are given to him.

Scene Three

Ozidi is angry with Orua citizens for neglecting their elected king. He abuses them. The people gather to discuss what Ozidi has said. Ofe tells them he will show them how to give Temugedege the ultimate tribute.

Scene Four

Bebeareowei, the state crier, summons Orua citizens to the square to discuss gifts and tributes to the king.

Scene Five

Orea, Ozidi's wife, tries to prevent him from joining his comrades to raid neighboring states for gifts to the king. She fears he might be killed even before they have a child.

Ozidi refuses to listen to her and rushes off to join in the raid.

Scene Six
Led by Ofe, Oguaran, Azezabife and Agbogidi, the Orua warriors kill their own man, Ozidi. They are unable to cut off his head because no cutlass can cut through him whether dead or alive.

Scene Seven
Messengers find out how Ozidi could be vulnerable to a cut, from Orea.

Scene Eight
Ozidi is decapitated and Ofe carries the head to Orua.

Scene Nine
Ozidi's head is presented to Temugedege as a tribute. Orea carries the head and weeps over it. Temugedege runs away from the house, imploring Orea to go with him to escape death. Orea refuses. Temugedege leaves alone. Orea tries to commit suicide but she is stopped by an old woman who tells her she is carrying a child in her. The old woman leads Orea to her mother, Oreame.

ACT 2
The story-teller narrates that Orea gave birth to a son in the seventh month of her pregnancy.

Scene One
Playmates tease Orea's son, Boy, for having no name and for not knowing who his father is.

Scene Two
Boy comes to his mother and grandmother asking them his name and the whereabouts of his father. Oreame tells him he has a father who is caught up by events in a far away city called Orua. She promises him she would take him there some day.

Scene Three

Oreame takes Boy to the forests for a test. She turns into a hill and then into a leopard. Boy is scared. Oreame chides him for being a coward.

Scene Four

Boy is tested again by Oreame who turns first into a young girl and later to a python. In the latter form she is so severely beaten by Boy that she has to seek hot water massage for some time.

Scene Five

Oreame takes Boy to Bouakarakarabiri, the old man of the forest, to get protective "mortar and pestle charm" for Boy. At the end of the exercise Boy is beyond the harm of any weapon.

Scene Six

Boy learns his father is dead. Oreame tells him he has to find out the fact about his father's life or death by himself. Boy enters a complete state of possession in which he discovers who he is—Ozidi.

Scene Seven

Oreame takes the young Ozidi to a blacksmith to get a sword. A seven-pronged sword is made for him because the ordinary sword cannot withstand Ozidi's strength.

ACT 3
Scene One

Ozidi, Orea, Oreame and attendants come to Orua and stay at the outskirts. Ozidi meets his uncle, Temugedege, who is living under an umbrella tree in the bush. Ozidi decides that they should clear the bush and raise again the compound of his fathers.

Scene Two

Ewiri tells Ofe and his companions that the murdered Ozidi has a son who has just come home with his mother and grandmother. Ofe and the men decide to arm themselves against Ozidi (the son), but only in self defense.

Scene Three

Ozidi and his attendant set out for the great market that is far away and shared by many communities. They are sent there by Oreame and Orea so that Ozidi may find out for himself the truth about his Father's death. Ozidi waits at the crossroads to get directions from market women. While he waits he falls asleep, spreadeagled across the road. Three women stumble Over him. Ozidi kicks one of them. The women are angry and threaten Ozidi with punishment from their powerful husbands who had killed Ozidi, the father. Ozidi springs to his feet and strips the women of their upper dresses. He tells them to inform their husbands what Ozidi, the son of the man they murdered, has done to them.

Scene Four

Ofe, Azezabife, Oguaran and their friend, Agbogidi, are gathered at Azezabife's compound, fuming aloud over what Ozidi had done to their wives. They decide to confront Ozidi in single combats. Azezabife is to challenge him first.

Scene Five

It is the day of battle between Ozidi and Azezabife. Oreame wakes Ozidi up and makes him go to the shrine to pray. Then she carries out a ritual on Ozidi before he leaves for the battle.

Scene Six

The combat takes place and Ozidi is victorious over Azezabife.

Scene Seven

Ozidi has won several more fights. Ofe and the remaining enemies debate what to do with him. Oreame cries out Ozidi's challenge to Ofe. Ofe tries to evade it but the citizens urge him to fight and not to allow the trouble to engulf all the people.

Scene Eight
Ozidi and Ofe fight for three days without a victor. On the fourth day, Oreame intervenes with her magical powers and Ozidi kills Ofe. The people are overwhelmed at the sight of Ozidi with Ofe's head and they rush away.

ACT 4
Scene One
Ozidi is restless and tells his mother strange dreams he has had about the people he killed in combat and about his dream fight with the Scrotum king. They want to send for Oreame but Ewiri comes to explain the meaning of the dream: Ozidi needs a wife. Ewiri also reveals that Tebesonoma 'of the seven heads' has challenged Ozidi to a fight to decide who is strongest in town and forest. Ozidi accepts the challenge.

Scene Two
Tebesonoma is victorious over Ozidi and his attendants. He binds them in a rope and carries them away to the forest. Ozidi cries involuntarily for his mother. Oreame appears and Tebesonoma is transfixed to one place. Oreame frees Ozidi and his men. It is discovered that it is Ewiri who had tricked them into a fight Oreame tells them to fight, however, because the place cannot contain two champions. Ozidi cuts off six of the seven heads of Tebesonoma. Tebesonoma begs to be left to live with the remaining head. Oreame refuses and Ozidi kills Tebesonoma. Tebesonoma tells them that his sister has just given birth to a Son who will avenge his unfair death.

Scene Three
Ozidi and Oreame meet Tebesonoma's sister. She is very hospitable but Oreame rejects her hospitality. Ozidi, however, does not want to kill her and her son. Oreame is

furious with him, and slaps him with her fan to rouse his powers; Oreame and Ozidi kill both mother and child and vanish.

Scene Four

Ozidi snatches away Odogu's wife as the latter is washing clothes by the beach. The woman seeks to know the source of Ozidi's power. Ozidi in anger pulls her out of the house to sacrifice her to the shrine she tries to defile. Orea hears the woman's cry and tells Ozidi to leave the woman alone.

Scene Five

Odogu the Ugly and Ozidi fight over the abduction of the former's wife. None is victor over the other for the two are equally matched: they have maternal witches supporting them and they have the charms given by the old wizard of the forest Bouakarakarabiri. Bouakarakarabiri intervenes to end the stalemate. He tells the witches that whoever gets a particular leaf from the hill will win. Oreame and Azema run for the leaf. Oreame succeeds in getting it first. She squeezes the herb into Ozidi's eyes. Ozidi rises in a renewed fury and cuts down Odogu. But he is dazed by the same herb Oreame squeezes into his eyes so that he also turns on her and kills her.

ACT 5
A Twin Scene

Engarando, the smallpox king, and his entourage— Cold, Cough, Headache, Spots, Fever—are on the beach of Orua. They dock at Ozidi's section. Orea and Ozidi are still mourning Oreame. Ozidi who has been out walking in the night rain has a cold. He has some rashes and a headache. Meanwhile Cold, Headache, Spots and Fever laugh at their success over Ozidi.

Neighbors tell Orea she and her entire house need to go through a purification ceremony, and they go away as Ozidi lies tossing on the bed. Orea prays to Tamara and then proceeds to scrub off what she thinks as a "mere riot of yaws." Smallpox king is angry that he is called Yaws, "common yaws" and takes his retinue out of Ozidi's dock. He lays it down that no member of his train should ever set foot on the soil of these ignorant people.

The Cassava Ghost by Ezenta Eze

Main characters of the play: Tina, wife of the late Kosoko and leader of Women Improvement Union of Nagase; Kamanu, leader of the Amalgamated Workers' Union, an underground movement; Dr. Akri, physician and former leader of the Liberation Party; Governor General and Colonial administrator; Mrs. London, wife of Governor General and Tunde, Tina's house boy.

ACT ONE
Scene One

It is the eve of the third anniversary of Kosoko's assassination. Tina receives the news that all over the country women are rioting against the colonial administration. Kamanu wants women and men to unite to fight the administration with one front. Tina is reluctant because she feels men have become cowards and she fears they might betray the cause just as they had betrayed her husband, Kosoko. Kamanu shows Tina a letter which the government is writing to Tina to talk peace with her, and tells her it is a trick to disorganize the women. Tina promises not to settle with the government till she discusses it with Kamanu.

Scene Two

Dr. Akri brings the expected government letter to Tina. The letter is a temporary suspension of the tax on women and a call for dialogue. Tina accuses Akri of betraying her husband and the natives who had hoped in him. Dr Akri tries to clear his name to a non-plussed Tina. Tina points out that the demand of the women now exceeds what the government intends to grant; women want not only the imposed taxation to be revoked but to have equal rights in representation in the government and in the legislative council. No sooner does Dr. Akri leave than policemen come to arrest Tina.

ACT TWO
Scene One
Tina is confined in a male prison but she finds life there pleasant because those in charge of her, though they ostensibly are loyal to the government for whom they work, are secret members of the liberation movement. Kamanu reveals government plans to exile Tina, but consoles her with his counter-plan—demand for Tina's release and immediate self-government for the country, refusal of which will make Kamanu's underground movement go into action.

Scene Two
Governor General is agitated. He is angry with his wife and his father-in-law for their bad influence over him. His wife, Mrs. London, is insistent that Governor General crush the insurrection with the army and police. Governor General gets the letter asking for release of Tina or face destruction of himself and the empire. He disagrees with his wife and decides to call for negotiation with the rebels. It is only when this fails he will use his armed forces. His wife is unhappy with the decision and threatens to pack her things and go away. Governor General gets a telegram that one of his officers, Mr. Peterson, has been murdered.

ACT THREE
Scene One
Paul broods over the death of his pregnant young wife from whom he had hoped to get a child to carry on his name. He puts the blame on Tina, who had begun the trouble, and not the police who actually shot his wife to death. He wonders why God hates him to visit him with scenes of death—first his father, then his mother, and now his wife. Peter and Mark try to console him.

Scene Two

The Governors of the North, East and West and Dr. Akri meet with Governor General to discuss the situation in the country. Governor General also discloses that the police and army have mutinied. Governor General and the members of his Council are arrested in their meeting by Kamanu and the rebels. Governor General accepts responsibility for everything and asks that all others at the meeting be allowed to go. Kamanu denies him this. Tina comes and takes over the command from Kamanu and Governor General and his men are put on trial. The expected letter from the Colonial Secretary granting immediate preparations for independence to Nagase through discussion with the Liberation Party arrives. Dr. Akri is overwhelmed by the turn of events and he commits suicide. The Imperial flag is lowered and that of Nagase is raised amidst Jubilant cries.

Langbodo by Wale Ogunyemi

Main characters: Aramonda, Kako, Efo Iye, Elegbede, Olohun Iyo, Imodoye and Young Akara Oogun—all hunters.

FIRST MOVEMENT

The king sends seven seasoned hunters on a perilous journey through the "Forest of a Thousand Daemons" to Mount Langbodo. The purpose is to get a certain unnamed object from the king of that place, for the possession of it spares a nation the horrors of war, disease and famine; it brings fame, peace and well-being. The hunters set out, meeting a number of problems on the way—from family, trees and birds. They lose one of their members, Efo Iye.

SECOND MOVEMENT

The hunters are still on the journey to Mount Langbodo. They come into encounters with terrible beings—ghommid, a creature God created to cause mishap in the world and the lunatic of heaven. In their encounter with the ghommid, they lose Imodoye who decides to be the ghommid's disciple. The First Medium attempts to mislead and drown them, but they are, except for Elegbede, saved by the Second Medium. They arrive in a land where they are well received. They soon abuse the hospitality shown by making love to married women in the place, including the Chief's favorite wife. The enraged inhabitants declare war on them. Aramonda and Kako are killed, and the others flee. Imodoye rejoins the remaining hunters and leads them to Mount Langbodo. There the king gives them an elephant tusk, a symbol of peace and plenty, and tells them that love of one another and the experiences they had on the journey will teach them how to build a united country. Just as the hunters are about to celebrate their achievement, two of them are swept away in a tornado, leaving only Akara Oogun. First Medium appears, mesmerizes Akara Oogun and takes the tusk from him. Akara Oogun finds himself with his people and appeals to them to help take the object, for which six of his companions had lost their lives, from First Medium, but his people simply jeer at him.

Shadows in the Horizon: A Play About the Combustibility of Private Property by Kole Omotoso
Principal Characters: Hon. Clement Bamigbade, merchant, trader, politician; Prof. Kofo Orimoogunje, Professor of hi-rated studies; Capt. Patient Atewolara, retired security man; Bibilari, worker in a canning factory and Alogbo, worker on a construction site.

ACT ONE
There is a revolt of workers against their propertied masters. The wealthy men, Bamigbade, Orimoogunje, and Atewolara, are gathering their belongings and are on the run. They meet on a layby on a motorway and there decide on what to do to stem the revolt. Orimoogunje writes a petition to the workers on behalf of the other rich men. The central idea of the petition is that the revolting servants must assume their responsibilities to their masters so that "servants and

masters all" can then sit down to discuss grievances. Atewolara and Bamigbade take the petition to the workers.

ACT TWO

While waiting for his colleagues to return, Orimoogunje plans different strategies to use to kill them so that he can claim all their wealth. He weighs different options— shooting and poison—and chooses the latter because it can kill both at the same time quietly. Orimoogunje is distracted from his thought by a prayer group; when he recovers from it he is confronted by Bibilari and Alogbo who, pretending to be starving people, disarm Orimoogunje from the gun he is wielding at them. Bamigbade and Atewolara return and disarm Bibilari and Alogbo; the latter flee and the former arrest Orimoogunje for trying to steal their wealth. Atewolara strangles Orimoogunje and they share the dead man's property.

ACT THREE

Placard-carrying demonstrators are shouting and singing slogans. Bamigbade and Atewolara are under a public inquiry, Bibilari and Alogbo presiding. Bamigbade, with strong evidence against him, is condemned to death; Atewolara is spared and assumes his military office. Indeed, Atewolara deceives the revolting people and becomes the new leader, decreeing that all public property be placed at his disposal. He bans the Workers' Union of Bibilari and Alogbo.

ACT FOUR

Atewolara, now robed in purple is in power and different classes of people—traditional rulers, market women, intellectuals—all come to pay their loyalty to him, except the Workers' Union. When the leaders of the Union, Bibilari and Alogbo, come it is to abuse and accuse Atewolara. When they leave Atewolara sends his security men to deal with them. Bibilari and Alogbo are killed but in the confrontation with the workers one of the security men is killed too. The workers and security men join hands in solidarity and set Atewolara's throne and property in flames. The workers promise to rebuild.

The Chattering and the Song, by Femi Osofisan
Main characters: Sontri, Yajin, Funlola, Mokan, Leje.

PROLOGUE
It is the aftermath of a wild party. Sontri and Yajin are engaged in a dance game of riddles which ends in a declaration of marital intentions between them. Yajin breaks her engagement with Sontri's friend, Mokan.

PART ONE
It is the festivity that goes on on the eve of Yajin's marriage to Sontri. Sontri, Yajin and Mokan have become friends again—ostensibly. Sontri has become a member of the Farmers' Movement. Sontri is angry with Funlola who has come to plait Yajin's hair for driving off his weaver birds. Yajin, Mokan, Funlola and Leje decide to put on a play by Sontri as a part of the celebrations. The play is about a confrontation between Latoye, a rebel, and a king, Alafin Abiodun.

PART TWO
The playlet takes place, with Sontri playing Alafin Abiodun, Leje the role of Latoye, and Mokan that of Aresa, chief of police guards. Mokan (Aresa), under the inspiration of Leje (Latoye), leads the guards to seize Sontri (Alafin Abiodun) and his wives. Mokan stops acting and turns the play into reality; he uses the play as a cloak to revenge on Sontri and Yajin. He handcuffs them and reveals to them that he is in the secret police, the "Special Squad" set up to combat internal insurrection. Sontri and Yajin are arrested for belonging to the Farmers' Movement that wants to seize power and proclaim a new republic.

EPILOGUE

Funlola and Leje are together, an hour after the events of Part Two. Funlola accuses Leje of belonging to the Secret Police and wants him out of their house. Leje reveals he is indeed Osongongon, the leader of the Farmers' Movement, and has no connection with Mokan. He is concerned with recruiting capable hands for the Movement and wants Funlola to be a part of the Movement. They pledge to work together. There is a singing of the Farmers' Anthem.

IF by Ola Rotimi

Main Characters: Papa, Mama, Dr. Hamidu Gidado, Chinwe, Onyema, Banji, Akpan, Betty, Landlord.

HAPPENINGS I

It is an apartment building in which there are many tenants. On the eve of an election the Landlord sends out letters to some of the tenants telling them he cannot allow them to be his tenants anymore. All the tenants gather and decide to reject both the recent increase of rent and the "quit" notice and to take the matter to court. They see the Landlord's action as a political blackmail because he had told them to vote for him in the coming election and had requested that they take an oath—both of which they had rejected. Hamidu points out that the tenants, as the oppressed, must unite and use their votes as tools for freedom from the capitalist oppressor. They need solidarity. And if votes fail to free them, then "mass struggle becomes imperative." Papa is given the duty of writing the letter of rejection to the Landlord. Akpan and Banji become disciples of Hamidu in reading *Das Kapital* and accepting Karl Marx's teachings. The young boy, Onyema, also sees more meaning in the life of helping others led by followers of Marx and Lenin than in the behavior of those who believe in God and the bible. Mama, Papa's wife, is seriously sick and her groans disrupt the ongoing bible class, children's class and Hamidu's political dictation to Akpan.

HAPPENINGS II

Mama is taken to Dr. Dokubo's house for observation. Mama insists that she will hold her 40th wedding anniversary the following day. Adiagha and Akpan quarrel over poverty, and Adiagha leaves her husband, taking their child and things with her. Chinwe puts the blame of the separation of the couple on Hamidu and Banji for teaching Akpan wrong ideas about Marxism and socialism instead of telling him how to cater for his family. Kalada, the poor boy who cannot go to college for lack of financial support, gets some money from Onyema; Onyema also promises to seek help for him from Chinwe, Hamidu and Banji.

HAPPENINGS III

Akpan turns to drink to wipe out the memory of his deserted wife after fourteen years of marriage. We learn that Onyema is an asthmatic patient who needs extra care because of his tender age. Exposure to cold and severe emotional upset could bring a fatal sudden attack to him.

HAPPENINGS IV

It is election day and the 40th wedding anniversary of Papa and Mama. It is also Mama's birthday and the day she passed Higher Elementary Teaching some 35 years ago. A choir comes to sing at the anniversary; gifts are presented. Onyema leads his group of children—New Nigeria Youths' Brigade—to perform before the gathering. They recite in unison "the enemies of our land:" political profiteers, intellectual swindlers, foreign business puppets, those who take bribes, the rich who keep the country divided and poor so they can be in power, tribalists, nepotists, and those who, by words and deeds, pull back the social, economic and political calendar of Nigeria. They also point out that the only way to build a great nation is through self-reliance and self-help. Akpan narrates his dream of the FLF, the Final Liberation Front, winning the elections, of his advancing professionally, of joining the FLF and becoming a governor and of his dedicating a school to Papa and Mama. Landlord attends the celebrations with a gift for Mama; he also tells the people to vote for his party, the Patriotic People's Party. Garuba, the deaf and dumb ex-boxer, grabs the parcel from the Landlord, shows it to Mama, and then dumps it contemptuously at the Landlord's feet. Garuba is restrained from beating the Landlord who carries his gift and leaves. At the end of the party, Mama and Papa are accompanied to the airport; Mama is leaving for Lagos for medical treatment. Landlord returns with policemen and thugs. Garuba, and Betty who tries to intervene, are forcibly led away; Onyema is thrown against a boulder where he crouches helplessly, seething with rage and loathing.

HAPPENINGS V
Late hours of the night, Onyema is still on the same spot the Landlord had thrown him—motionless. Mama is unable to go to Lagos due to cancelled flights. PPP wins the elections. Hamidu discovers Onyema's body. He is rushed to the hospital on foot by Hamidu, Garuba and Betty because no taxi works late at night and no one to call to give them a ride.

HAPPENINGS VI
We learn that Onyema is dead. Papa is so shaken by it that he speaks to no one now; he only gazes at the ceiling. Bible Class Group and children come to console Chinwe and others for Onyema's death and to pray. Papa's door is kicked open to speak to the children. He emerges, back to the people, talking volubly, as if addressing the bare walls. The sympathizers go away, Hamidu forgives Papa for his behavior but rejects his apparent new philosophy—"Blessed are they in these times who feel nothing, see nothing, hear nothing, but keep existing!"[2] Hamidu joins the funeral procession affirming his belief that people need to survive together.

Old Wines Are Tasty, by Zulu Sofola
Main characters: Okebuno, Okolo—political rivals, and
Iyese, Odogwu, Ogbelani and Onishe—members of the
town council.

ACT I
Scene 1
Okebuno comes to his place of birth, Olona, from
Lagos to represent his political party and to begin his
campaign. He is getting some opposition already but he
thinks he will get the people's votes if he gives them food,
wine and money. He insists on holding a party towards this
end even when told that his political opponent, Okolo, is
poisoning the minds of the townspeople.

Scene 2
Okolo and his supporters try to buy the elders to their
side by pointing out to Odogwu that people from Lagos have
no respect for elders, and that Okebuno has just been
imposed on them without prior consultation. They try to
discourage Odogwu from attending Okebuno's party.

Scene 3
Okolo's supporters are so dazzled by the enormous
preparations for the party that they tell Okolo the futility of
fighting against Okebuno. Okolo insists on a fight pointing
out he knows the "right buttons" to press. Elders arrive at
the party but Okebuno does not greet them with their titles.
Moreover, they are not placed at the high table and they are
angry. They tell Okebuno that a man who does not know
how to behave to elders cannot represent them in Lagos.
They abandon the party for home.

Scene 4
The people in Okebuno's house wait anxiously for him
to come from the banquet to another party at home. But
neither Okebuno nor the townspeople appear. Akuagwu
returns to tell them what happened and how he had gone to
the elders to plead with them. The elders have set a

condition before Okebuno can meet with them again—he must first be initiated into manhood.

ACT II
Scene 1

Okolo is with the elders. He further inflames the wrath of the elders against his rival, Okebuno. The elders are baffled at the disrespect of Okebuno to them and try to attribute such behavior to those educated in Western ways. Okebuno comes to them to ask forgiveness, but when he is asked to speak through an interpreter—though he speaks his language eloquently—because he is a non-initiate, he loses his temper and attacks the elders verbally. He is fined.

Scene 2

Okebuno's people are waiting anxiously for their son to come back from the elders. They try to put the blame on Okolo and his relatives for what is happening to their son. The infuriated Akuagwu, Okebuno's uncle, returns to tell the family what took place in the elders' home. Okebuno comes home only to face another fierce attack, from his family this time. He drives out of the house in his car in a fury.

ACT III
Scene 1

Okolo and his supporters are meeting at the place where Okebuno's banquet with the elders had failed. Okolo plans to go to the Party's headquarters in Lagos to tell them the way things are at home. Okebuno and his supporters uncover how Okolo had turned the elders against them. Okebuno and Okolo exchange insults and draw daggers to fight. One of the elders is called to separate them and he is informed of Okolo's machination. He goes home to speak to the other elders.

Scene 2

At Okebuno's house, his people are worried about his whereabouts. They put pressure on Akuagwu to find Okebuno for them. Okebuno storms in to question his mother about his paternal roots; someone had told him he was an illegitimate son. Okebuno decides to abandon his plans and family and go to Lagos alone. This makes tempers flare up, in which Akuagwu slaps Okebuno. Okebuno drives out wildly and inattentively and crashes into a tree.

Farewell to Babylon by Bode Sowande
Main characters: Field Marshal, Moniran, Kaago, Onita, Kasa, Jolomi, Dansaki, Majidun.

Part One: Patience
Jolomi, a female officer of the State Security, is learning to behave like a farmer under the watchful and critical eyes of Moniran, Head of the State Security, and Kaago, Commissioner of Counter-Insurgency. The purpose of the training is to infiltrate the farmers' enclave and stop their revolt. Kaago wants to crush the revolt with brute force while Moniran thinks the anarchy is so widespread that intelligence is needed to crush all the anarchists, dissidents, ideologues, and farmers. There is a hint that Moniran is against the dictatorship of Field Marshal, although he works for him and he is seen as his most loyal friend. So also is Kasa.

Dr. Onita is in prison for meeting with the dissident farmers and for his published book. Chief Majidun, a business magnate, finds his way into the farmers' enclave to "talk business" with the farmers. He wants to buy all the farmers' land, but the farmers hold him hostage till their man, Seriki, held in jail, is released. Oduloju, one of the farmers, is suspicious of Jolomi and the farmers decide to watch her closely; Dansaki also hopes to make her his wife.

Dr. Onita's cell increases in number to include Yulli, Seriki and Cookie. They tell the stories of their life: one common aspect of their arrest is that they have been accused of anti-government activities. They unite in singing and story telling and in the anguish of torture and imprisonment.

Part Two: Countdown
Seriki is released from imprisonment in exchange for Majidun. He brings to the farmers a photograph of Dansaki taken as he lay "naked ... on the mat in a pose of lust, fast asleep." Jolomi is the suspect and she is brought in as she tries to escape. The farmers decide to change camp to reorganize. Jolomi is branded with tribal marks and held hostage.

Field Marshal takes a trip outside the country. Moniran and Kasa decide that he must not be allowed back. Majidun is arrested by Moniran. Cookie, a drug addict and prisoner, kills Onita in jail. Kasa and Moniran stage a coup d'etat that topples Field Marshal; his close associates, like Kaago, are arrested, ready for a "purge" of bad government officials. The farmers are given an unconditional pardon by the new Eagle of State, Major Kasa; they are given back their land and invited to a dialogue with the new government. The farmers give Jolomi back to Moniran.

Death and the King's Horseman by Wole Soyinka
Main Characters: Elesin, horseman of the king; Iyaloja, 'mother' of the market; Simon Pilkings, District Officer; Olunde, eldest son of Elesin.

1
Elesin goes to the market place to be among women on the eve of his death. He affirms his readiness to join his ancestors when the time comes; he is going to keep his friend and master, the deceased king, company in death just as he had done in life. When Elesin feigns indignation with the market women for not giving him new robes, they quickly adorn him with rich clothes and dance round him. Suddenly something catches his attention—a beautiful young girl. He asks about her and he is told she is betrothed to Iyaloja's son. But Elesin must have her as his new bride. Fearing to arouse the anger of a death-bound man, Iyaloja and the women allow Elesin to have the girl as wife.

2

Simon Pilkings and his wife Jane are practicing dance steps for a colonial club ball. They are costumed in Egungun attire, the dress of the cult of the dead. Amusa is horrified. He is unable to deliver his message orally, so he writes it in a notebook for the Pilkingses; Elesin is "to commit death ... as a result of native custom ..." Simon Pilkings understands that Amusa is referring to a ritual murder in which Elesin will "simply die" without being killed by someone. The king had died the previous month and it is time for the burial ceremony in which Elesin must die so as to accompany him to heaven. Simon Pilkings instructs Amusa to arrest and lock up Elesin.

3

Sergeant Amusa and two policemen meet stiff opposition by Iyaloja and the women as they come to arrest Elesin. Girls mimic them and they go away, their mission unfulfilled. Elesin emerges from among the fold of women, bearing a cloth of a "virgin stain"—an indication that he has consummated his marriage to the new bride. As he hears the drum-beats and the chant of the Praise-singer, Elesin progressively enters into a trance.

4

The Pilkingses are at the Masque with the visiting Prince and other colonial officials. They are interrupted by a note from Amusa complaining about the behavior of the market women. Simon Pilkings goes with Amusa and other policemen towards Elesin's place. Meanwhile, Olunde, Elesin's eldest son who is studying medicine in Britain, shows up before Mrs. Pilkings at the masque. He is not happy with her at her desecration of an ancestral mask, and asks to see Mr. Pilkings. He tells Mrs. Pilkings he has come home to bury his father, Elesin. Mrs. Pilkings is astonished that he knows about it and tells him that Mr. Pilkings has gone to prevent Elesin from committing suicide. Olunde hears the drum rise to a crescendo and tells her his father is dead. Mrs. Pilkings is so surprised at his calm acceptance of suicide that she screams. Simon Pilkings returns with the arrested Elesin. Father and son are shocked at the sight of each other. Olunde repudiates his father.

5

Elesin is imprisoned, his wrists chained together. His recent bride is imprisoned with him in the same cell. Two guards are with them inside the cell. Pilkings is outside, by the window of the cell and holds some conversation with Elesin. Elesin rebukes Pilkings for preventing him from doing his duty and tells him the peace of the world is shattered forever. Iyaloja comes to see Elesin and rebukes him for the abomination he has brought on the world by his betrayal. Women come bearing an object covered in cloth, and Iyaloja asks Elesin to perform his duty. It is opened before Elesin; it is the body of Olunde, who has taken his father's place, "because he could not bear to let honor fly out of doors." Elesin stands rock-still at the sight, his eyes glued to the body of his son. Then with a sudden movement, he strangles himself with his chains. Elesin's recent bride performs some ritual on him; she is comforted and led away by Iyaloja who tells her to turn her attention only to the "unborn" in her now.

Kongi's Harvest by Wole Soyinka

Main characters: Oba Danlola, a traditional ruler; Daodu, heir to Danlola's throne; Segi, a courtesan and Kongi's ex-mistress; Kongi, President of Isma; Organizing Secretary.

Hemlock

The detained Oba Danlola and his retinue are doing a royal dance in desecration of the National anthem, much to the disapproval of the superintendent. In anger the superintendent stops the royal drums and threatens to put them in different sections of the camp. We learn that Kongi wants to "eat the first of the New Yam," a duty that belongs to Oba Danlola.

First Part

An assembly of men, the Reformed Aweri Fraternity, is in session. Having replaced the traditional conclave of elders, the Ogbo Aweri, members of the Reformed Aweri Fraternity are discussing what image to assume when they appear in public for the first time the following day.

Meanwhile Daodu and Segi are dancing. Kongi's secretary comes to warn Daodu about his uncle, Danlola, being "a pain in the neck" although he is in detention.

Kongi appears at the session of the hungry Reformed Aweri Fraternity and tells the members he is assuming the image of "a benevolent father of the nation". He orders them to begin disputation and later, a planning session, on that subject. He goes away and the Secretary tells the Fraternity that Oba Danlola is the stumbling block towards realizing this image because he has refused to publicly submit the New Yam to Kongi. The Secretary is looking for whatever way is possible to persuade Oba Danlola to bring the New Yam to Kongi in his own hands.

A member of the fraternity advises the Secretary for a fee, to make a deal with Oba Danlola: let Kongi grant amnesty to condemned prisoners for Danlola's presentation of the New Yam to Kongi. Kongi agrees and Daodu goes to persuade Oba Danlola. One of the condemned prisoners escapes and Kongi revokes the reprieve. Kongi demands that the escapee be brought back "alive if possible—if not, ANY OTHER WAY!"

Second Part

It is the day of the New Yam festival. Daodu learns Danlola is going to be absent at the celebrations, breaking his promise to Daodu. Danlola's reason is that Kongi has broken his promise also. Daodu persuades him to attend by telling him that Segi, the daughter of the escaped prisoner, will be at the festival, and that she wants the Harvest to be held.

Men from Daodu's Farm Settlement and the Women's Corps, led by Segi, are present at the celebrations. So also are the Carpenters' Brigade, traditional rulers and the Reformed Aweri Fraternity. The Secretary is uneasy at the presence of Segi and Daodu's men. Kongi arrives and Danlola presents the Yam to him. Gun shots are heard and the Secretary reports to Segi that her father has been killed. The New Yam is pounded; Kongi gives his speech and he is presented with his meal in a copper salver. Segi opens the dish for him and in it is found the head of an old man. There is confusion in the gathering in which Kongi is left in speechless terror.

Hangover

It is near dawn after the festival. Kongi Square is still littered with the debris that followed the scramble of the festival. The Secretary, Dende and Danlola—all carrying a few emergency rations—are escaping from their country, heading towards the border.

Opera Wonyosi by Wole Soyinka

Principal Characters: Dee-Jay, Anikura, De Madam, Capt. Macheath, Inspector Brown, Emperor Boky, Col. Moses, Polly.

Scene I

There is an impending imperial coronation of Emperor Boky in the Central African Republic and Anikura, King of Beggars administering to his beggars' establishment, Home from Home for the Homeless, mostly made up of Nigerian exiles from the Nigerian Civil War. He has costumes that "represent the five types of misery most likely to touch people's hearts," so that when people see the beggars in such form they give them money. These categories of beggars are: the cheerful cripple, the war casualty, the Taphy-Psychotic—an idiot made so through flogging, Victim of Modern Industry—Fibrositosis—and the blind man. To this Anikura adds a new one—that of the Good Man Ruined by Kindness. Meanwhile, Anikura and his wife, De Madam, are concerned that their daughter Polly has taken an ill-reputed man, Capt. Macheath, alias Mack the Knife, as her latest boy friend.

Scene II
Polly and Mack wed in a stable that is furnished by stolen goods. Mack's fellow thieves are the principal attendants at the wedding. Prophet Jarubabel and Inspector Brown, all criminals in their various callings, are present at the wedding, though uninvited.

Scene III
Boky proclaims himself a revolutionary and pays homage to his "mother country," France, for the motto, "liberté. Egalité. Franternité." He compares himself to Napoleon and calls Idi Amin, the Dictator of Uganda, his friend to whom he sends an aide for execution. He points out that Idi Amin is also his rival in acquisition of unmerited titles. To outclass Idi Amin, once and for all, he has decided to crown himself Emperor, the "black Napoleon."

Brown comes to report to Boky that school children are causing a minor unrest in the city on the eve of Boky's coronation. He asks for the children to be brought to him and he executes all of them to "emulate the worthy example" of King Herod. He also warns that all Nigerians in his country would be expelled without notice and compensation if any disturbance occurs.

Scene IV
Brown searches Anikura's establishment to arrest the habituees so as to prevent them from appearing during the imperial coronation. Anikura threatens to send out thousands of the poor to disrupt the grace of the coronation unless Macheath is arrested and shot by Brown. Anikura asks why Brown does not make the streets safe so that innocent citizens will not be murdered.

Scene V
Mack and members of his gang are holding a board meeting. Mack tells them he should go into hiding because

Brown is out for him. Polly is to assume chairmanship of the group in the interim. Polly tells all the thieves to dress well and appear like businessmen, all in lace. When Mack comes out of hiding he would wear the most expensive lace in the market—Wonyosi. Polly reports that in the new image, the gang has already bought shares of a marble factory supported by fifteen African Heads of State. While still discussing business, Brown and his officers raid Mack's enclave. Mack and his men escape.

Part Two
Scene VI
Mack is with Sukie in a whore house. De Madam, Polly's mother, finds out where Mack is. Mack leaves Sukie's room because her rich customer would soon come. Mack is to return before one in the morning. De Madam makes a deal with Sukie to let her know when Mack would return to Sukie's room.

Scene VII
Mack is in jail. He tries to bribe the warder, Dogo, with his Wonyosi so as to escape. Dogo is at first reluctant but later sets his own terms—a thousand dollars in raw cash, after all he has two wives and seven children to cater for. Polly and the gang come to visit Mack, but Lucy, Mack's pregnant second wife, comes with them and gives Polly a rough time. Mack tells his gang he needs a thousand dollars and tells Lucy he would be shot unless she helps him out. The gang succeeds in buying a stay of execution and a retrial for Mack from the Deputy Chief Justice.

Scene VIII
Anikura and his wife are unhappy about Mack's release. They decide to call in the help of the military in the person of Col. Moses. Anikura suggests that Col. Moses issue a decree, backdated, abolishing the right of appeal from Special Tribunals. Col. Moses refuses but Anikura and his beggars blackmail him into decreeing that "Macheath ... shall die."

Scene IX

It is Boky's coronation day, and Macheath's death is to add color to the splendor and pageantry. Everyone, from the hospital patient to the student, is interested in watching the public execution of Macheath. Mack is wheeled to the execution spot where priests of the various religions try to claim him. They all abandon him when Mack tells them he has no property left for them to claim. Just as the firing squad is about to take position, the newly crowned Emperor Boky gives general amnesty to all criminals, except political ones, in honor of his coronation. Mack is saved and Polly and the gang gather around him. Emperor Boky appears in his splendor and everyone, including Anikura and Mack, joins a procession after the Emperor's chariot that is drawn by four stalwarts.

The Strong Breed by Wole Soyinka

Main Characters: Eman, a stranger; Sunma, Jaguna's daughter; Ifada, an idiot; Jaguna, Oroge.

It is the eve of New Year and villagers are preparing for a festival in the night. Sunma is urging Eman to leave the village, if only for that night. A girl and Ifada play in front of Eman's house with an effigy which the girl claims to be her "carrier." Sunma is angry at the presence of both the girl and Ifada. Sunma tells Eman that the villagers are cruel and that they should go away. When the last lorry leaves and Eman would not go away, Sunma tells him that someday he might wish he had left.

Ifada is kidnapped by two men while playing with the girl. He escapes and comes to Eman's house. Eman opens the door for the distraught Ifada, much to the raging warning and protests of Sunma. Jaguna, Oroge and villagers come to Eman's house and tell him to release Ifada. They tell him Ifada has become a carrier of "the evil of the old year" and that by harboring him, Eman's house has become contaminated and should be burned down, but they would not burn down Eman's house if he releases Ifada without causing any trouble. No carrier ever returns to the village that offers him; if he does he is stoned to death. Ifada is forcibly removed from Eman's house, but he returns a short while. Sunma who had been forced out of Eman's house when she refused to cooperate with her father in dealing with Eman, returns. She learns from Ifada's presence and pointing that Eman has been taken away. She goes looking for him. Eman, naked down to the waist and adorned in the manner of a carrier, escapes and hides. The villagers, led by Jaguna and Oroge, are after him. Eman is thirsty and decides to go to a stream nearby. He falls into a reverie of his past life in which we learn that Eman is a descendant of a "carrier" family and that he is a widower. He had left his father and village after his wife died and when he also felt he was not meant to live the life of a carrier. He is brought back to the real life situation by the villagers searching for him. We once more see Eman in his past as a young carrier in training, his fight with his tutor over his girl friend, and later wife, Omae, and his disappearance from his village. Eman is again startled from his reverie, this time by a girl. Eman sends her for a drink but she slips out to betray him to the elders. Eman escapes. The villagers now know what he wants, so they send men to guard all the wells, leaving the route open to the stream only. Eman again has a vision in which he sees his father carrying the boat as a carrier to the stream. This dream merges with reality as Eman himself goes towards the stream to slake his thirst. This time Eman is caught and sacrificed as a carrier but with a difference: the people cannot curse him; they flee from him and the priests who sacrifice him.

Appendix C

Glossary

Alarinjo

This is the traditional Yoruba travelling theatre which first emerged from the *Egungun* (ancestral masquerade). It began when a king made an unpopular political decision and his councillors wanted to thwart his effort by using masked actors to act as ghosts. The strategy succeeded until it was betrayed by one of the councillors. The king captured the "ghosts" and surprised his councillors by making the "ghosts" a permanent band of palace entertainers. This story of the "Ghost Catcher" was re-enacted thrice annually at Oyo, an ancient Yoruba city. Hubert Ogunde was greatly influenced by the Alarinjo Theatre, not only in music but in the political proclivity of his theatre. (Joel Adedeji, "'Alarinjo': The Traditional Yoruba Travelling Theatre" in *Theatre in Africa*, pp 27-51) In the Alarinjo, audience participation is limited; a barrier exists between actor and audience not by use of the proscenium but by the religious taboo that surrounds the actor. The audience can hear the actors but cannot see them because they are masked. They can look at the masked actors but cannot touch them. The religious barrier renders impossible a complete rapport between stage and audience (Ebun Clark).

Bori

Here one treads the thin line between drama and ritual in some African traditional performances. It is a form of Hausa drama therapy. Bori performances occur most often during family or community crisis or transition: serious illness, epidemics, marriages, periods of national instability. They are usually held, when public, in an open area where all the local *masu bori* (owners of bori) and whoever else may wish to attend, gather. At one end of this "theatre" space sit the male musicians, not themselves intiates but professional specialists in the unique music of bori and the theme-melodies of the *iskoki* (spirits) or *aljannu* (jinns).   The musical instruments include a *garaya* (two-stringed plucked lute), *gora* (calabash rattles) and *k'warya* (inverted half-clabashes beaten with wooden sticks).   When the musicians begin to play the song of a particular spirit the woman associated with the spirit, costumed, moves into the performance area and dances.   Soon she assumes the demeanor of the spirit and her movements, voice, words, knowledge and power will be those of the spirit "riding" her. "If Malam Alhaji, she will cough and stoop, reading from an imagined Qu'ran, like an aged religious scholar; if the fever-bearing Dan Cladima ('the Prince'), she will walk with noble dignity, sit on a mat and mime the proceedings of a royal court; if, on the other hand, the rural Hunter Ja-Ba-Fari ('Neither-Red-nor-White'), the half-African, half-Arab spirit of madness, she will eat dirt and, either arousingly or grotesquely, mime copulation." It is at this point that the audience enter into the performance and make direct appeals to the spirit, and the spirit may converse with the spectators, foretell individual fates, offer guidance in personal conduct or issue orders.   (Andre Horn, "Ritual, Drama and the Theatrical: the Case of *Bori* Spirit Mediumship" in *Drama and Theatre in Nigeria*, pp. 181-202)

But *Bori* is more than this. It has assumed a powerful socio-political theatre role as Michael Onwuejeogwu tells us:

From 1950, with the rise in nationalism, the development of political parties in Hausaland, and the redefinition of the concept of freedom and individualism, Bori again took a new trend. The *Magajiya* [Bori cult leader] and her followers became the core organization of the women's wing of political parties and rallies. These women now use bori dance and music not only to win more clients but also to win over members for the political parties they support. These women, under the leadership of the *Magajiya*, are mostly practising prostitutes,new divorcees, those waiting to be granted a divorce, runaway girls, and the new girls from the rural areas seeking fortune and excitement in the urban areas. ("The cult of the Bori Spirits among the Hausa" in *Man in Africa*, pp. 279-306)

Coup d'etat

Often referred to simply as coup in Nigeria, this is the military practice of forcibly wrenching away leadership of the country from constitutionally and democratically elected politicians. Usually the constitution or most part of it is suspended as the military aristocracy settles in power and rules by issuing decrees. Some of these coups have popular support when they come to rescue the nation from near-anarchy politics and bloodshed. But they attract public anger when they outlive their salvific mission and engulf themselves in unparalleled corruption and maladministration. In thirty-one years of existence as a self-governing nation, Nigeria has had eight ruler, six of them military. Here is a comparative table:

Date	Military	Civil
Oct. 1, 1960		Sir Abubakar Tafawa Balewa
Jan. 15, 1966	Major-General Johnson Aguiyi-Ironsi	
July 29, 1966	Colonel Yakubu Gowon	
July 29, 1975	Brigadier Murtala Mohammed	
Feb. 13, 1976	Lieutenant-General Olusegun Obasanjo	

Oct. 1, 1979   President   Shehu
                                            Shagari
Dec. 31, 1983   Major-General
                 Mohammadu Buhari
Aug. 27, 1985   Major-General Ibrahim
                 Babangida
Nigeria is projected to return to full civil rule in October,
1992.

Egungun
Egungun (ancestral masquerade) is a ritual and theatrical
presentation organized by members of the Egungun Society–
a secret society for intiates only. The Society is responsible
for the ritual worship of an ancestor and of "organizing the
ceremony of the materialization of the ancestor as a costumed
figure." Annual Egungun festivals exist in which different
Egungun groups compete, competitions that have helped
improve the general style and form of each group.   A
significant breakthrough, says Ogunba, is the emergence of
the profane element with its increased interest in the sketch
or "revue": the prostitute with prominent breasts and hips
moving about the play-ground seductively and sometimes
grotesquely; the police officer marching about the arena,
officious, cruel and insincere; the foreigner, usually white,
authoritarian, his pointed nose high up in the sky. There are
also maskers playing the bishop, sometimes with his choir
boys and girls, usually with an exaggerated appearance of
holiness. Another frequent type is the couple who get
married in the western mode and go about arm in arm,
clinging to each other as if inseparable, though this conjugal
felicity is more of appearance than reality. (Oyin Ogunba,
Theatre in Africa, p. 23; and Joel Adedeji, p. 32). Wole
Soyinka's *Death and the King's Horseman* deals partly with
the Egungun. Note the socio-political arguments that arise in
the play between Olunde and Jane over the use/misuse of the
Egungun costumes.

FESTAC

In 1977, the Second World Black and African Festival of Arts and Culture was held in Nigeria. Popularly referred to as *Festac 77* or simply *Festac*, seventy-five nations from the various continents participated in it. Among its principal aims were to bring to light the diverse contributions of black and African peoples to the universal currents of thought and arts; to promote black and African artists, performers and writers and facilitate their world acceptance and their access to world outlets; and to facilitate a periodic "return to origin" in Africa by black artists, writers and performers uprooted to other continents. Festival events included Art Exhibitions, Dances, Music, Drama, Films, Literature and the Colloquium. Nigeria's entry in drama was Wale Ogunyemi's *Langbodo*. The next festival will be held in Ethiopia.

Guerrilla Theatre

The Guerrilla Theatre in Nigeria was the experiment of Wole Soyinka at Ife. Its purpose was overtly political. It was made up of satiric sketches put together and presented by theatre artists from the University of Ife (now Obafemi Awolowo University) during political campaigns and electioneering. The sketches were loosely scripted, allowing much room for improvisation. Usually, members of the group would block a street and one of them would announce to the people in the manner of an indigenous town-crier that an important theatrical event was about to take place. Then as the crowd, ignorant of what was going to happen gathered, the Guerrilla theatre artists would quickly present powerful sketches dealing with political impropriety and social corruption of some identifiable political figures and social elites. Its avowedly radical political attacks made the group to always be on the run and to attract government displeasure. The Guerrilla Theatre never really got the desired audience and therefore not quite successful because the sketches were written and performed in English before a predominantly indigenous Yoruba audience that could not actually follow the meaning of the presentation and because there was no attempt made to involve the actors and the audience in a critique of the productions. (Yemi Ogunbiyi, *Drama and Theatre in Nigeria*, pp. 45-46)   But what survives of these sketches gathered in *Before the Blackout* shows the creative boldness of an unusually stubborn artist ready to struggle with a hungry lion to save his pet rabbit from being devoured.   It is this selfless patriotism, perhaps the prodding from an incubus, that would later goad Soyinka into trying to save Nigeria from a bloody civil war.   This time the hungry lion almost ate the owner along with his pet rabbit.

The Ibadan-Ife Group
A group of brilliant radical critics and scholars, most of them fully bearded, young academics mostly from the universities of Ibadan and Ife who believe that art must have an ideological   perspective,   namely   Marxist,   socialist, progressive.   Often referred to as angry young men, the group "terrorized" through critical condemnation any artist of stature, especially playwrights, who did not follow Marxist canons in the creative process.   Their celebrated case is the scathing condemnation of Wole Soyinka's *Death and the King's   Horseman*   for   the   playwright's   "nostalgic patronizing" of myth and ritual, his "falsification of history to   suit   his   reactionary   mind",   his   unalloyed,   naive "celebration of a backward custom", his total, deliberate acceptance of the "feudalistic metaphysics which is an antidote to human progress.   In a rebuttal, Soyinka condemns the Marxist approach to literature as narrow, simplistic and "flawed by the contrived insertions of Pavlovian codes from elementary Marxist texts."   He goes on to point out that the "truly creative writer who is properly uninhibited by ideological winds, *chooses* ... when to question accepted History ...; when to appropriate Ritual for ideological statements ... and equally, when to 'epochalise' History   for   its   mythopoeic   resourcefulness   ...."   (Wole Soyinka, *Art, Dialogue and Outrage*, pp. 110-131) Biodun Jeyifo, Femi Osofisan, G. G. Darah, O. Onoge and Kole Omotoso are the cornerstone of the Ibadan-Ife Group.

Negritude
As coined by Aimé Cesaire, "Negritude is the simple
recognition of the fact of being black, and the acceptance of
this fact, of our destiny as black people, of our history, and
our culture." Over the years, the term has generated a
multiplicity of meanings but in its immediate reference,
Negritude refers to the literary and ideological movement of
French-speaking black intellectuals, which took form as a
distinctive and significant aspect of the comprehensive
reaction of the black man to the colonial situation, a situation
that was felt and perceived by black people in Africa and in
the New World as a state of global subjection to the political,
social and moral domination of the West. (Abiola Irele, *The
African Experience in Literature and Ideology*, p. 67).
Among those who contributed to the development of the
concept are Leopold Sedar Senghor, Birago Diop, Jean-Paul
Sartre and Cheikh Hamidou Kane.

Obatala
Obatala is the Yoruba god of creation. He moulds the forms
but it is Olodumare, the Supreme Being, who gives the
breath of life. Obatala's creative activity then is essentially
formal, and plastic. Like Ogun, Obatala is said to have also
fallen to the "fumes of wine; this craftsman's fingers lost
their control" and he moulded deformed beings. (Wole
Soyinka) The worship of Obatala has important
consequences for the development of Yoruba ritual drama
and finally the emergence of the theatre, says Professor Joel
Adedeji. All the stock-characters of the first recorded
beginnings of the Yoruba theatre (*Alarinjo*) are caricatures of
humanity believed to have been created by the archdivinity
Orisa-nla (another name for *Obatala*) when he was thus
under the influence of wine. These stock-characters are the
hunchback, the albino, the leper, the prognathus, the dwarf
and the cripple. They are called *eni Orisa* (those of the
Deity). The impetus to create has been identified with the
worshippers of *Obatala*. Ologbin Ologbojo, founder of the
Alarinjo theatre was a worshipper of Obatala. It is said that
it was on account of his hybrid son–half-man, half-ape–that

he invented masks and costumes to masquerade his son's unusual features and established the theatre as a permanent part of court entertainments. (Joel Adedeji, "'Alarinjo': The Traditional Yoruba Travelling Theatre" in *Theatre in Africa*, pp. 27-51)

Ogun
Ogun is the Yoruba god of iron and steel. He has been made popular in theatre mostly through the writings of Wole Soyinka. Soyinka describes Ogun as the "god of creativity, guardian of the road, god of metallic lore and artistry. Explorer, hunter, god of war, Custodian of the sacred oath." Ogun looms large in Soyinka's "The Fourth Stage"–a theory of the origin of tragedy among the Yoruba people of Nigeria. According to this theory, the gods were unhappy and felt incomplete because of their separation from men; what Soyinka calls the "anguish of severance" or "the principle of complementarity"–that is, the desire for divinities to constantly experience the human in them and a parallel human desire to be godlike. The interaction between the spiritual and material essences brings a "cosmic totality", a unity of being. The gods had physically experienced life on earth and human companionship; some default, some sin brought an end to the happy relationship and the gods withdrew from men. The sin created a barrier, "the chthonic realm", between gods and men. It was Ogun's fate to be the only god to undertake the selfless act of battling the forces of the chthonic realm, bridge the gap between man and god, thereby restoring the fulness of being (the principle of complementarity) to both men and gods. Ogun is thus the first actor in Yoruba drama and his pathway, his bridge over "the gulf of transition" is what Soyinka calls "the fourth stage". Ogun's tragic individuality is also seen when inebriated before going on a battle, he slaughtered both his enemies and his supporters. "The erstwhile hero of the transitional abyss" found himself alone. (*Art, Dialogue & Outrage*, pp. 21-34)

Theatre for Development
Also called *Popular Theatre for Development*, this experiment uses theatre as a vehicle for promoting social awareness among the rural communities. The Katsina-Ala Project of Benue State and the Samaru Community Theatre of the Ahmadu Bello University are examples of *Theatre for Development*. They use theatre to educate the people about health, agriculture, education, cooperatives and self-development. The real focus is the active participation and involvement in the theatrical process by the people themselves. At the University of Benin Peter Ukpokodu experimented with drama therapy. The defining yardstick in these experiments is the conscious use of the performing arts to bring about or reinforce a process of social change and of changes in self-concept, attitude, awareness and behavior. Tar Ahura, Salihu Bappa, Oga Abah are proponents of *Theatre for Development*. In its eclectic wastefulness, Babangida's MAMSER (a slogan for ill-defined development programs) has this type of theatrical experiment under its aegis too.

Turu
A traditional dance drama performed by the Hausa of Northern Nigeria. It is meant to entertain mostly the royalty and its invitees. It is usually performed when there is a royal installation or when a new chief is being turbanned. Variable of this performance are the *Wasan Gauta* which is an elaborate dramatic performance for the royalty and the *Wawan Sarki*, the King's Fool.

NOTES

CHAPTER 1

[1] This is a theological interpretation of the history of Israel, especially of the purported Covenant Israel entered with God that made the former God's people. He, God, fought Israel's wars, using her to whip other nations when they transgressed. Apart from the *Old Testament*, see John Bright's *A History of Israel* (London: SCM Press Ltd., 1972), pp. 130-139; 144-151.

[2] Michael Crowder, *The Story of Nigeria* (London: Faber and Faber, 1962), p. 19.

[3] Crowder, p. 19.

[4] Federal Ministry of Information, Nigeria, *Nigeria Handbook, 1978-1979* (Lagos, Nigeria: Third Press International, 1979), pp. 29-30.

[5] Crowder, p. 21.

[6] Crowder, p. 46.

7 *The Movement of Transition* (Ibadan: Ibadan University Press, 1975), p. 1.

8 For synopsis of this play, see Appendix B.

9 Femi Osofisan, "Tiger on Stage: Wole Soyinka and Nigerian Theatre" in *Theatre in Africa*, ed. Oyin Ogunba and Abiola Irele (Ibadan: Ibadan University Press, 1978), p. 166.

10 Wole Soyinka, *Death and the King's Horseman* (New York and London: Norton and Company, 1975), p. 6.

11 "The African Traditional View of Man" *Orita: Ibadan Journal of Religious Studies*, VI, 2, December 1972, p. 104.

12 I am here indebted to Prof. J. A. Adedeji, widely acclaimed for his research on the "Alarinjo Theatre," for his series of lectures on that subject at the University of Ibadan, Nigeria, during the 1974-75 academic year.

13 A paraphrase of J. O. Awolalu's lectures on "African Traditional Religion" in May 1975, at the University of Ibadan.

14 Awolalu, May, 1975.

15 J. P. Clark, *Ozidi* (London and Ibadan: Oxford University Press, 1966), no page. See "Note" to the play. Also see *The Ozidi Saga* (Ibadan: Oxford University Press and Ibadan University Press, 1977), p. ix.

16 *The Ozidi Saga*, p. ix.

17 *The Ozidi Saga*, p. xxxii.

18 *The Ozidi Saga*, p. xxxiii.

19 Wole Soyinka, "The Fourth Stage" in *The Morality of Art*, ed. D. W. Jefferson (London: Routledge and Kegan Paul, 1969), pp. 119-134.

20 Janheinz Jahn has a list of at least eighteen meanings of Negritude, ranging from its concept as "Instrument" through "Style," "Attitude," "Being," "Race" to "Sum of all Values". See *A History of Neo-African Literature* (London: Faber and Faber Ltd., 1966), pp. 251-252.

21 R. N. Egudu, *Modern African Poetry and the African Predicament* (London and Basingstoke: The Macmillan Press Ltd., 1978), pp. 30-31.

22 Ngugi wa Thiong'o, *Homecoming* (London: Heinemann, 1972), pp. 81-82. It is important to read these pages and to note that the policy of assimilation was not total. Other writers like E. R Braithwaite and V. S. Naipaul have pointed out the African "consciousness" that remained, especially in "genuine African cultural survivals in names of certain foods and in the practice of various religious cults..."

23 This English translation of the French original is by Abiola Irele in "Negritude—Philosophy of African Being" in *Nigeria Magazine*, Nos. 122-123, 197, p. 1.

24 Irele, p. 5.

25 Oyin Ogunba, *The Movement of Transition* (Ibadan: Ibadan University Press, 1975), p. 7.

26 Wole Soyinka, *The Man Died* (London: Rex Collings, 1972), p. 18.

CHAPTER 2

1 Robert Smith gives an interesting account of this sudden change of events. There was a battle between the Nupes and the Oyos and the former were winning, to the extent that the Oyo king was in danger of being killed or captured. In order to protect the King, a warrior "exchanged clothes with him and drew on himself the concentrated fire of the Nupe bowmen. His dead body, transfixed by their arrows, remained upright, his teeth set as in a grin. The Nupe, supposing themselves to be opposed by a supernatural being, fled in terror from

the field, leaving their king a prisoner of the Oyo." See *Kingdoms of the Yoruba* (Norwich: Methuen and Co., Ltd., 1976), p. 43.

2 Smith, p. 43.

3 Joel Adedeji, "'Alarinjo': The Traditional Yoruba Travelling Theatre" in *Theatre in Africa*, ed. Oyin Ogunba and Abiola Irele (Ibadan: Ibadan University Press, 1978), p. 28.

4 Adedeji, p. 28.

5 Adedeji, pp. 28, 50.

6 Smith, p. 43.

7 Smith, pp. 43-44.

8 Adedeji, p. 29.

9 Smith, p. 44.

10 Adedeji, p. 29.

11 J. P Clark, *The Ozidi Saga* (Ibadan: Ibadan University Press and Oxford University Press, 1977), p. ix.

12 Clark, p. xx.

13 Clark, p. xx.

14 Clark, p. xx.

15 Clark, p. 389.

16 Martin Banham and Clive Wake, *African Theatre Today* (London: Pitman Publishing Ltd., 1976), p. 9.

17 *The Missionary Impact on Modern Nigeria* (London: Longmans, 1966), p. 242.

[18] Ayandele, p. 242.

[19] Ayandele, p. 243.

[20] Ayandele, p. 244.

[21] Ayandele, p. 245.

[22] Ayandele, p. 246.

[23] Ayandele, pp. 246-248.

[24] Ayandele, pp. 249-251.

[25] African Church, *Report of Proceedings of the African Church Organization for Lagos and Yorubaland 1901-1908* (Liverpool, 1910), p. 91. Also see *The Missionary Impact on Modern Nigeria*, pp. 263-264.

[26] *Nigeria: Background to Nationalism* (Los Angeles: University of California Press, 1963), p. 426.

[27] *Hubert Ogunde: The Making of Nigerian Theatre* (Oxford: Oxford University Press, 1979), p. 79. Also see her articles "Ogunde Theatre: The Rise of Contemporary Professional Theatre in Nigeria 1946-72" and "The Nigerian Theatre and the Nationalist Movement" in *Nigeria Magazine*, Nos. 115-116, 1975. Most of my ideas concerning Hubert Ogunde are based on these works and on lectures by J. A. Adedeji at the University of Ibadan, 1974/75 academic year.

[28] *West African Pilot*, July 25, 1947, Editorial page.

[29] *West African Pilot*, July 9, 1947, Editorial page.

[30] Ebun Clark's translation in *Hubert Ogunde: The Making of Nigerian Theatre*, p. 89.

[31] Ebun Clark, "The Hubert Ogunde Theatre Company," Diss. University of Leeds 1974, pp. 257-259.

32 *Nigeria: Background to Nationalism*, pp. 258-259.

33 *Hubert Ogunde: The Making of Nigerian Theatre*, pp. 89-90.

34 Martin Banham and Clive Wake, p. 10.

35 Ayandele, pp. 248-249.

36 Ayandele, p. 325.

37 *Hubert Ogunde: The Making of Nigerian Theatre*, p. 83.

38 *Hubert Ogunde: The Making of Nigerian Theatre*, p. 85.

39 G. O. Olusanya, *The Second World War and Politics in Nigeria 1939-53* (Lagos: University of Lagos Press and Evans Brothers Ltd., 1973), p. 118.

40 *Hubert Ogunde: The Making of Nigerian Theatre*, p. 86.

41 G. O. Olusanya, p. 118.

42 I reiterate that much of the material on Hubert Ogunde is available exclusively to Ebun Clark who has made it available to the public through her M.Phil. dissertation (which includes some translation of some of the plays), her book on Hubert Ogunde and her articles. Professor J.A. Adedeji, himself a distinguished scholar on Ogunde, told me in a conversation on April 23, 1991, that what Ogunde had as written portions of his plays usually appeared in program notes printed by Pacific Press. They contained the synopsis, scenarios and songs of the particular production.

43 *Hubert Ogunde: The Making of Nigerian Theatre*, p. 58.

44 *Hubert Ogunde: The Making of Nigerian Theatre*, pp. 58-59. Though *Yoruba Ronu* was composed in 1963, the more appropriate date is 1964 since it was that year it became available for public consumption.

45 *Daily Times*, Thursday, April 2, 1964, p. 1.

46 *West African Pilot*, Thursday, April 2 1964, Editorial page.

47 Oduduwa is the progenitor of the Yoruba people.

48 "Ogunde Theatre: The Rise of Contemporary Professional Theatre in Nigeria 1946-72" in *Nigeria Magazine*, Nos. 115-116, 1975, pp. 20-21.

49 G. O. Olusanya's yet unpublished paper entitled "Olaniwun Adunni Oluwole—Nationalist Pioneer of Women's Liberation Movement and Religious Leader," pp. 11-13. It will be published by the University of Ibadan. As Ebun Clark points out, "Olusanya was originally not aware of her theatre career which spanned from the mid forties to 1954." *Hubert Ogunde: The Making of Nigerian Theatre*, p. 92.

CHAPTER 3

1 See the discussion of Adunni Oluwole in the penultimate paragraph of Chapter 2.

2 Most of the ideas here and elsewhere are from the editorial comments, "The Heroes of Nigeria," in *Nigerian Opinion*, 6, Nos. 8-10 (August-October, 1970), 69-70. The editorial is explicitly on the independence anniversary, but it contains implicit reference to Independence. The interpretation of the events as they apply to 1960 is mine.

3 *Nigerian Opinion*, pp. 69-70.

4 Page references in this chapter, unless otherwise indicated, are to Wole Soyinka's *Before the Blackout*, Orisun Acting Editions (Ibadan: n.p., n.d.). Oftentimes, dramatic sketches, as in *Before the Blackout* are not given the critical examination accorded to drama per se. But the nature of this study—a sort of excursion into Nigerian and African socio-political situations through art (drama)—demands that these sketches be given some detailed consideration. They assume the function as it were of the Monet paintings—highly impressionistic, allowing a filling-in of details both through interpretation and history. Indeed, the mark of this chapter is its great reliance on history to

corroborate the sketches. Drama per se, even when technically innovative, often "expresses" its own view, and by so doing, taints the audience with its prejudice. Dramatic sketches liberate the audience from such confinement allowing him to interpret messages by himself through available means, sensually and/or intellectually, and as in this chapter, historically. Professor J.A. Adedeji informed me in an academic discussion on April 23, 1991, that the actual date for *Before the Blackout* is 1965. In 1964 Soyinka had written *The New Republican* and some of the sketches in this were repeated in *Before the Blackout*.

5 N.B.C. has since changed its name to F.R.C.N. (Federal Radio Corporation of Nigeria).

6 This is in pidgin. A free translation, without regard to rhyme, might read as follows:
Let me confess, I can even shout it out
When there is trouble
Principle—a word that sounds so good—
Must yield to compromise, which is by far better (than adhering to principle)
That golden slice of national cake
Is sweeter than any woman
Must a donkey work for the monkey to reap the benefit?
My friends I'm only human.
The point here is that the speaker of the stanza is not ashamed to abandon following laid down principles when he sees trouble looming. In such a situation it is better to compromise with the author of the threat—here a government agent.than be deprived of a share of the national wealth—that national wealth that yields more pleasure in having than in love-making. The understanding here is that one takes from, and not gives to, the nation. Only fools do things for the sake of others. The speaker realizes he is only a human being—a foxy one at that.

7 M. R. Ofoegbu, "Programme-Oriented System for Nigeria," in *Nigerian Opinion*, p. 74.

8 *Headlines*, No. 73 (April 1979), pp. 2-4, 8.

9 *Daily Times*, Editorial, August 26, 1964, p. 3.

10 Zulu Sofola, *Old Wines Are Tasty* (Ibadan: University Press Limited, 1981), pp. 13-16, 21.

11 *Headlines*, p. 4.

12 Zulu Sofola, pp. 39-40.

13 *Headlines*, p. 4.

14 *Headlines*, pp. 1-4, 8.

15 M. R. Ofoegbu, "Programme-Oriented Political System for Nigeria," in *Nigerian Opinion*, pp. 74-78, from which much of the material given is taken.

16 Ofoegbu, p. 76.

17 Ofoegbu, p. 77.

18 *Headlines*, p. 8.

19 *Before the Blackout*, pp. 11, 73-75. Also see Ofoegbu, p. 75.

20 Ofoegbu, p. 74.

21 See note 6 above.

22 Tayo Akpata, "Intellectuals in Contemporary Nigerian Politics," *Nigerian Opinion*, 2, No. 12 (December 1966), 141.

23 "The Writer in a Modern African State," *When the Man Died*, ed. John Agetua (Benin City: B. N. C., 1975), p. 30. The essay first appeared in *L'Afrique Actuelle*, No. 19 (June 1967) pp. 5-7.

24 Peter Enahoro, *How to be a Nigerian* (Lagos: Daily Times of Nigeria Ltd., 1966), p. ix.

25 Enahoro, p. 3.

26 Enahoro, p. 27.

[27] Ime Ikiddeh, *Blind Cyclop in Ten One-Act Plays*, ed. Cosmo Pieterse (London: Heinemann Educational Books ,1968 , p. 123.

[28] Kole Omotoso, *Shadows in the Horizon* (Ibadan: Sketch Publ. Co., 1977), pp. 4-5.

[29] *Farewell to Babylon* (London Drumbeat, 1979), p. 73.

CHAPTER 4

[1] Sonny Oti, *The Old Masters* (Ibadan: Oxford University Press, 1973), p. 10.

[2] Wole Soyinka, *The Lion and the Jewel*, in *Collected Plays 2* (London: Oxford University Press, 1974), p. 22.

[3] *Before the Blackout*, p. 75.

[4] James Ene Henshaw, *This is Our Chance* (London: University of London Press, 1956), p. 19.

[5] Zulu Sofola, *Old Wines Are Tasty* (Ibadan: University Press Limited, 1981), p. 35.

[6] E. A. Ayandele, *The Missionary Impact on Modern Nigeria* (London: Longmans, 1966), p. 73. Similarly, one could refer to Archbishop Makarios who led Cyprus to independence. In a limited way, Archbishop Desmond Tutu, a Nobel Laureate, plays such a role in South Africa.

[7] The commander-in-chief (of the army).

[8] A. F. Ajayi and R. Smith, *Yoruba Warfare in the 19th Century* (Cambridge: Cambridge University Press, 1964), p. 67. Also see the plays: Ola Rotimi, *Kurunmi* (Ibadan: Oxford University Press, 1971) and Wale Ogunyemi, *Ijaye War* (Ibadan: Orisun, 1970).

[9] *The Swamp Dwellers* in *Collected Plays 1* (London: Oxford University Press, 1973), pp. 93-94.

10 Oyin Ogunba, *The Movement of Transition* (Ibadan: Ibadan University Press, 1975), p. 20.

11 Wole Soyinka, *The Trials of Brother Jero* in *Collected Plays 2* (London: Oxford University Press, 1974), p. 145.

12 Wole Soyinka, *Jero's Metamorphosis* in *Collected Plays 2* (London: Oxford University Press, 1974), pp. 181-2.

13 Femi Osofisan, *The Chattering and the Song* (Ibadan: Ibadan University Press, 1977), pp. 56-57. The play will be discussed in its Socialist/Marxist dimension in the chapter on Man and the Masses.

14 Wole Soyinka, *Kongi's Harvest* in *Collected Plays 2* p. 96.

15 *This is Our Chance*, p. 35.

16 *The Lion and the Jewel*, pp. 9-10.

17 Femi Osofisan, *Kolera Kolej* (Ibadan: New Horn Press, 1975), pp. 81-82.

18 Native doctors, who mix sorcery with religious practices, and are thought capable of doing harm/good through magical means.

19 Kole Omotoso, *Shadows in the Horizon* (Ibadan: Sketch Publishing Company, 1977), p. 17.

20 *The Road* in *Collected Plays 1*, p. 149.

21 Wole Soyinka, *A Dance of the Forests* in *Collected Plays 1*, pp. 50-51.

22 This play will be more thoroughly examined under Chapter 5.

23 *The Chattering and the Song*, p. 18.

24 Following the enumeration I made at the beginning of this chapter, I would have discussed the armed forces before the artist but it

has now dawned on me, especially with the last coup d'etat (August 27, 1985) in Nigeria, that the armed forces have occupied such a prominent position that a separate chapter be devoted to them, just as the professional political leaders have been treated to a chapter of their own. The Armed Forces and the Nigerian Civil War will be discussed in the next chapter then. The evidence from Nigerian drama is that they are found lacking in leadership qualities. Why? See Chapter 5.

24 *The Strong Breed* in *Collected Plays l*, pp. 142, 118.

26 *The Writing of Wole Soyinka* (London: Heinemann, 1973), p. 54. It should be noted also that Eman is actually a stranger; the scapegoat is always a stranger in Yoruba culture (conversation with Prof. J.A. Adedeji at the University of Kansas, April 23, 1991).

27 Oyin Ogunba, *The Movement of Transition* (Ibadan: Ibadan University Press, 1975), p. 115. Prof. J.A. Adedeji gives a penetrating insight on the artist by pointing out the relationship between Eman and Ifada. Eman's creativity is linked to Ifada's. Ifada is actually the artist by his origin; he owes his being to the creator-god Obatala, also referred to as Orisha. Ifada is "eni-orisha"—one who belongs to Orisha—and therefore inheres in that god's creative attribute. Eman, more than any other reason, qualifies as an artist because he takes Ifada's place. There is an absorption here into Obatala's creative powers. (Conversation with J.A. Adedeji on April 23, 1991, at the University of Kansas, Lawrence.)

28 Bode Sowande, *The Night Before* in *Farewell to Babylon* (London: Longman, 1979), pp. 46-47.

CHAPTER 5

1 Chinua Achebe, *Morning Yet on Creation Day* (London: Heinemann Educational Books, 1975), pp. 78-79.

2 Wole Soyinka, "The Writer in a Modern African State," *When the Man Died,* ed. John Agetua (Benin City: Bendel Newspaper Corporation, 1975), p. 30. But the essay first appeared in *L'Afrique Actuelle*, No. 19 (June 1967), pp. 5-7.

3 On December 31, 1983, soldiers again staged a take-over of the government. Another coup d'etat took place in August 1985. At the moment of writing this book the soldiers are still running the government and there has been at least two known coup attempts against the military rule of Gen. Ibrahim Babangida. The carnage in these coups has been enormous.

4 Claude E. Welch, Jr. *Soldier and State in Africa* (Evanston: Northwestern University Press, 1970), pp. 17-18.

5 *Nigerian Opinion*, 3, Nos. 10 & 11 (October-November, 1967), 246.

6 *Nigerian Opinion*, p. 247.

7 NCNC (National Council of Nigerian Citizens), Action Group and NPC (Northern People's Congress) were political parties of the First Republic.

8 *Nigerian Opinion*, p. 247.

9 Elechi Amadi, *Peppersoup and The Road to Ibadan* (Ibadan: Onibonoje Publishers, 1977), p. 89. The *Road to Ibadan* could indeed be Amadi's personal diary and observation. He was a Captain in the Nigerian Army during the Nigerian Civil War, 1967-1970.

10 Gordon Tialobi, *Full-Cycle* in *Nine African Plays for Radio*, eds. Gwyneth Henderson and C. Pieterse (London: Heinemann, 1973), p. 149.

11 *Monkey on the Tree*, in *African Plays for Playing*, ed. Michael Etherton (London: Heinemann, 1976), p. 9. The playwright is now married to John Hunwick and both are at Northwestern University. Husband and wife were once activists.

12 Rasheed Gbadamosi, *Echoes from the Lagoon* (Ibadan: Onibonoje Publishers, 1972), pp. 10-11.

13 Wole Soyinka, *Madmen and Specialists* in *Collected Plays 2* (London: Oxford University Press, 1974), pp. 239-240. In the summer of 1970, Soyinka was invited by Lloyd Richard as a Writer-in-

Residence at the Eugene O'Neill Memorial Theatre in Waterford, Connecticut. It was there he wrote the first version of *Madmen and Specialists*. In August that same year, Soyinka directed the play at the same theatre with members of UTAC (University Theatre Arts Company) from the University of Ibadan, Nigeria. The Company was dissolved in 1971 when Soyinka left Nigeria. (Conversation with Prof. J.A. Adedeji, April 23, 1991, at the University of Kansas).

14 Bode Sowande, *The Night Before* in *Farewell to Babylon and Other Plays* (London: Longman, 1979), pp. 7-8.

CHAPTER 6

1 Bode Sowande, *Farewell to Babylon and Other Plays* (London: Longman Drumbeat, 1979).

2 Wole Soyinka, *Kongi's Harvest* in *Collected Plays 2* (London: Oxford University Press, 1974).

3 Wole Soyinka, *Opera Wonyosi* (Bloomington: Indiana University Press, 1981). By the time we come to *A Play of Giants* (1984), even the United Nations Organization in New York is held hostage by Africa's most powerful dictators.

4 *Isaiah* 13:1-14:23; 21:1-10; *Jeremiah*, 50:1-51:64. *Encyclopaedia Britannica*, 1983 ed., Vol. 2, pp. 554-556. *The New Columbia Encyclopedia*, 1975 ed., pp. 202-23.

5 *The New Columbia Encyclopedia*, p. 1989.

6 Wole Soyinka, *Before the Blackout*, pp. 14-21. Prof. J.A. Adedeji also gives an interesting interpretation of Asagbefo. Asa=hawk; gbe=snatch; fo=fly. Thus, the hawk flies away with something snatched. On another level, Asagbefo means "we will snatch something," or "we will take care of somebody/something" (in the negative aspect of it). Whatever interpretation, the element of power, of use of force is there.

7 I am here indebted to Prof. Dapo Adelugba, Dean of the Faculty of Arts, University of Ibadan, Nigeria, for his analysis in a paper he

presented at a Soyinka symposium at the University of Ibadan, April
1973.

8 Page numbering is from *Kongi's Harvest* in *Collected Plays 2*.

9 In 1970, *Kongi's Harvest* was made into a film by Calpenny-
Nigerian Films. In the film version, Kongi was killed in the coup
d'etat led by Daodu-Segi citadel but the Nigerian government insisted
that it was untenable for an African head of State to be so killed. The
censor board had to prevail on Soyinka if the film was to be released.
(Conversation with Prof. J.A. Adedeji, April 23, 1991, in Lawrence,
Kansas. Adedeji had a major acting role in the film).

10 Gerald Moore, in *Wole Soyinka* (London: Evans, 1971), p. 68,
identifies Kwame Nkrumah as Kongi, while Oyin Ogunba identifies
Banda as Kongi. Ogunba attributes the statement: 'I want him back—
alive if possible. If not, ANY OTHER WAY!' to Banda, when the
latter learned that Mr. Chipembere, his former Minister of Education in
Malawi, had escaped from detention. Ogunba argues that the
playwright himself had "said that it is this particular statement ...
which provoked him to write *Kongi's Harvest*. Ogunba's *The
Movement of Transition* (Ibadan: Ibadan University Press, 1975), p.
191.

11 After his ouster, the country reverted to its former name,
Central African Republic.

12 Michael Etherton explains that the title plays on the meanings
of the.word 'opera' in Yoruba and English: "Accented thus: Òpèrá, it
means in Yoruba 'The fool buys..' In English it refers to a very
elaborate and expensive form of opera in which every word is sung to
the accompaniment of a large orchestra Wonyosi was a very expensive
type of lace (it cost about $1000 a meter!) for which there was a craze at
this time in Nigerian high society." *The Development of African
Drama* (London: Hutchinson University Library for Africa, 1982), p.
269.

13 While it is easy to recall that Uganda and Central African
Republic were dictatorships, it is not so easy to recall that of Nigeria
because it never reached the proportion of the former. But Soyinka
believes that Nigeria of the period he writes, that is, Nigeria of the
Military regime of the 70's was one of dictatorship. He has devoted a

whole book of historical accuracy to his experience of dictatorship in
The Man Died (London: Rex Collins, 1972) and from this I quote to
show he believes Nigeria was a dictatorship at this time:

> I experience this solidarity only with such of my people as share in
> this humiliation of tyranny. I exclude and ignore all others.
> Whatever the factors that made a dictatorship inevitable in the first
> place, those factors no longer exist. The present dictatorship is a
> degrading imposition. It is additionally humiliating because, in
> my knowledge and yours, this dictatorship has exceeded a thousand-
> fold in brutish arrogance, in repressiveness, in material corruption
> and in systematic reversal of all original revolutionary purposes the
> worst excesses of the pre-1966 government of civilians. This is a
> shameful admission but it is the truth (p. 15).

14 *Farewell to Babylon*, p. 57.

CHAPTER 7

1 See Chapter 2

2 Ebrahim N. Hussein, *Kinjeketile* (Dar es Salaam: Oxford
University Press, 1970). See also: Ngugi wa Thiong'o and Micere
Mugo, *The Trial of Dedan Kimathi* (London: Heinemann Educational
Books, 1977). Athol Fugard, *Sizwe Bansi is Dead* and *The Island* (New
York: Viking Press, 1976).

3 Frantz Fanon, *The Wretched of the Earth* (New York, U.S.A.
and Harmondsworth, England: Penguin Books, 1967). The Preface is
by Jean-Paul Sartre. See also Paulo Freire, *Pedagogy of the Oppressed*
(Harmondsworth: Penguin Education, 1972).

4 Page numbers, except otherwise indicated, are to Ezenta E. Eze,
The Cassava Ghost (Benin City: Ethiope Publishing Corporation,
1974). The play is based on the Aba Market Women riot of 1929
against a Nigerian Colonial Government imposition of an unpopular
tax.

5 *The Wretched of the Earth*, pp. 15-16.

6 *The Wretched of the Earth*, p. 28.

7 *The Wretched of the Earth,* p. 16.

8 *The Wretched of the Earth,* pp. 16-17.

9 *Pedagogy of the Oppressed,* pp. 31-33.

10 Black magic or sorcery.

11 *Pedagogy of the Oppressed,* p. 22.

12 *Pedagogy of the Oppressed,* p. 21.

13 An insult to the country. The idea is "let me defecate on my country."

CHAPTER 8

1 John Agetua, *Six Nigerian Writers* (Benin City, Nigeria: Bendel Newspapers Corporation, n.d.), p. 14.

2 *Six Nigerian Writers,* p. 16.

3 The name given to the Marxist playwrights, critics and literary men who are mostly academicians of the Universities of Ibadan and Ife. The two universities are located in the same state, and within a short distance of each other.

4 Wole Soyinka's Foreword to his play *Opera Wonyosi* (Bloomington: Indiana University Press, 1981), n.p.

5 *Six Nigerian Writers,* p. 52.

6 *Six Nigerian Writers,* p. 52.

7 Foreword to *Opera Wonyosi.*

8 David Craig, ed., *Marxists on Literature: An Anthology* (Middlesex: Penguin Books, 1975), pp. 207-213.

[9] Barrington Moore Jr., *Soviet Politics—The Dilemma of Power* (Cambridge, Mass.: Harvard University Press, 1950), pp. 20-37, 40, 222-223. Also see, William H. Harris and Judith S. Levey, eds., *The New Columbia Encyclopedia* (New York and London: Columbia University Press, 1975), pp. 1708-1709.

[10] *Nigerian Opinion*, 3, Nos. 10 and 11 (Oct.-Nov., 1967), p. 247.

[11] Paul H. Landis, *Social Control* (Chicago: Lippincott Co., 1956), pp. 416-433.

[12] *Six Nigerian Writers*, p. 16.

[13] Programme Notes to the First Production in Femi Osofisan's *Once Upon Four Robbers* (Ibadan: BIO Educational Services Ltd., 1980), n.p.

[14] Page references here are to Femi Osofisan's *The Chattering and the Song* (Ibadan: Ibadan University Press, 1977).

[15] Though the Farmers' Anthem may appear isolated in the text, it is not so in production. The song engages the audience in a lively participatory atmosphere. Prof. Adedeji, who was Head of the Department of Theatre Arts, University of Ibadan, Nigeria, when the play was first produced, informed me that the charismatic Osofisan gave out programs containing the song to every audience member and taught people the anthem before the play started. At the end of the play when the song was raised, everyone in the entire building joined in it and sang it as they left the stage and the auditorium. Seen in this light, the Farmers' Anthem assumes a central role not at first perceived. It also shows the great theatrical feeling of Osofisan; after all, the test of a successful play is in the production, not in the text.

[16] Page references are to *Shadows in the Horizon* (Ibadan Sketch Pub. Co., Ltd., 1977).

CHAPTER 9

[1] Christian Chukwunedu Aguolu, *Nigerian Civil War, 1967-1970: An Annotated Bibliography* (Boston, Mass.: G. K. Hall and Co., 1973), p. viii.

[2] For details, see Chapter 7.

[3] These plays have been treated in detail in previous chapters.

[4] Preface to Wale Ogunyemi's *Langbodo* (Lagos, Nigeria: Thomas Nelson (Nigeria) Limited, 1979), n.p. to the Preface. Henceforth, all page references to the play use the 1979 publication.

[5] Ogun is the Yoruba (a Nigerian tribe) god of war, of metallic art; he is also the patron of hunters.

[6] Sango is the god of fury, the god of thunder and of lightning.

[7] Greetings to an Oba (king).

[8] First Medium explains what "Sharo" and "Bori" are:
Sharo is a public test of strength and endurance after which one may take one's beloved. There is physical torture but maturity is attained through braving pain and enduring discomfort for love. Bori is a cult of spirit possession based on ancient pre-Islamic Hausa religion ... (p. 48).

[9] Preface to the play, n.p.

[10] Africa Journal Limited and the International Festival Committee, *FESTAC 77* (London: Kirkman House and Lagos: 13 Hawkesworth Road, 1977), p. 136.

[11] The FESTAC presentation of *Langbodo* was not the first production of the play. The Theatre Department of the University of Ibadan had presented it two years before FESTAC.

CHAPTER 10

[1] *The Movement of Transition* (Ibadan: Ibadan University Press, 1975), p. 70.

[2] E. Clark, "Ogunde Theatre: The Rise of Contemporary Professional Theatre in Nigeria 1946-1972" in *Nigeria Magazine*, 115-116, 1975, p. 17.

[3] Jonathan Robertson, "Art in Revolution," in *New Theatre Magazine*, vol. xi, No. 2, n.d., p. 17.

[4] Karl Marx, "Letter to Ferdinand Lassalle" and Friedrich Engels, "Letter to Ferdinand Lassalle" in Bernard F. Dukore's *Dramatic Theory and Criticism* (New York: Holt, Rinehart & Winston, Inc., 1974), pp. 797-801.

[5] *Daily Times* (of Nigeria), Thursday, July 31, 1975, p. 24. And *Sunday Times*, August 3, 1975, p. 9. The quote from Shakespeare's *As You Like It* becomes more meaningful when examined with the circumstances surrounding the chief characters: i) Gen. Gowon, like the rightful Duke, is ousted in a coup; ii) Gen. Gowon, like the Duke, goes into exile. It is noteworthy that it is to Britain he goes; iii) There is an attempt to reinstate Gen. Gowon to the throne. While that of Gowon fails, that of the Duke succeeds, through a change of heart of the usurper.
The question one may ask is, whether by quoting from *As You Like It*, General Gowon was planning on his return to power even as he seems to accept the fate of the player—a necessary entrance and a necessary exit. The answer is beyond the scope of this study.

[6] For a detailed treatment of *The Cassava Ghost*, see Chapter 7. Also see *The Cassava Ghost*, p. 8.

[7] *The Cassava Ghost*, p. 9.

[8] See Chapter 9.

[9] *Langbodo*, p. 69.

[10] See Chapter 8.

[11] See Chapter 2.

[12] Preface to *Langbodo*, n.p.

[13] *The Old Masters*, p. 10.

APPENDIX B

[1] In the edition I used, scene iv is misnumbered Scene iii while Scene v is Scene iv. See pages 112-132 of *The Road to Ibadan* (Ibadan: Onibonoje Publishers, 1977).

[2] In the production of the play I attended at the University of Ibadan, 1979, the playwright-director made up Papa in his final appearance to be blind and deaf. Papa had cotton swabs stuck to both ears.

BIBLIOGRAPHY

Primary Sources

Plays

Amadi, Elechi. *Peppersoup and the Road to Ibadan.*
    Ibadan: Onibonoje Publishers, 1977.

Clark, John Pepper. *Ozidi* Ibadan: Oxford University
    Press, 1966.

Etherton, Michael, ed. *African Plays for Playing 2.* Ibadan:
    Heinemann Educational Books Ltd., 1976.

Eze, Ezenta. *The Cassava Ghost.* Benin City: Ethiope
    Publishing Corporation, 1974.

Gbadamosi, Rasheed. *Echoes from the Lagoon.* Ibadan:
    Onibonoje Publishers, 1973.

Henderson, Gwyneth, and Cosmo Pieterse, eds. *Nine African Plays for Radio.* London: Heinemann Educational Books Ltd., 1973.

Ogunyemi, Wale. *Langbodo.* Lagos: Thomas Nelson (Nigeria) Limited, 1979.

Omotoso, Kole. *Shadows in the Horizon.* Ibadan: Sketch Publishing Company Ltd., 1977.

Osofisan, Femi. *The Chattering and the Song.* Ibadan: Ibadan University Press, 1977.

Osofisan, Femi. *Once Upon Four Robbers.* Ibadan: BIO Educational Services Ltd., 1980.

Oti, Sonny. *The Old Masters.* Ibadan: Oxford University Press, 1977.

Rotimi, Ola. *If.* Ibadan: Heinemann Educational Books (Nigeria) Ltd., 1983.

Sofola, Zulu. *Old Wines Are Tasty.* Ibadan: University Press Limited, 1981.

Sowande, Bode. *Farewell to Babylon and Other Plays.* Harlow, Essex: Longman Drumbeat, 1979.

Soyinka, Wole. *Before the Blackout.* Ibadan: Orisun, n.d.

Soyinka, Wole. *Collected Plays 1.* London: Oxford University Press, 1973.

Soyinka, Wole. *Collected Plays 2.* London: Oxford University Press, 1974.

Soyinka, Wole. *Death and the King's Horseman.* New York and London: W.W. Norton & Company, 1975.

Soyinka, Wole. Opera Wonyosi. Bloomington: Indiana University Press, 1981.

Secondary Sources

I. *Plays*

Fatunde, Tunde. *No Food, No Country.* Benin City: Adena Publishers, 1985.

Fatunde, Tunde. *No More Oil Boom And Blood and Sweat.* Benin City: Adena Publishers, 1985.

Fugard, Athol *Sizwe Bansi is Dead* and *The Island.* New York: The Viking Press, 1976.

Henshaw, James Ene. *Dinner for Promotion.* London: University of London Press, 1967.

Henshaw, James Ene. *This is Our Chance.* London: University of London Press, 1956.

Hussein, Ebrahim N. *Kinjeketile.* Dar es Salaam: Oxford University Press, 1970.

Nasiru, Akanji. *Come Let Us Reason Together.* Ijebu-Ode: Shebiotimo Publications, 1987.

Nasiru, Akanji. *Our Survival.* London: Macmillan Publishers, 1985.

Ngugi, wa Thiong'o, and Micere Githae Mugo. *The Trial of Dedan* Kimathi. London: Heinemann Educational Books Ltd., 1977.

Ogunyemi, Wale. *Eniyan.* Ibadan: Ibadan University Press, 1987.

Ogunyemi, Wale. *Ijaye War*. Ibadan: Orisun, 1970.

Onwueme, Tess A. *The Broken Calabash*. Owerri: Totan Publishers, 1984.

Onwueme, Tess A. *The Desert Encroaches*. Owerri: Heins Nigeria Publishers, 1985.

Osofisan, Femi. *Eshu and the Vagabond Minstrels*. Ibadan: New Horn Press, 1988.

Osofisan, Femi. *Who's Afraid of Solarin?* Ile-Ife, Nigeria: Ogunbiyi Printing Works, 1978.

Osofisan, Femi. Morountodun and Other Plays. Lagos: Longman, 1982.

Pieterse, Cosmo, ed. *Ten One-Act Plays*. London: Heinemann Educational Books, Ltd., 1968.

Rotimi, Ola. *The Gods are not to Blame*. London: Oxford University Press, 1971.

Rotimi, Ola. *Kurunmi*. Ibadan: Oxford University Press, 1971.

Rotimi, Ola. *Our Husband Has Gone Mad Again*. Ibadan: Oxford University Press, 1977.

Rotimi, Ola. *Ovonramwen Nogbaisi*. Ibadan: Oxford University Press, 1974.

Sofola, Zulu. *King Emene*. Ibadan: Heinemann Educational Books Ltd., 1974.

Sofola, Zulu. *The Sweet Trap*. Ibadan: Oxford University Press, 1977.

Sofola, Zulu. *Wedlock of the Gods*. Ibadan: Evans Brothers Limited, 1972.

Soyinka, Wole. *A Play of Giants*. London: Methuen, 1984.

Soyinka, Wole. *Requiem for a Futurologist*. London: Rex Collings, 1985.

Ukala, Sam. *The Log in Your Eye*. Ibadan: University Press, 1986.

II. *Books*

Achebe, Chinua. *Morning yet on Creation Day*. Garden City, New York: Anchor Press/Doubleday, 1975.

Africa Journal Limited and International Festival Committee. *FESTAC '77*. London: Kirkman House and Lagos: 13 Hawkesworth Road, 1977.

African Church. *Report of Proceedings of the African Church Organization for Lagos and Yorubaland* 1901-1908. Liverpool 1910.

Adelugba, Dapo, ed. *Before Our Very Eyes*. Ibadan: Spectrum Books, 1987.

Agetua, John. *Six Nigerian Writers*. Benin City: Bendel Newspapers Corporation, n.d.

Agetua, John. *When the Man Died*. Benin City: Bendel Newspapers Corporation, 1975.

Aguolu, Christian Chukwunedu. *Nigerian Civil War*, 1967-70: An Annotated Bibliography. Boston, Mass.: G. K. Hall and Co., 1973.

Ajayi, A. F. and R. Smith. *Yoruba Warfare in the 19th Century.* Cambridge: Cambridge University Press, 1964.

Angoff, Charles, and John Povey. *African Writing Today.* New York: Maryland Books, 1969.

Ayandele, E. A. *The Missionary Impact on Modern Nigeria 1842-1914.* London: Longmans, Green & Co., Ltd., 1966.

Baldwin, Claudia. *Nigerian Literature: A Bibliography of Criticism, 1952-1976.* Boston, Mass.: G. K. Hall and Co., 1980.

Banham, Martin, and Clive Wake. *African Theatre Today.* London: Pitman Publishing Ltd., 1976.

Beier, Ulli, ed. *Introduction to African Literature.* London: Longman, 1979.

Booth, James. *Writers and Politics in Nigeria.* London: Hodder and Stoughton, 1981.

Bright, John. *A History of Israel.* London: SCM Press Ltd., 1972.

Cadigan, Rufus J. "Richard Billinger, Hanns Johst and Eberhard Moeller: Three Representative National Socialist Playwrights." Diss. Kansas, 1979.

Clark, Ebun. *Hubert Ogunde: The Making of Nigerian Theatre.* Oxford University Press, 1979.

Clark, John Pepper. *The Ozidi Saga.* Ibadan: Oxford University Press and Ibadan University Press, 1977.

Coleman, James S. *Nigeria: Background to Nationalism.* Los Angeles: University of California Press, 1963.

Cook, David. *African Literature: A Critical View*. London: Longman, 1977.

Craig, David, ed. *Marxists on Literature: An Anthology*. Hammondsworth: Penguin Books, 1975.

Crowder, Michael. *The Story of Nigeria*. London: Faber and Faber, 1962.

Dathorne, O. R. *African Literature in the 20th Century*. Minneapolis: University of Minnesota Press, 1975.

Dukore, Bernard F. *Dramatic Theory and Criticism*. New York: Holt Rinehart and Winston, Inc., 1974.

Durverger, Maurice. *The Study of Politics*. Harmondsworth: Nelson, 1972.

Egudu, R. N. *Modern African Poetry and the African Predicament.*London: The Macmillan Press, Ltd., 1978.

Enahoro, Peter. *How to be a Nigerian*. Lagos: Daily Times Ltd., 1966.

Etherton, Michael. *The Development of African Drama*. London: Hutchinson & Co. (Publishers) Ltd., 1982.

Fagunwa, D. O. *The Forest of a Thousand Daemons*. Trans. Wole Soyinka. London: Thomas Nelson and Sons, Ltd., 1968.

Fanon, Frantz. *The Wretched of the Earth*. Harmondsworth: Penguin Books Ltd., 1967.

Federal Ministry of Information, Nigeria. *Nigeria Handbook 1978-79*. Lagos: Third Press International, 1979.

Flint, John E. *Nigeria and Ghana.* Englewood Cliffs, New Jersey: Prentice-Hall, Inc., 1966.

Freire, Paulo. *Pedagogy of the Oppressed.* Trans. Myra Bergman Ramos. Harmondsworth: Penguin Books Ltds., 1972.

Graham-White, Anthony. *The Drama of Black Africa.* New York: Samuel French, 1974.

Harrison, Paul Carter, ed. *Totem Voices.* New York: Grove Press, 1989.

Heywood, Christopher, ed. *Perspectives on African Literature.* London: Heinemann Educational Books, 1971.

Irele, Abiola. *The African Experience in Literature and Ideology.* London: Heinemann, 1981.

Jahn, Janheinz. *A History of Neo-African Literature.* Trans.Oliver Coburn and Ursula Lehrburger. London: Faber and Faber, 1968.

Jefferson, D. W., ed. *The Morality of Art.* London: Routledge and Kegan Paul, 1969.

Jones, Eldred Durosimi. *The Writing of Wole Soyinka.* London: Heinemann Educational Books Ltd., 1973.

Katrak, Ketu H. *Wole Soyinka and Modern Tragedy.* New York: Greenwood Press, 1986.

Killam, G. D. *African Writers on African Writing.* Evanston: Northwestern University Press, 1973.

Kohn, Hans and Wallace Sokolsky. *African Nationalism in the 20th Century.* Princeton, N.J.: Van Nostrand, 1965.

Landis, Paul H. *Social Control*. Chicago: Lippincott Co., 1956.

Lichtheim, George. *Marxism*. London: Routledge and Kegan Paul, 1964.

Manning, Patrick. *Slavery and African Life*. Cambridge: Cambridge University Press, 1990.

Moore, Gerald. *Twelve African Writers*. Bloomington: Indiana University Press, 1980.

Moore, Gerald. *Wole Soyinka*. London: Evans, 1971.

Moore, Barrington Jr., *Soviet-Politics—The Dilemma of Power*. Cambridge, Mass.: Harvard University Press, 1950.

Ngugi, wa Thiong'o. *Homecoming*. London: Heinemann Educational Books, Ltd., 1972.

Ogueri, Eze. *African Nationalism and Military Ascendancy*. New York: Conch, 1976.

Ogunba, Oyin. *The Movement of Transition*. Ibadan: Ibadan University Press, 1975.

Ogunba, Oyin and Abiola Irele, eds. *Theatre in Africa*. Ibadan: Ibadan University Press, 1978.

Ogunbiyi, Yemi, ed. *Drama and Theatre in Nigeria: A Critical Source Book*. Lagos: Nigeria Magazine, 1981.

Olusanya, G. O. *The Second World War and Politics in Nigeria 1939-53*. Lagos: University of Lagos Press and Evans Brothers Ltd. 1973.

Osofisan, Femi. *Kolera Kolej*. Ibadan: New Horn Press, 1975.

Pieterse, Cosmo, and Donald Munro, eds. *Protest and Conflict in African Literature.* New York: Africana Publishing Corporation, 1969.

Roberts, Andrew, ed. *The Colonial Moment in Africa.* Cambridge: Cambridge University Press, 1990.

Sannes, G. W. *African 'Primitives': Function and Form in African Masks and Figures.* London: Faber and Faber, 1970.

Smith, Robert. *Kingdoms of the Yoruba.* Norwich: Methuen and Co., Ltd., 1976.

Soyinka, Wole. *Art, Dialogue and Outrage.* Ibadan: New Horn Press, 1988.

Soyinka, Wole. *The Man Died.* London: Rex Collings, 1972.

Traore, Bakary. *The Black African Theatre and its Social Functions.* Trans. Dapo Adelugba. Ibadan: Ibadan University Press, 1972.

Welch, Calude E. Jr. *Soldier and State in Africa.* Evanston: Northwestern University Press, 1970.

III. *Journals*

Adedeji, J. A. "Indigenous Drama at the Festival." *Nigeria Magazine*, Nos. 115-116 (1975), pp. 3-8.

Akpata, Tayo. "Intellectuals in Contemporary Nigerian Politics." *Nigerian Opinion*, 2, No. 12 (1966), 139-142.

Antola, Esko. "The Roots of Domestic Military Interventions in Black Africa " *Instant Research on Peace and Violence*, V, No. 4 (1975), 207-221.

Awolalu, J. O. "The African Traditional View of Man." *Orita: Ibadan Journal of Religious Studies,* VI, No. 2 (1972), 104.

Bettlestone, J. "A New Racialism?" *Nigerian Opinion,* 3, Nos. 10-11 (1967), 243-244.

Clark, Ebun. "The Nigerian Theatre and the Nationalist Movement." *Nigeria Magazine,* Nos. 115-116 (1975), pp. 24-33.

Clark, Ebun. "Ogunde Theatre: The Rise of Contemporary Professional Theatre in Nigeria 1946-72." *Nigeria Magazine,* Nos. 115-116 (1975), pp. 9-24.

"Drama in the New Nigeria." Editorial. *West African Pilot,* 21 February 1951.

"The Heroes of Nigeria." Editorial. *Nigerian Opinion,* 6, Nos. 8-10 (1970), 69-70.

Ibikunle, Supo. "Electioneering with Tears in 1964." *Headlines,* No. 73, April 1979, pp. 1-4, 8.

Idahosa, Paul E. "The Changing Gears of Politics." *New Nigerian,* 31 March 1979, Saturday Extra, p. 4.

Irele, Abiola. "Negritude—Philosophy of African Being." *Nigeria Magazine,* Nos. 122-123 (1977), pp. 1-5.

"Nigerian Theatre in the Making." Editorial. *West African Pilot,* 9 July 1947.

O'Connell, James. "Nigeria: The Politics of Majorities and Minorities." *Nigerian Opinion,* 3, No. 7 (1967), 216-218.

O. D. "The Military and Politics." *Nigerian Opinion,* 3, Nos. 10-11 (1967), 245-252.

Ofoegbu, M. R. "Programme-Oriented Political System for Nigeria." *Nigerian Opinion*, 6, Nos. 8-10 (1970), 74-83.

Omotoso, Kole. "The Festival of African Art and Culture (FESTAC) and Africa's Crisis of Self-Definition." *Africa Currents*, No. 5, (1976), pp. 22-26.

"Truth is Bitter." Editorial. *West African Pilot*, 2, April 1964.

Ugonna, Nnabuenyi. "Ezeigboezue: An Igbo Masquerade Play." *Nigeria Magazine*, No. 114 74), pp. 22-33.

Williams, Bayo. "The Paradox of a Nation." *Newswatch*, October 1985, pp. 7-13.

INDEX

English, 2, 7, 12, 13
Enugu Miners, 39
Equatorial Guinea, 121
Ethiopia, 121
Europe (European), 4, 25, 26, 27, 29, 32
Eze Ezenta, 143, 144, 149, 152, 155, 158, 211

Fanon, Frantz, xi, xiv, 44, 143, 145
Farewell to Babylon, 65, 118, 122, 124-130, 134, 202, 205, 208, 238-239
Fatunde Tunde, xiii, xviii, 17
FESTAC '77 (Second World Black and African Festival of Arts and Culture), xv, 196-197, 253
Findlay, Robert, vi-vii, xxii
First Republic, The, 44, 50, 63
Fodio, Uthman dan, 4
Fourth Stage, The, 12, 256
France (French), 3, 13, 14, 15
Freire, Paulo, xiv, 143, 149
Fulani, 4
Full-Cycle, 103, 105, 106

Gbadamosi, Rasheed, 103, 109, 111, 211-212
Germany, 3, 51
Ghana, 109, 121, 134
Ghost actors, 21, 22
Ghost catcher, 22, 24
Gowon, Yakubu, 129, 136, 171, 202, 251
Guerrilla Theatre, xvi, 253-254
Guinea Coast, 4
Greek, 12

Hamlet, 23
Hausa, 4, 205, 250, 251, 257
Henshaw, James Ene, 73, 87
Herbert Macaulay, 29 32, 33-34
Horn, Andre, 250
How to be a Nigerian, 62, 63-64

Ibadan-Ife Group, The, 254
Iboland (Igbo), viii, 4, 5, 205
If, 165,205, 208, 233-235
Ife (Ile-Ife), viii, 4, 6, 253, 254
Ijaw (Ijo), 10, 11, 12, 22, 23 ,24
Ijaye War, xxi, 78
Independence, 5, 13, 15, 43, 44, 61, 62, 96, 142, 162

DATE DUE